Francis Hutcheson

PHILOSOPHICAL
WRITINGS

The Lion and Unicorn staircase at the Old College, Glasgow University (Mirrorpix/Alamy)

FRANCIS
HUTCHESON
PHILOSOPHICAL WRITINGS

ESSAYS ON

Ethics, Taste, Laughter,
Politics, Economics

Edited and introduced by
ROBIN DOWNIE

JOHN DONALD

First published by Everyman 1994
This edition first published in Great Britain in 2019 by
John Donald, an imprint of Birlinn Ltd

West Newington House
10 Newington Road
Edinburgh
EH9 1QS

www.birlinn.co.uk

ISBN: 978 1 910900 34 5

Preliminary material copyright © Robin Downie 1994, 2019

British Library Cataloguing-in-Publication Data
A catalogue record for this book is available on request from the British Library

Printed and bound in the United Kingdom by Clays Ltd, Elcograf S.p.A.

CONTENTS

CONTENTS

PREFACE

Philosophical interest in the Scottish Enlightenment was at one time limited to Book 1 of Hume's *Treatise on Human Nature*, which was understood as an early version of logical positivism. But, since the second half of the twentieth century, interest in the Scottish Enlightenment has been growing, and editions and detailed analyses of its philosophers have appeared. As far as Francis Hutcheson is concerned there are now scholarly editions of his works edited by Knud Haakonssen and others, and there are also many detailed commentaries on these works. I list at least some of them in my bibliography. These works are for specialists. But there are many non-specialist philosophers who none the less would like to read for themselves the central themes in Hutcheson's writings. This selection is for them.

There are three distinctive features of Hutcheson's writings which I have tried to capture in my selections. First, his stress on the sentient side to human nature and its centrality in moral and aesthetic judgements represents a new and original departure for the philosophy of that period. It is a theme which continues to the present.

Secondly, although claims to historical priority are always contentious, there is a case for maintaining that his was the first philosophical treatise since Aristotle dealing in a perceptive way with questions of aesthetics and taste. And it is less contentious that Hutcheson's three essays on laughter are still of interest. In our contemporary world many people are offended by some types of humour such as satire or caricature. Hutcheson offers an analysis of the moral rights and wrongs of humour. Certainly, his essays on laughter represent a totally new, original and insightful departure for philosophy. Moreover, as I try to bring out in my selection, many of the celebrated economic ideas of Adam Smith are to be found in Hutcheson's works. Smith, of course, was one of Hutcheson's students and always retained an admiration for him. In sum, Hutcheson made original contributions to philosophy of contemporary relevance,

and has had a large influence on both the philosophy and economics
of his successors, such as David Hume and Adam Smith. Indeed, he is
mentioned not unfavourably by Kant.

Thirdly, and perhaps most importantly, his influence extended
internationally to the practical politics of North America. Hutcheson's
belief that natural rights belong equally to all led him to reject any form
of slavery. This had an appeal to the abolitionist movement in North
America, so it is not surprising that he was a highly influential and
respected philosopher in eighteenth-century America. I have selected
texts to bring out that Hutcheson's appeal and influence extended beyond
what we would nowadays think of as professional philosophy and are
relevant to the political movements of his time, and indeed of our time.
There cannot be many philosophers who are read by presidents of the
United States, but consider the entry of 16 January 1756 in the diary
of John Adams of Massachusetts, the second president of the United
States: 'A fine morning. A large white frost upon the ground. Reading
Hutcheson's *Introduction to Moral Philosophy*.' It is also arguable that
Thomas Jefferson, the third president, was influenced by Hutcheson,
specifically in his approach to the Revolution of 1776. I have said that
my selection is for the mainstream philosopher rather than the historical
specialist. Perhaps it is unrealistic to say it is also for presidents! But I
hope at least that it will be of interest to political theorists and economists
as well as philosophers.

Robin Downie
University of Glasgow, 2019

NOTE ON THE AUTHOR AND EDITOR

FRANCIS HUTCHESON was born 8 August 1694 in Drumalig in Northern Ireland, the second son of John Hutcheson, an Irish Presbyterian minister of Scottish parentage. After early education in Northern Ireland he attended Glasgow University where he studied philosophy and theology. On his return to Ireland in about 1717 he was licensed as a preacher but soon turned to an academic career. He was invited to Dublin to run a 'dissenting academy', i.e. an academy for those not eligible for the Irish University. This period (1721–9) was the most productive in Hutcheson's life. The works he wrote then constitute his major achievement and he continued to revise them until the end of his life. In 1730 he took up the Chair of Moral Philosophy at Glasgow University where he played an important role as a teacher and in liberalising the University. His influence on the Scottish Enlightenment and on thinkers and institutions in Europe and North America was enormous. He married in 1725 and was survived by a son who became Professor of Chemistry at Trinity College, Dublin. Hutcheson died of a fever in 1746 on a visit to Dublin where he is buried.

ROBIN DOWNIE is Emeritus Professor of Moral Philosophy at the University of Glasgow, where his predecessors include Francis Hutcheson, Adam Smith and Thomas Reid. In his many writings on the history and theory of moral philosophy, the arts, and the philosophy of medicine he has attempted to follow the example of his distinguished predecessors and reach the non-specialist reader.

ACKNOWLEDGEMENTS

For the Everyman edition (1994)
I owe an intellectual debt to the Hutcheson scholarship of Professors Peter Kivy, Bernard Peach and David Raphael. In particular, the teaching of David Raphael first created my interest in the British Moralists. The staff of the Special Collections at Glasgow University Library were helpful and prompt in answering my questions and obtaining editions for me. My colleague Elizabeth Telfer helped me to clarify the Introduction, and Professor David Walker advised me on Hutcheson's jurisprudence. I am grateful to Natalina Bertoli, Carol Johnson and Andrea Henry for steering the book through the editorial processes, and to Lydia Rohmer and Carla Fassetta for help with proofs. Hilary Laurie and Dr David Berman of Everyman Library drew my attention to the need for a selection from Francis Hutcheson which would be usable by the non-specialist interested in the thought of the early eighteenth century. I hope the selection fulfils this need.

For the John Donald edition (2019)
Since 1994 many studies have appeared on different periods of Scottish philosophy, and on individual philosophers including Hutcheson, and the *Journal of Scottish Philosophy* has published many scholarly articles. I am indebted to this research, but especially to the scholarship and enthusiasm of my colleague Professor Alexander Broadie. I would also like to thank the Scottish publisher Birlinn for agreeing that there is a continuing need for an easily available selection of the major writings of Francis Hutcheson.

INTRODUCTION

Why Read Hutcheson?

Francis Hutcheson lived from 1694 to 1746. What is his relevance today? Why should we read him in the twenty-first century? The importance of Hutcheson can be judged in three ways: by his influence on philosophical thought; by the impact of his thought on issues and events beyond philosophy; by the inspiration of his life devoted to the courageous delivery of just and liberal causes. In terms of these criteria, Hutcheson is a major philosopher because through his writings and his personal teaching he exerted an enormous influence on several spheres of life. Indeed, whereas Hume is in some respects a greater philosopher than Hutcheson, it cannot be said that he exerted a greater influence. Hume's influence is largely confined to the sphere of what is now called 'professional philosophy', whereas Hutcheson's influence went beyond professional philosophy and extended to political movements in North America, to improvements in the teaching and organisation of Scottish universities and to the Scottish Enlightenment more generally. In all cases his influence was a liberalising one. It is not possible in a short introduction to do justice to Hutcheson's enormous influence on so many areas of intellectual and institutional life – and indeed, despite the important pioneering research of Professor Caroline Robbins, Professor Peter Kivy, Professor David Fate Norton, Professor M. A. Stewart, Professor Knud Haakonssen and many others, the full extent of Hutcheson's influence has not yet been fully documented. It will be convenient in this brief account of Hutcheson's influence to look first at his influence on Hume, Adam Smith, and Scottish life and letters more generally, to touch on his influence on Kant, and finally to say something about his great influence on North America.

According to the philosopher A. N. Prior, 'There is little or nothing in Hume's moral philosophy that cannot be traced to Hutcheson . . .'[1]

Norman Kemp Smith drew attention to what he saw as the more fundamental influence on Hume's foundational theory of knowledge. Kemp Smith was concerned to reject what was the prevailing interpretation of Hume – that he was a radical sceptic, working out to their negative conclusions the empiricist premises of John Locke and George Berkeley. This view gained currency in philosophical circles through the 'common-sense' philosophy of Thomas Reid and, more popularly, through the philosophy of James Beattie. Kemp Smith rejects this interpretation and argues that Hume is a consistent naturalist. According to Kemp Smith (and this is his main thesis) Hume was profoundly influenced by Hutcheson's view that 'judgments of moral approval and disapproval . . . are based not on rational insight or on evidence but solely on feeling; and what "opened up to [him] a new Scene of Thought, which transported him beyond Measure" was the discovery that this point of view could be carried over into the theoretical domain, and could there be employed in the solution of the chief problems to which Locke and Berkeley had drawn attention, but to which they had not been able to give a satisfactory solution.'[2] Kemp Smith develops this thesis in some detail in his Introduction, and since then it has become a widely accepted interpretation of Hume. More recently doubts have been expressed both about Kemp Smith's interpretation of Hutcheson and also about the kind of influence which Hutcheson exerted on Hume. But whatever the details of the influence – and these can never be known – there can be no dispute about the general claim that Hume was profoundly influenced by Hutcheson. Indeed, it is clear from Hume's letters to Hutcheson that he was anxious to please the older philosopher and modified and qualified some of his own writing with the explicit aim of gaining Hutcheson's approval. He never succeeded in this, and in a letter expressed hurt surprise that Hutcheson did not support him in his candidature for the Chair of Ethical Philosophy in Edinburgh around 1745.

The truth is that the two men had very different views on the nature of philosophy. Hume saw himself as applying what in his *Enquiry* he called 'a new philosophical microscope'[3] with the aim of making ideas clearer through analysis, or, as the full title of the *Treatise* suggests, of making 'an attempt to introduce the experimental method of reasoning into moral subjects'. It is therefore not surprising that Hutcheson found

Hume's philosophy lacking in warmth in the cause of virtue. On the other hand, Hutcheson saw himself as a 'friend to virtue' in the sense that he aimed in his writings and his personal teaching to encourage people to live a good life, which for Hutcheson was the life of benevolence and right reason. This difference might be put in twentieth-century terminology if we say that Hutcheson attributed a strongly normative function to moral philosophy, whereas Hume saw it as 'meta-ethics'. Hume's view of moral philosophy is the one which dominated in the first two thirds of the last century – perhaps one reason for the decline in interest in Hutcheson – whereas there now seems to be a partial return to normative moral philosophy – perhaps one reason for the revival of interest in Hutcheson. But there can be no doubt that, despite the temperamental and philosophical differences between the two men, Hutcheson exerted an enormous influence on Hume.

On the other hand it is not surprising that Hutcheson exerted a great influence on Adam Smith, since Adam Smith attended his lectures, the two men were temperamentally more similar than Hutcheson and Hume, and Hutcheson was noted as an influential teacher. Smith was indebted to Hutcheson in a general and in a more specific respect. In general terms Smith's philosophical position is much influenced by Hutcheson in that he makes natural liberty, utility, and naturalism the key ideas in his philosophy. Smith also follows Hutcheson in making immediate sense and feeling key ideas, and in stressing that moral judgement is disinterested. On the other hand, he seems to reject Hutcheson's view that benevolence is the whole of virtue, for he allows that self-love can be a motive for virtuous actions.[4] But, whatever the differences of detail in their respective treatments of moral philosophy, the general tone of the two philosophers is similar, as distinct from the tone of Hume's moral philosophy. Unlike Hume, but like Hutcheson, Smith is warm in the cause of virtue.

Turning now to the more specific influence we find, as Edwin Cannan pointed out at the end of the nineteenth century and as has been documented in detail by W. R. Scott and others, that the main influence on Smith's theory of price and value is in Hutcheson's own theory of these matters, a theory which was almost certainly outlined in the lectures which Smith attended. Whereas the relationship between Hume and Hutcheson seems to have ended on a sour note,

Smith generously acknowledges his teacher. In a letter to the Principal of Glasgow University dated 16 November 1787, accepting the post of Lord Rector, Smith writes of having been appointed to the Chair of Moral Philosophy, 'to which the abilities and Virtues of the never to be forgotten Dr Hutcheson had given a superior degree of illustration'.

Hutcheson wrote his four major treatises before taking up the Chair of Moral Philosophy at Glasgow in 1730. He worked on *A System of Moral Philosophy* from 1734–7, but seems to have abandoned the project by 1740, describing it as 'a confused book'. He gives two reasons for this situation in a letter of 15 June 1741 to his friend Thom Drennan. The first is 'an incapacity of mind for such close thinking and composition as I once had', and the second is 'more avocations, by too numerous an acquaintance than you can imagine'. It is the second explanation which is more likely to be accurate, for Hutcheson's energies were being taken up with numerous committees and with his passion to liberalise the University through teaching and through committee work.

Hutcheson's philosophical influence extended far beyond the cloisters of Glasgow University. The first two treatises, on aesthetics and ethics, were published together in 1725. I shall quote the full title, which summarises the themes: *An Inquiry into the Original of Our Ideas of Beauty and Virtue; in Two Treatises, in which the Principles of the late Earl of Shaftesbury are explain'd and defended, against the Author of the 'Fable of the Bees': and the Ideas of Moral Good and Evil are establish'd, according to the Sentiments of the Antient Moralists. With an Attempt to introduce a Mathematical Calculation in subjects of Morality.* You could be forgiven for thinking that someone who writes a book with a title of that length is not going to get into the best-seller lists. In fact, Hutcheson's writings went through many editions in his lifetime, were translated into French and German, and exerted an enormous influence not only on the Scottish Enlightenment but more widely in Europe and America. It is known, for example, that he exerted considerable influence on the development of the aesthetic and the moral ideas of Kant. Indeed, Kant's aesthetics has as its starting point the Hutchesonian idea that there can be disinterested feeling. And while Kant dismisses the appeal to 'moral feeling' in the *Groundwork of the Metaphysic of Morals* (1785), he is less scathing of this view and Hutcheson's connection with it than he is of other 'heteronomous' systems. Indeed, in his *Critique of Practical*

Reason (1788) when he is discussing what he calls the 'indemonstrable' foundations of other practical principles, Kant writes 'In this respect, under the name of "moral feeling", Hutcheson and others have provided a start toward some excellent observations.'[5]

I shall turn now to Hutcheson's influence on areas outside professional philosophy. One such area is painting in the eighteenth century. The Scottish Enlightenment is usually depicted as a period where reason was stressed. While this is true, the period also stressed the centrality of sentiment, of human nature. Hutcheson laid the foundations of this doctrine of human nature, a doctrine which was to influence the portraiture of Allan Ramsay. In Ramsay's portraits we see real people looking at us out of the canvas. Hutcheson's aesthetics had a more specific influence on the painting of the period which is best understood in terms of his aesthetic theory. He argued (Treatise I, pp. 23–4) that a painting could be beautiful even if the original subject was not.

Hutcheson's ideas were readily accepted in North America. One reason for this was that his work was widely available. For example, *A Short Introduction to Moral Philosophy* was frequently imported until an American edition was published in Philadelphia in 1788. The author of the first American textbook of philosophy – Samuel Johnson of Yale – borrowed many of Hutcheson's ideas from *A Short Introduction*. Professor David Fate Norton traces the dissemination of Hutcheson's philosophy through the activity of various North American disciples such as Francis Alison who emigrated from Scotland about 1735. Alison became Vice-Provost and Professor of Moral Philosophy at the Philadelphia Academy and through his teaching and the teaching of his students Hutcheson's ideas were widely disseminated.[6]

As already indicated, it was Hutcheson's political ideas which appealed most. The rights of resistance to the tyranny of a magistrate had been maintained by Hutcheson as early as the *Inquiry* and his belief that natural rights belong equally to all leads him to reject any form of slavery: 'Nature makes none masters, none slaves . . .' (*Short Introduction*, p. 168; see also *System*, p. 190). This had an appeal to the abolitionist movement in America. Basically restrained in style and an advocate of right reason, Hutcheson's warmth in the cause of virtue was nevertheless able to catch the imagination of the North Americans. It is not surprising that, as N. Fiering reports, 'Hutcheson was probably the most influential and respected moral philosopher in eighteenth-century America.[7]

There is a tradition in which philosophers are seen as possessing both the courage and the skill to stand up to oppressive and unreasonable authority. Socrates is the outstanding example, but Hutcheson can offer a similar inspiration by the way he both stood up to unreasonable authority and skilfully circumvented it. Even as a student he was politically active and was one of the ringleaders who took the University of Glasgow to court in 1717 over the students' right to elect their own rector. But he influenced his students also by his manner of teaching. He taught in English, which was a new departure. His colleague William Leechman says in his biographical preface to the *System* that Hutcheson 'displayed a fervent and persuasive eloquence which was irresistible' and that 'his happy talent of speaking with ease, with propriety and spirit, rendered him one of the most masterly and engaging teachers that has appeared in our age'. This aspect of Hutcheson is linked to the points which emerged when we compared Hutcheson and Hume. In his teaching as in his writing Hutcheson was an enthusiast for virtue and saw his mission as that of moulding the character of his students. Indeed, there is evidence that he helped students of all faculties with advice, friendship, and even financial assistance.

Turning now to Hutcheson's wider influence on academic life we find that soon after his first arrival at the University of Glasgow he was placed on many committees. His main battles were with bigoted clergy who were exerting an undue influence on university teaching. It is easy nowadays, when the power of the clergy in universities is minimal, to underestimate their dominance in eighteenth-century Scotland. But Hutcheson succeeded in securing the election of his (liberal) candidates for the Chairs of Divinity (William Leechman) and Greek (James Moor). Without these efforts on the part of Hutcheson Glasgow University would have degenerated into a sectarian college.

Hutcheson is often said to be 'the father of the Scottish Enlightenment'. There is a sense in which this is true. By his teaching, and especially his celebration of Greek philosophers such as the Stoics, he did create a culture in Scotland in which ideas could flourish more easily. Soon after he was appointed to the Chair at Glasgow he was called a 'new light'. On the other hand, it is important not to exaggerate the Scottishness of

all this. Hutcheson's main ideas were published before he took up the
Chair in Glasgow, and many of them are developed forms of the ideas
of Shaftesbury who in turn is influenced by Hellenic ideals. Moreover,
not dissimilar ideas were being worked out by Bishop Butler in England.
What Hutcheson undoubtedly did do, however, was to import these
progressive and liberal ideas into an oppressive institutional situation
and succeed by the inspiration of his teaching (and a certain amount of
behind-the-scenes political manoeuvring) in developing and spreading
them throughout Scotland. W. R. Scott sums up Hutcheson's achievement
as follows: 'That Hutcheson was a Philosopher of the Enlightenment
constitutes his chief claim upon posterity. This single title unites his
liberalising influence in the University, his efforts towards a higher
standard of culture among the clergy, and his eclectically popular type
of thought.'[8]

To this it must be added that more recent research has revealed the
international influence of Hutcheson in Europe and North America. This
influence included but extended beyond philosophy, law and economics
to affect actual social and political institutions. What in Hutcheson's
background and education enabled him to exert such an impressive and
lasting international influence?

Hutcheson's Life

Francis Hutcheson was born on 8 August 1694, in Drumalig in Northern
Ireland, the second son of John Hutcheson, an Irish Presbyterian minister
of Scottish parentage. Francis received a good classical education, and
when he was fourteen years old he was sent to Killyleagh in Co. Down
where there was a 'dissenting academy', i.e. an academy for those not
eligible for the Irish University. The death of his grandfather, Alexander,
eased the financial constraints on the Hutcheson family and in 1711
Francis matriculated at the University of Glasgow where he obtained an
MA. His subjects included classics, mathematics, moral philosophy and
logic. He then studied theology. On his return to Ireland in about 1717
he was licensed as a preacher. It cannot be said that he was an unqualified
success, mainly because he emphasised the benevolence of God, a doctrine
that did not appeal to the orthodox among the Irish Presbyterians.

It is reported in Stuart's *History of Armagh* that on an occasion when
he had replaced his indisposed father as a preacher one of the elders

complained to his, doubtless mortified, father as follows: 'We a' feel muckle wae for your mishap, Reverend Sir, but it canna be concealed. Your silly loon, Frank, has fashed a' the congregation wi' his idle cackle; for he has been babbling this 'oor aboot a gude and benevolent God, and that the sauls o' the heathens themsels will gang to Heeven, if they follow the licht o' their ain consciences. Not a word does the daft boy ken, speer, nor say aboot the gude auld comfortable doctrines o' election, reprobation, original sin and faith. Hoot mon, awa' wi' sic a fellow.'[9]

In the early 1720s Hutcheson began a career that was to prove much more congenial to his personality and appropriate to his intellectual gifts. He was invited to Dublin by a group of Presbyterians to run a 'dissenting academy' of the kind he himself had earlier attended. This period (1721–9) was the most productive, and perhaps the happiest, in Hutcheson's life. He was fortunate in becoming acquainted with Lord Molesworth and his circle, around 1722–3. Lord Molesworth was particularly interested in Lord Shaftesbury's works, and in Shaftesbury (Anthony Ashley Cooper, 3rd Earl of Shaftesbury) Hutcheson found a philosopher who was especially congenial to him. Through the Molesworth circle Hutcheson made several friends, such as Edward Synge, later Lord Bishop of Elphin, and James Arbuckle, essayist, with whom he discussed his work and whom he influenced. During the years 1725–8 he produced two works, each in two parts: *An Inquiry into the Original of Our Ideas of Beauty and Virtue* (London, 1725), and *An Essay on the Nature and Conduct of the Passions and Affections, with Illustrations on the Moral Sense* (London and Dublin, 1728). Hutcheson referred to *An Inquiry Concerning Beauty* as Treatise I, *An Inquiry Concerning Virtue* as Treatise II, *An Essay on the Passions* as Treatise III, and *Illustrations on the Moral Sense* as Treatise IV. He also published in the *Dublin Journal* in 1725–6 *Reflections upon Laughter* and *Remarks upon the Fable of the Bees*. These were a series of letters written under pseudonyms and reprinted in *Hibernicus's Letters* (1729).

Lord Molesworth died in 1725 and the breaking up of this circle seems to have removed the incentive to publish philosophy for Edward Synge and James Arbuckle. But Hutcheson was fortunate to have been taken up by a patron who was even more influential than Lord Molesworth. This was Lord Carteret, later Lord Granville, who became Lord Lieutenant of Ireland and was a man of wide reading and culture.

Dean Swift, who was the centre of Lord Carteret's Vice-Regal Court in Dublin, says of him that he had 'more Greek, Latin and Philosophy, than properly became a person of his rank'. Hutcheson's serious personality did not fit him for this circle, although he was appreciated by Carteret. During this period Hutcheson was introduced to Archbishop King, who defended Hutcheson against charges that he taught youth without subscribing to ecclesiastical canons.

In 1730 Hutcheson was invited to take up the Chair of Moral Philosophy at Glasgow University where he played an important part in liberalising the University, and became an influential teacher. His main writings at Glasgow were *A System of Moral Philosophy*, written around 1733–7, but published posthumously (London 1755), and his 'Compends' or works written in Latin and developed from his lectures. The most important of the 'Compends' was translated into English, probably by Hutcheson himself (Glasgow, 1747). All his works went through numerous editions in the eighteenth century and were translated into French and German.

As a Professor at Glasgow Hutcheson was much involved in committee work and in the numerous political intrigues of the various professorial factions. He was particularly concerned to improve the standards of teaching and to develop a humane Hellenic spirit of learning. Gradually, the liberalising influence of Hutcheson prevailed, especially after the appointments of William Leechman, Hutcheson's friend and later his biographer, as Professor of Divinity in 1743, and James Moor as Professor of Greek in 1746.

During his period in Dublin he had married a Miss Mary Wilson with whom he lived happily until his death on 8 August 1746 when he was on a visit to Dublin. He is buried in St Mary's Churchyard, Dublin. One child survived out of seven. He also was called Francis, became a physician and in 1760 Professor of Chemistry at Trinity College, Dublin. He was responsible for the posthumous publication of his father's *System*. He is also known as a composer of music, and some of his compositions are in the Library of Trinity College, Dublin.

Background to Hutcheson's Thought

The philosophical context in which Hutcheson was writing can be characterised both negatively and positively: he was reacting against certain sets of ideas and he was positively influenced by others. I shall begin with the ideas against which he was reacting and which he criticised. First there was the philosophy of Thomas Hobbes, which was seen as offering a radically egoistical view of human nature. The general run of subsequent thinking was against Hobbes, but he had one very successful follower – Bernard de Mandeville, whose *Fable of the Bees* (1714, 1723) was widely discussed in the eighteenth century. The theme of the book was that public benefits, such as prosperity, the arts, commerce and so on, are the result of private vices such as envy, fraud, and self-interest. The satirical nature of the book made it both widely accessible to the educated reader and an irritant to the high-minded philosopher. Hutcheson consistently attacks the ideas of Hobbes, stressing that human nature has benevolent as well as egoistic impulses.

The second set of ideas derived from the writings of the Rationalists, such as Samuel Clarke, William Wollaston, and later, Richard Price. They too opposed Hobbes but held that it could be shown by reason that morality was founded on the nature of things. Clarke, for example, used mathematical analogies and argued that rightness was 'fitting' to a situation in the same sort of way that two triangles might be congruent. Hutcheson devotes a great deal of his writings to criticising this position. Perhaps the clue to his own position is provided in William Leechman's biography prefacing the *System*. Leechman writes:

> It was his opinion in this early part of his life, and he never saw cause to alter it, that as some subjects from their nature are capable of demonstrative evidence, so others admit of only a probable one.

Morals was one of the subjects which admits of only probable reasoning and therefore the rationalists were to be rejected as unsound, and indeed dangerous to morality. (It is worth noting, however, that Hutcheson himself attempts in the first two editions of his *Inquiry* 'to introduce a mathematical calculation on subjects of morality'. But this is an attempt to use mathematics to work out the implications in complex situations of what the moral sense had already pronounced as right or wrong, rather than an attempt to establish an analogy between mathematical and moral truth.)

The third negative influence on Hutcheson, or ideas against which he was reacting, were the ideas of the Presbyterians. Presbyterianism in Scotland and Ireland was dominated by Calvinism, a doctrine with a pessimism about human nature exceeding that of Hobbes. According to the Westminster Confession of Faith (1647) human nature is 'disabled and made opposite to all Good, and wholly inclined to all Evil'. The believers in this doctrine were politically and institutionally powerful, and Hutcheson was obliged to proceed with caution in his opposition to it.

On the positive side and much more to Hutcheson's taste were the views of Shaftesbury (Anthony Ashley Cooper, 3rd Earl of Shaftesbury). Shaftesbury's main work, containing essays written over several years, was entitled *Characteristics of Men, Manners, Opinions, Times*, and in it he appeals to psychological experience as a foundation for morals. His psychology is quite different from that of Hobbes, however, in that he insists that we have social impulses which are expressed in our sense of benevolence, beauty, and justice, and that these are not reducible to self-interest, but form a harmonious system. Moreover, he holds that we have a 'reflex sense' which can reflect on our affections and passions, and in this context he introduces the term 'moral sense' which Hutcheson made central to his own thinking.

Another contemporary influence on Hutcheson was that of John Locke. Locke's epistemology is all-pervasive. For example, we shall see (p. 14) that there is a lack of clarity as to whether our idea of beauty is a Lockean primary or secondary quality. Hutcheson's later works have similarities to those of Joseph Butler but it is debatable whether Butler influenced Hutcheson or vice versa.

In addition to these contemporary philosophical ideas which were to provide the general context for Hutcheson's thinking we must remember that his own education was in the great classics of philosophy. He frequently acknowledges his debts to Cicero, Marcus Aurelius and Aristotle, and in his aesthetic writings he frequently quotes Horace. Indeed, in the portrait of Hutcheson by Allan Ramsay, Hutcheson is portrayed as holding a book by Cicero: *De Finibus* (*Concerning Ends*). This book stresses the importance of harmony among the elements of human nature, of society and of government. These ideas were central in Hutcheson's political and social thinking, and indeed to Allan Ramsay's approach to portrait painting.

The positive and negative influences I have so far mentioned were influences on Hutcheson as a mature philosopher but it is reasonable to consider the influences which might have affected him as an undergraduate at Glasgow University. The professor of moral philosophy who was in post when Hutcheson was a student was Gershom Carmichael (1672–1729). Carmichael belonged to the natural law tradition in moral philosophy of which Grotius, Pufendorf and Barbeyrac are the best-known exponents in the modern period. It is not clear whether Hutcheson attended Carmichael's lectures but he certainly later taught courses along the jurisprudential lines of Carmichael, which suggests the influence of his predecessor. Indeed, in his 'Compends' of 1742 (translated as *A Short Introduction to Moral Philosophy*) and in his posthumously published *System of Moral Philosophy* (1755), he tried unsuccessfully to combine the ideas of his Dublin moral sense writings with the natural law theories of writers such as Carmichael. He was aware of his failure to make a convincing synthesis, describing his *System* as a 'confused book'. Hence, while Carmichael may have had some influence on him, Hutcheson's preferred position – and his main contribution – is the one developed in Dublin and revised in his Glasgow periods. I shall now look in more detail at the works he wrote in his Dublin period.

Aesthetics

It is not difficult to present a superficial account of Hutcheson's aesthetics: 'the word beauty is taken for the idea raised in us, and a sense of beauty for our power of receiving this idea' (Treatise I, p. 10).* This invites the question of what quality in objects excites the idea of beauty. The answer which Hutcheson gives is that 'the figures which excite in us the ideas of beauty seem to be those in which there is uniformity amidst variety' (Treatise I, p. 15). At least, that is Hutcheson's account of absolute or original beauty, or 'that beauty which we perceive in objects without comparison to anything external' (Treatise I, p. 14). Hutcheson also recognises what he calls 'relative or comparative beauty' or 'that which we perceive in objects commonly considered as imitations or resemblances to something else' (Treatise I, p. 14).

* Page references are to this edition.

The greatest source of absolute or original beauty is nature, in which 'there is a surprising uniformity amidst an almost infinite variety' (Treatise I, p. 16). But absolute beauty can also be found in theorems of mathematics, in science or metaphysics, and in art thought of as pure form, especially in music which is the art nearest to pure form. A great deal of the beauty of art, however, is imitative. This is most clearly plausible of visual art but Hutcheson holds that it is true of literature, and even music has its imitative aspects. It has already been noted that Hutcheson was deeply read in Greek philosophy and his account of imitation is probably influenced by Plato, who held in the *Republic* that literature and even music can imitate qualities of character such as courage or cowardice. Hutcheson is probably also influenced in his doctrine of imitation by Aristotle's *Poetics*.

It should be noted that relative or imitative beauty can exist even where the original being imitated does not have absolute beauty. In other words, the beauty of what is relative or imitative consists in its *relation* to an original. Indeed, imitative beauty can exist even where the original is ugly or morally bad. As Hutcheson says 'we have more lively ideas of imperfect men with all their passions, than of morally perfect heroes such as really never occur to our observation, and of which consequently we cannot judge exactly as to their agreement with the copy' (Treatise I, p. 24). In this passage Hutcheson is consciously avoiding the temptation to judge art in terms of the morally didactic. His ideas have influenced Allan Ramsay in his paintings. Ramsay refers to Hogarth's example of a toad – the essence of ugliness – but a toad can be the subject of a beautiful painting, and indeed is beautiful in the eyes of the female toad.[10] Nevertheless, he is aware of the moral significance of art and beauty. This is apparent in his *Reflections upon Laughter* and Section VI of *An Inquiry Concerning the Original of Our Ideas of Virtue or Moral Good*. For example, in the third of the *Reflections upon Laughter* he discusses the morally good and bad uses of ridicule in writing and conversation, and in Section VI of *An Inquiry Concerning the Original of Our Ideas of Virtue or Moral Good* he links the 'external beauty of persons' with moral qualities. 'Let us consider the characters of beauty which are commonly admired in countenances, and we shall find them to be sweetness, mildness, majesty, dignity, veracity, humility, tenderness, good-nature . . .' (Treatise II, p. 104).

He is probably influenced by his classical background in this blurring
of the distinction between moral and aesthetic qualities in persons. The
Greek word *kalos* means 'beautiful' but it is also the chief adjective for
distinctively moral praise in our sense of moral. It expresses admiration,
especially of conduct which is courageous or gracious. Another Greek
word, *agathos*, means good in an everyday way, what we might regard
as 'decent behaviour'. In a roughly similar way an action in our culture
can sometimes be called beautiful if it is very praiseworthy. Indeed, in
the English language we have assorted terms which blur the distinction
between the good and the beautiful. For example, someone might be
said to have a 'nice face' or situations might be described as 'ugly'. In
such cases there is some ambiguity as to whether the judgement is one of
aesthetics or ethics. But the ambiguity goes deeper than language. Our
assumptions about someone's moral character are often affected by our
reactions to their appearance. This is the point Hutcheson is making.

It should also be noted that Hutcheson distinguished different
categories of beauty. Within the species of beauty there is (as we have
seen) absolute beauty and relative beauty or, as he also calls it, imitation.
But he also recognises harmony and design as forms of beauty. Indeed, he
goes wider than beauty in his identification of other species of aesthetic
appreciation, or 'the pleasures of the imagination' as the eighteenth
century often described aesthetic appreciation. For example, he follows
Addison (*Spectator*, No 142)* when Addison discusses 'Grandeur' and
'Novelty'. These are not forms of the idea of beauty because they are not
caused by the necessary 'unity amidst variety', but they have something
important in common with the sense of beauty – they are appreciated
for their own sakes. He therefore includes them as species of the genus
'aesthetic appreciation'. It is arguable that Hutcheson could also have
included appreciation of comedy in the genus of aesthetic appreciation.
If we stress the spontaneity of humour and its disinterested nature then
it could be included as a 'pleasure of the imagination'. But Hutcheson
did not so include it, perhaps because in the context in which he was
writing the *Reflections upon Laughter* he was concerned with criticising

---

* The *Spectator* was a periodical conducted by Joseph Addison and Richard Steele from 1711
to 1712. It appeared daily and its papers were mainly concerned with manners, morals and
literature.

Hobbes and with the usefulness and moral purposes of laughter, which distinguish it from the central cases of the 'pleasures of the imagination'.

In sum, then, Hutcheson distinguishes within the genus 'aesthetic experience' or 'the pleasures of the imagination' different species, such as 'grandeur', 'novelty' and 'beauty'. The species 'beauty' includes 'harmony', 'design', 'absolute beauty' and 'relative or imitative beauty', all of which are based on 'unity in variety'.

His views on the types of aesthetic experience may be summarised in a diagram as shown.

An evaluation of Hutcheson's aesthetics must proceed at two levels: it must consider the plausibility of his account of what produces the idea of beauty – our awareness of 'unity amidst variety'; and at a more abstract level it must consider whether he is convincing in suggesting that we have an aesthetic sense which apprehends the idea of beauty.

As regards the first point it might be questioned whether the idea of unity amidst variety is clear or at all developed as expressed by Hutcheson. It is a familiar neo-classic idea which derives from Aristotle. For Aristotle, art does not copy nature but rather it presents unified wholes as nature does. Works of art are structured in a manner comparable to

Aesthetic experience or 'the pleasures of the imagination'

| 'grandeur' | 'novelty' | 'beauty' |

| harmony | design | absolute beauty | relative or imitative beauty |

unity in variety

that exhibited by living things. Beauty for Aristotle is a matter of size and order. This idea, which is developed in Aristotle's *Poetics* (1450b 34–36), is the source of the neoclassic conception adopted by Hutcheson that beauty is unity amidst variety. But Hutcheson uses the criterion in a confused way, suggesting that 'unity' and 'variety' are two properties which can vary independently of each other. Thus he is led to reach the absurd conclusion (Treatise I, p. 15) that a square is more beautiful than a triangle because, although the two shapes equally display unity, the square has greater variety, presumably because it has more sides. But if 'unity in variety' is to be at all helpful in the explanation of aesthetic appreciation it must be regarded as in some complex way constitutive of our total experience of beauty; the units cannot helpfully be seen as independent variables which cause the idea in varying degrees.

Even if we ignore the problems attached to Hutcheson's use of the idea of 'unity amidst variety' there remains the question of whether Hutcheson stresses too much the formal side to beauty; painting, poetry and music have a content as well as a form. And what for Hutcheson is the pure or absolute beauty of sunsets, for example, impresses by striking colours rather than by any formal properties. Indeed, it is doubtful what sense can be attached to the idea of unity as applied to such objects as sunsets, unless one holds, as Hutcheson probably did, that sunsets are God's artefacts. It is interesting to note that Hutcheson himself seems also to use the test of 'liveliness' or 'passion' or the ability to arouse strong feelings as a criterion of beauty (Treatise I, p. 24), and this kind of criterion is perhaps more appropriate for such objects as sunsets than unity amidst variety.

Turning now to the more abstract level, we must assess Hutcheson's claim that there is an aesthetic sense which apprehends the idea of beauty. As has been indicated already, Hutcheson is influenced by Shaftesbury in his introduction of a special sense of beauty. By a 'sense' he means 'a determination of the mind, to receive any idea from the presence of an object which occurs to us independent on our will' (Treatise II, p. 71). We can call this the 'perceptual model' of aesthetic appreciation. Before exploring some of the ambiguities attached to the perceptual model we should note three undoubted merits which it possesses.

The first is that one important feature of aesthetic appreciation has been captured by the perceptual model (and as we shall see later, the same merit is to be found in the parallel account of the moral sense). That feature is the disinterested nature of aesthetic appreciation. When we survey a striking sunset or a great work of art we feel that some quality is being forced upon us 'independent on our will'. We are, as it were, taken out of ourselves. We should note that for Hutcheson aesthetic appreciation is *disinterested* for a second reason, namely that aesthetic objects – the various forms of beauty, along with the appreciation of grandeur and novelty – are enjoyed for their own sakes rather than for their consequences.

The third merit of the perceptual model is that it enables aesthetic appreciation to be depicted as basic to human nature. Insofar as our awareness of beauty is determined by a sense independent of our will then it must be an essential component of human nature. The eighteenth century strongly (and correctly) believed that there were some essential or universal features of human nature, and Hutcheson's perceptual model of aesthetic appreciation enables him to explain why our sense of beauty is one of these universal features.

Nevertheless there are at least two difficulties attached to Hutcheson's use of the perceptual model. The first concerns variations in the 'standard of taste', and the second concerns Hutcheson's use of John Locke's epistemological apparatus.

If there is an unchanging and universal nature which is the common ground for judgements of taste, how can there be variation in our judgements of what is beautiful? Hutcheson is fully aware of the fact that such variations exist, but he makes a familiar move to minimise the extent of variation. He admits that 'men may have different fancies of beauty' but explains that away by saying: 'yet uniformity be the universal foundation of our approbation of any form whatsoever as beautiful' (Treatise I, p. 35). In other words, the underlying standard of taste (uniformity amidst variety) is universal, but it may take different forms in different cultural contexts. There are merits in this familiar move, but the danger is that the standard of taste becomes trivialised because it becomes so general and diluted that any object or work can be said to possess 'unity amidst variety'.

The second move which Hutcheson makes to explain deviations from the 'standard of taste' is to invoke the doctrine of the association of ideas. This doctrine was used by Hobbes in *Leviathan* (1651) and John

Locke took up the idea in his *Essay Concerning Human Understanding* (4th edition, 1700). Hutcheson would be familiar with the doctrine as expressed by Hobbes and Locke, and he appeals to it as an explanation of 'the apparent diversity of fancies in the sense of beauty [which] makes men have an aversion to objects of beauty, and a liking to others void of it, but under different conceptions than those of beauty or deformity' (Treatise I, p. 36). In other words, if your first experience of the beauty of (say) the poetry of Wordsworth was in the classroom of a tyrannical teacher you may fail to appreciate its beauty because of its bad associations. Hutcheson in fact is suspicious of custom, association, and even education because they may obscure the universal aesthetic awareness which is part of our human nature. It should be noted here, although it belongs to the history of aesthetics in the later eighteenth century, that the doctrine of the association of ideas which is used by Hutcheson to explain *deviations* from the universal standard of taste was itself to become the *foundation* of taste in such writers as Joseph Priestly in the *Course of Lectures in Oratory and Criticism* (1777) and Archibald Alison in *Essays on the Nature and Principles of Taste* (1790).

The second difficulty which faces Hutcheson's perceptual model concerns its basis in Locke's epistemological apparatus. I shall say nothing about the difficulties in Locke's distinctions as such, although the interpretation of them is to this day controversial, but confine the discussion to the use Hutcheson makes of the distinction. It should be noted that similar issues arise for both the idea of beauty and the idea of moral good.

Locke holds that 'Whatsoever the mind perceives *in itself* or is the immediate object of perception, thought or understanding, that I call *idea*; and the power to produce any idea in our mind, I call *quality* of the subject wherein that power is.'[11] Locke then goes on to distinguish the ideas of primary and secondary qualities. Basically Locke's point seems to be that the ideas of primary qualities resemble the qualities in the objects which produce the ideas, while the ideas of secondary qualities do not resemble what produces them. For example, the idea of length resembles the actual quality of length in the object which produces the idea, whereas the ideas of cold, hot, sweet etc. are produced by qualities in the object (perhaps molecular motion) which do not resemble the ideas. Does Hutcheson hold that the idea of beauty is more like the idea of a primary or a secondary quality? The answer is by no means clear and Hutcheson is so ambiguous that he must be allowed to speak for himself:

> let it be observed that by absolute or original beauty is not understood any quality supposed to be in the object which should of itself be beautiful, without relation to any mind which perceives it. For beauty, like other names of sensible ideas, properly denotes the perception of some mind; so cold, hot, sweet, bitter, denote the sensations in our minds, to which perhaps there is no resemblance in the objects which excite these ideas in us, however we generally imagine otherwise. The ideas of beauty and harmony, being excited upon our perception of some primary quality, and having relation to figure and time, may indeed have a nearer resemblance to objects than these sensations, which seem not so much any pictures of objects as modifications of the perceiving mind; and yet, were there no mind with a sense of beauty to contemplate objects, I see not how they could be called beautiful. (Treatise I, p. 14)

I am not sure that in the end it is possible to derive a consistent position from Hutcheson's words, but a possible interpretation is as follows. The experience of beauty is a subjective experience, like a sweet taste, but there are features of the objective situation (perhaps 'unity amidst variety') which cause the idea or experience of beauty and which that idea in a way pictures or resembles.

The obscurity of Hutcheson's position is compounded by the fact that he frequently refers to beauty as a pleasure or as giving rise to a pleasure (Treatise I, pp. 10–12). A possible interpretation of Hutcheson's position on this issue, although others are possible, is that beauty and pleasure are not two ideas causally connected – it is not that the idea of beauty causes pleasure – but rather that one and the same idea (caused by 'unity amidst variety') can be described from two different points of view – as the idea of beauty or the idea of pleasure.

A final feature of Hutcheson's aesthetics should be noted: God provides the underpinning to many of the doctrines. For example, Hutcheson is not content to leave it as an ultimate fact about human nature that we find aesthetic pleasure in unity amidst variety. God has made us with the useful curiosity to find unity amidst the variety of creation. But this curiosity is the foundation of both scientific investigation and aesthetic appreciation. The pleasures of aesthetic appreciation and scientific inquiry are therefore united, thanks to the provision of a benevolent God.

Despite the many obscurities in Hutcheson's aesthetic writing his work has important merits: that he saw aesthetic awareness as some kind of pleasurable but disinterested feeling; that he distinguished different categories of beauty and more widely of aesthetic appreciation; that in a subtle rather than in a crude way, he saw the moral dimension to aesthetics; that he saw aesthetic appreciation as basic to human nature.

Moral Philosophy

Hutcheson recognises that there are three kinds of 'good', which he characterises as natural good – as in the possession of houses, lands, gardens, vineyards, health, strength and sagacity – aesthetic good – as in the appreciation of objects of beauty – and moral good – as in the possession of honesty, faith, generosity, kindness, and so on. These three kinds of good have some features in common: they are all pleasurable (and their opposites painful), judgements involving them are all immediately certain, involuntary or for us necessary, and in the end lacking in the possibility of rational justification. In other words, just as the sweetness of sugar is a taste forced on us immediately and involuntarily, because it is simply a fact about our nature that we so respond to its taste, so our judgements about aesthetic and moral good are immediate and involuntary expressions of the sort of nature we have as human beings. Of course, as we have seen in the preceding discussion of Hutcheson's aesthetics, it is possible for custom and association to distort the natural judgements that flow from universal human nature.

Hutcheson's position has several implications. First, if our judgements of moral good (or aesthetic good) are immediate and involuntary then they cannot be based on rational deliberation about what is in our own interests. In other words, positions such as those of Hobbes or Mandeville are ruled out, and Hutcheson is at pains to demonstrate that we can approve or disapprove in cases where our own interests are not at all affected. It might be thought that he has made a dangerous concession to philosophies of self-interest by his insistence that good of any kind is pleasurable. Does this mean that Hutcheson is some kind of egoistic hedonist? It does not. Hutcheson is insistent that the fact that we obtain pleasure from performing an action does not mean that we perform it in order to obtain the pleasure. We have certain natural inclinations and these are the primary springs of action, and in acting from these natural motives (such as benevolence) we obtain pleasure. It is simply an ultimate fact about human nature that we desire the good or well-being of our fellows and obtain pleasure when we act on these benevolent motives. Thus, Hutcheson rejects the views of Hobbes and Mandeville that human nature is driven only by motives of self-interest. It is also worth noting on this topic that he deserves some of the credit which is generally given to Bishop Butler (1692–1752) for exposing the basic weakness in psychological egoism.

The second implication of Hutcheson's position is that the theories of the rationalists must be rejected. Accordingly, Hutcheson devotes a great deal of argument to undermining the theories of several rationalists, such as Samuel Clarke (1675–1729) and William Wollaston (1659–1724). Clarke tries to argue, using mathematical analogies, that morally right actions 'fit' situations in a manner analogous to that in which geometrical shapes fit one another. But Hutcheson points out that 'fitness' is relative to a given end – 'compassion is fit to make others happy, and unfit to make others miserable' (Treatise IV, p. 141) – and Clarke is attempting to use it in an absolute way. Hutcheson notes the absurdity of the 'absolutely fit'. It is worth noting that the confusion Hutcheson is referring to exists in the modern obsession with physical fitness. People say 'I'm not fit', but what is the end? Someone may be fit to run for a bus but not to climb a mountain. 'Fitness' in any sphere is relative to an end and is not an absolute term. Wollaston offers another sort of rationalism in terms of which moral virtue in action is like truth in statements and vice like falsity in statements. Hutcheson again makes fun of this suggestion, pointing out that actions can sometimes imply what is not the case without there being anything morally amiss in the situation, as 'to leave lights in a lodge, to make people conclude there is a watch kept' (Treatise IV, p. 143).

The third implication of Hutcheson's position is that moral virtue and vice must be antecedent to the commands of God. We approve the ends proposed by the Deity because we judge Him to be our benefactor. In other words, some judgement of moral good is presupposed prior to our approbation of divine ends. It is worth noting that whereas Hutcheson's view, that our judgements of moral good and evil do not presuppose divine commands, would not now excite much controversy in any except the most extreme religious circles they were highly controversial at the time (Treatise II, pp. 110–11).

Having noted some of the negative implications of Hutcheson's moral philosophy, let us now turn to his positive development of it. The central thesis of Hutcheson's moral philosophy may be expressed in his own words: '. . . we shall find that all exciting reasons presuppose instincts and affections, and the justifying presuppose a moral sense' (Treatise IV, p. 131). Let us first consider what Hutcheson means by 'exciting reasons'. In other words, let us consider his theory of motivation.

Whereas Hutcheson is not altogether consistent in his usage he tends to distinguish between 'instincts', 'propensities', 'appetites', or 'passions' on the one hand, and 'affections' on the other. Basically, his view is that the first list identifies springs of action which do not presuppose a prior belief about good and evil in their objects, whereas the affections, of which the most important are desire and aversion, do presuppose prior beliefs about a good to be obtained or evil avoided. But belief or reason can never on their own motivate us to act; instincts and affections (or desires) are required. Some desires are passionate and others are calm. Among the calm desires are calm general desires, of which the most important are self-love and benevolence. Self-love is directed to the long-term happiness of the agent, and calm general benevolence is directed towards the general happiness. These then are the springs of action, the 'exciting reasons', and Hutcheson makes it clear that these instincts and affections are not reducible to self-interest, and that they arise from human nature.

Hutcheson seems to be on the whole correct here. Obviously there is a motive of calm self-interest, but there is also a motive of benevolence which is basic to human nature and is not reducible to self-interest. We can feel genuine benevolence for our children, for our friends, and on occasion for the sufferings of others. Indeed, as Hutcheson says, we want our family or friends or country to be happy after we are dead.

The second part of Hutcheson's central thesis in ethics is that 'justifying reasons presuppose a moral sense'. The idea of the moral sense he takes over from Shaftesbury, but it cannot be said that he has a consistent account of what he means by it. A 'sense' is 'a determination of the mind, to receive any idea from the presence of an object which occurs to us, independent on our will' (Treatise II, p. 71). It follows that a sense must involve some sort of capacity to be able to respond immediately without calculation. Hutcheson is probably correct in suggesting that we have this capacity to respond to voluntary actions immediately without regard to our own interests or pleasure. It is much less obvious that what Hutcheson is identifying is best described as a 'sense', and indeed he is ambiguous on what he does mean by a moral sense.

The moral sense is not needed to detect motives such as benevolence; they are detected in common-sense ways. It is 'justifying reasons' which presuppose the moral sense. In other words, the moral sense is needed to attribute moral approval and love for the agents of benevolent actions. Now, as we have seen in the previous section, Hutcheson draws upon Locke's epistemology in an ambiguous way when he discusses our sense of beauty, and the same problems arise again over the moral sense. His opening definition of moral goodness as 'our idea of some quality apprehended in actions, which procures approbation' (Treatise II, p. 67) is ambiguous as between Locke's idea of a primary quality and his idea of a secondary quality. In terms of the first interpretation Hutcheson would be saying that there is a quality in action necessarily connected with benevolence which produces approbation. Our idea would then be an idea of a special sort of primary quality. On the second interpretation, the idea which procures approbation is simply benevolence itself, and it is just a fact about human nature that our idea of this benevolence procures approbation, just as it is a fact about human nature that a certain movement of molecules produces the taste of sweetness. It is plausible to argue that the second interpretation is what Hutcheson intended. For example, he argues:

> The perception of approbation or disapprobation arises in the observer, according as the affections of the agent are apprehended kind in their just degree, or deficient, or malicious. This approbation cannot be supposed

an image of anything external, more than the pleasures of harmony, of taste, of smell. (Treatise IV, p. 146)

In other words, the prevailing tendency of Hutcheson's writing suggests that the perception of moral goodness by the moral sense is simply the experience of the pleasurable feeling of approbation. The dominant strand in his thinking is therefore better characterised in terms of moral sentiments than a moral sense. But it must always be remembered that Hutcheson is not consistent on this, especially in the *System*, where we find passages such as the following:

> when we admire the virtue of another, the whole excellence, or that quality which by nature we are determined to approve, is conceived to be in that other; we are pleased in the contemplation because the object is excellent, and the object is not judged to be therefore excellent because it gives us pleasure. (*System*, p. 149)

Doubts therefore remain as to whether Hutcheson had a consistent position.

Ambiguity of the kind just discussed has contributed to the contemporary revival of interest in Hutcheson. In particular, there has been discussion as to whether or not Hutcheson is what is called a 'moral realist' and whether or not he is a 'cognitivist'. Interesting and illuminating books and articles have been written on such questions and they certainly succeed in presenting Hutcheson in new ways. I shall not discuss such interpretations here, however, for they suffer from a serious disadvantage – that they discuss Hutcheson in terms of terminology which is itself as ambiguous as Hutcheson's own discussion. Thus, terms such as 'moral realist' or 'quasi-realist' or 'cognitivist' and 'non-cognitivist' are themselves radically unclear and subject to controversy in philosophical journals, so it is not necessarily helpful to speculate about whether Hutcheson was, say, a moral realist. As Hutcheson's contemporary, Bishop Berkeley, put it, 'we have first raised a dust, and then complain we cannot see'.[12]

We have seen that the features of action which produce our approbation or are 'justifying reasons' are ultimately benevolent motives or actions. But Hutcheson includes three different sorts of motivation under the heading of benevolence:

> Sometimes it denotes a calm, extensive affection, or good-will toward all beings capable of happiness or misery; sometimes, 2. a calm deliberate affection of the soul toward the happiness of certain smaller systems of individuals; . . . or, 3. the several kind particular passions of love, pity, sympathy, congratulation. (Treatise II, p. 88)

Hutcheson suggests that the first kind, 'universal benevolence', as he calls it, is the proper object of the moral sense and he supports this view with an explicitly utilitarian argument which enables him to employ a procedure to decide between competing claims if the types of benevolence were to conflict. He writes:

> In comparing the moral qualities of actions, in order to regulate our election among various actions proposed, or to find which of them has the greatest moral excellency, we are led by our moral sense of virtue to judge thus; that in equal degrees of happiness, expected to proceed from the action, the virtue is in proportion to the number of persons to whom the happiness shall extend (and here the dignity, or moral importance of persons, may compensate numbers); and in equal numbers, the virtue is as the quantity of the happiness, or natural good; or that the virtue is in a compound ratio of the quantity of good, and number of enjoyers . . . so that the action is best, which procures the greatest happiness for the greatest numbers; and that worst, which, in like manner, occasions misery. (Treatise II, p. 90)

Here we have what seems to be the first fully explicit articulation of the utilitarian doctrine, and, moreover, a formulation which shows a full appreciation of the possibility of its quantitative development. It cannot be over-emphasised that it was Hutcheson rather than Hume, Bentham or any other philosopher who explicitly formulated the principle of utility with a full understanding of its implications.

Indeed, Hutcheson went further and revealed the significance of what more recently has come to be known as 'rule utilitarianism'. Thus, Hutcheson introduces the concept of rights:

Whenever it appears to us, that a faculty of doing, demanding, or possessing any thing, universally allowed in certain circumstances, would on the whole tend to the general good, we say, that one in such circumstances has a right to do, possess, or demand that thing. (Treatise II, p. 112. See also pp. 90–1.)

In a familiar manner, although it is familiar only because later philosophers took up Hutcheson's ideas, he distinguishes between 'perfect rights', or those absolutely necessary to the public good, and 'imperfect rights', or those not absolutely necessary to the public good. These distinctions enable Hutcheson to explain many moral phenomena which do not immediately seem to be directly approved by the moral sense. Thus, he uses the indirect connection with the public good to explain rights to commerce, contracts, promises, marriage and others. Hutcheson's view, then, is that ultimately 'justifying reasons' refer to benevolent motives, and especially to those benevolent motives which involve 'universal benevolence', although there can be justifications referring to rights which are themselves justified in terms of public good. Hutcheson should be given much credit for this explicit and complex formulation of utilitarianism.

But does Hutcheson think that benevolent motives are reasons for approval, or that they cause approval? It cannot be said that he clearly distinguishes these two positions, but there is a case for saying that his position is nearer the latter than the former. The case consists firstly in the many passages in which he suggests the causal interpretation. For example 'what reason makes us approve the happiness of a system? Here we must recur to a sense or kind affections' (Treatise IV). Again, 'Or what end can be proposed, without presupposing instincts, desires, affections, or moral sense, it will not be easy to explain' (Treatise IV, p. 147). Hutcheson seems to be saying that it is simply a fact about human nature that we have certain instincts and affections, and that it is similarly a fact that we experience the unique pleasure of approbation when we perceive benevolent actions or good consequences. Certainly, this was the interpretation which Hume gave to Hutcheson; but it must be stressed again that Hutcheson does not consistently take this line.

There is a second argument for interpreting Hutcheson in this way: such an interpretation enables him to link 'exciting reasons' and 'justifying

reasons'. There is a possible view in moral philosophy in terms of which
a judgement of moral rightness is one thing and a reason or motivation
to act another. Hutcheson criticises the rationalists for adopting this
view, and so failing to show how our rational apprehension of fitness
and unfitness can motivate us to act (Treatise IV, pp. 129–31). In other
words, Hutcheson is criticising the rationalists for failing to link moral
judgement and action. But if we take Hutcheson to be inclining towards
the causal interpretation of the moral sense then we can see how he
would solve the difficulty he raises for the rationalists: the 'justification'
produced by the moral sense is in the end no more than the experience of
a certain sort of pleasurable approbation, and insofar as it is pleasurable
it will give rise to a desire to act in a certain manner. In linking 'exciting
reasons' and 'justifying reasons' in this way Hutcheson has provided a
plausible account of how moral approbation, or moral judgements, can
be practical or lead to action. The theory he provides is once again an
anticipation of the theory which Hume later adopts.

Hutcheson's account of moral motivation is confusing in that his
terminology is not consistent. It therefore may be helpful to provide a
diagram which offers a way of simplifying it and also connects motivation
with (what Hutcheson considers to be) justification.

How successful is Hutcheson's moral philosophy? There are many
ambiguities in all his works and possible inconsistencies between earlier
works and the later, but leaving these aside we have a theory with many
merits. He successfully distinguishes natural, aesthetic, and moral
good, and succeeds against Hobbes and Mandeville in establishing the
disinterested nature of moral judgements. Again, he provides a vigorous
and sustained attack on rationalism which is in the main persuasive.
Another achievement, a major one, is his formulation of utilitarianism
with a full awareness of how it can be developed, for example by
accommodating rights within it. In the end, therefore, Hutcheson's moral
theory has the merits and drawbacks of utilitarianism. For example, it has
the drawback of engulfing the whole of the moral life in the production
of happiness, or of attempting to make the one concept – benevolence –
include the whole of virtue. To take just one case of the distorting effect
of Hutcheson's analysis, he tries to analyse gratitude into benevolence
(Treatise II, pp. 100–01). Now, of course, gratitude may include a feeling
of benevolence, but clearly it includes other elements which are not

Hutcheson's Account of Motivation
and its necessary connection with the moral sense

'Exciting reasons presuppose instincts and affections and
the justifying presuppose a moral sense'
(TREATISE IV, p.131)

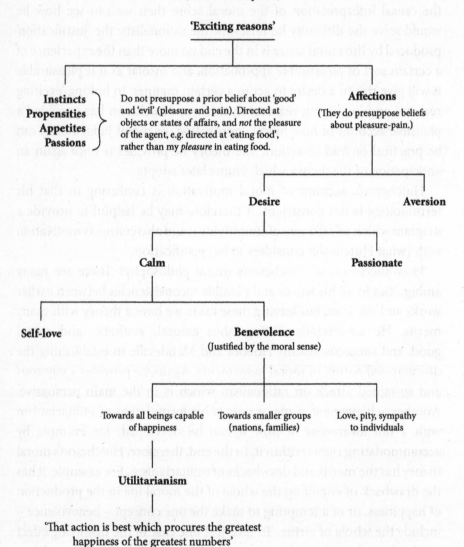

'Exciting reasons'

**Instincts
Propensities
Appetites
Passions** }
Do not presuppose a prior belief about 'good'
and 'evil' (pleasure and pain). Directed at
objects or states of affairs, and *not* the pleasure
of the agent, e.g. directed at 'eating food',
rather than my *pleasure* in eating food.

Affections
(They do presuppose beliefs
about pleasure-pain.)

Desire   **Aversion**

Calm   **Passionate**

Self-love   **Benevolence**
(Justified by the moral sense)

Towards all beings capable
of happiness

Towards smaller groups
(nations, families)

Love, pity, sympathy
to individuals

Utilitarianism

'That action is best which procures the greatest
happiness of the greatest numbers'
(p.90)

reducible to benevolence, such as a desire or an obligation to make a just requital for a favour. Hutcheson rightly criticises Hobbes for the distortions which result from the attempt to analyse every motive into self-interest, but he himself is guilty of at least some distortion in his attempt to show that benevolence is the whole of virtue. It may be that underlying Hutcheson's philosophical analysis of morality there remains the Christian ethic with which he had been brought up. Nevertheless, his achievements in moral philosophy are enormous and his contributions, which were admired very much by his contemporaries and successors in the eighteenth century, are due to be re-assessed.

Jurisprudence, Politics and Economics

Hutcheson is celebrated among philosophers for his aesthetics and ethics, but no less an authority on eighteenth-century Scotland than Professor Caroline Robbins claims that 'Hutcheson's most original contribution to eighteenth-century thought was undoubtedly made in the field of politics'.[13] Certainly, as we shall see in the next section, his main influence on North America was a political one. His major contributions to politics, jurisprudence and economics were made during his Glasgow period and are contained in his *System of Moral Philosophy* and in his *Short Introduction to Moral Philosophy*. There is little difference between the doctrines of the two works on politics, jurisprudence and economics, and I have extracted sections on Politics and Jurisprudence from the *Short Introduction* and sections on Politics and Economics from the *System*. The application of his general social theory to practical problems is very clear and simply argued. This may be partly because, as the Preface to the *Short Introduction* says, the work is not for the learned but for those anxious to study and discover the way of life which right reason requires. The social theory of the *System* is also clearly stated.

The key to Hutcheson's politics is his philosophical assumption that there must be a balance between natural liberty and natural law, and that this balance can be achieved by the principle of utility, or 'calm benevolence' directed to mankind in general and perceived by the moral sense:

. . . it was then right and just that any person should act, possess, or demand from others, in a certain manner, when his doing so tended either directly to the common interest of all, or to the interest of some part or some individual without occasioning any detriment to others. And hence we say in such cases that a man has a right thus to act, possess or demand. (*Short Introduction*, p. 155)

He distinguishes between the *precept* of a law – what is required or forbidden – and the *sanction* – the rewards or punishments. There are further distinctions between natural laws – discovered by reason – and positive laws – revealed only in writing. Some laws are more necessary than others for the survival of a society. Hutcheson makes an interesting jurisprudential point about law when he contrasts equity with strict law. The function of equity is 'the reasonable wise correction of any imperfection in the words of the law' (*Short Introduction*, p. 158). In other words, equity is a second order principle regulating the application of law in the light of reason.

Having provided us with an outline of his theory of law Hutcheson proceeds to consider the nature of rights. He devotes a good deal of attention to rights, presumably because it is through rights that natural law – God's will for his creatures – receives its practical application. He starts off firmly with what has become known as 'the liberal theory of rights':

> . . . all actions by which any one procures to himself or his friends any advantage, while he obstructs no advantage of others, must be lawful . . . we therefore deem that each man has a right to obtain for himself or his friends such advantages and enjoyments . . . which right is plainly established . . . by the general precept . . . enjoining and confirming whatever tends to the general good of all. (*Short Introduction*, pp. 160–1)

Now there is a certain ambiguity here, an ambiguity which is found in some other liberal political philosophers. Is Hutcheson justifying rights in terms of general utility or is he adhering to some version of natural rights theory? The passage just quoted sounds utilitarian, but further on in chapter 2 Hutcheson puts forward a view which is much more suggestive of the pure theory of natural rights:

> A right therefore may be defined, 'a faculty or claim established by law to act, or possess, or obtain something from others'; tho' the primary

notion of right is prior to that of a law, nor does it always include a reference to the most extensive interest of the whole of mankind. For by our natural sense of right and wrong, and our sympathy with others, we immediately approve any persons procuring to himself or his friends any advantages which are not hurtful to others, without any thought either about a law or the general interest of all. (*Short Introduction*, pp. 161–2)

In other contexts, however, Hutcheson comes down squarely in the utilitarian camp:

. . . no private right can hold against the general interest of all. For a regard to the most extensive advantage of the whole system ought to control and limit all the rights of individuals or of particular societies. (*Short Introduction*, p. 162)

This is what we might expect from the utilitarian tone of the *Inquiry Concerning Virtue*.

Following the distinctions he made in the *Inquiry*, he reminds us of the difference between perfect and imperfect rights, but more interesting is his distinction between rights which are alienable, and such as cannot be alienated or transferred. Alienable rights are those 'where the transfer can actually be made, and where some interest of society may often require that they should be transferred . . . Unless both these qualities concur, the right is to be deemed inalienable . . .' (*Short Introduction*, p. 164). There is an interesting conceptual question as to whether it is logically possible both to maintain utilitarianism and inalienable rights. This is another aspect of the ambiguity throughout Hutcheson's political philosophy as to whether he is a utilitarian or a natural rights theorist. But even if we decide that in the end he is a utilitarian it is the natural rights strand that exerted most influence in the American colonies. Thus, in his account of the State Hutcheson maintains a contract theory and is quite explicit about the natural right to rebellion if the contract is not kept (*System*, p. 195).

Natural liberty appears again when Hutcheson discusses the natural rights of the individual. The state of natural liberty, is 'that of those who are subjected to no human power' (p. 165).

Unlike Hobbes, Hutcheson holds that the state of nature is one of peace and goodwill. Moreover, in the state of nature 'all men are originally equal, and these natural rights equally belong to all' (*Short Introduction*, p. 168). Even a servant 'is to retain all the rights of mankind... excepting only that to his labours, which he has transferred to his master' (*System*, p. 189). And the slavery of the ancient world was 'horridly unjust' (*System*, p. 190). Hutcheson then goes on to use familiar considerations to persuade us of the advantages of political society (*Short Introduction*, p. 156; *System*, p. 191).

Another theme which occupies his political thought is *property*, which is a *real* as distinct from a *personal* right. Real rights terminate upon some certain definite goods, whereas personal rights terminate upon some person. The principal real right, he tells us, is property. Property can be original or derived. On the whole Hutcheson puts forward a balanced view of the acquisition and nature of property, using strictures like the following: 'that the natural fruits of no man's honourable or innocent labours should be intercepted' (*Short Introduction*, p. 171). While not opposing colonialism as such, Hutcheson sets limits to it. He makes the point that there cannot be a property right in an extensive territory held by only a small number of people. 'Nothing can be more opposite to the general good of mankind than that the rights, independency, and liberty of many neighbouring nations should be exposed to be trampled upon by the pride, luxury, ambition, or avarice of any nation' (*Short Introduction*, p. 173). Music to the ears of the settlers in North America! He sums up his theory of property as follows:

> Full property originally contains these several rights: first, that of retaining possession, 2. and next, that of taking all manner of use, 3. that also of excluding others from any use, 4., and lastly, that of transferring to others as the proprietor pleases ... But property is frequently limited by civil laws, and frequently by the deeds of some former proprietors (*Short Introduction*, p. 176; *System*, p. 193)

Hutcheson devotes a large chapter of the *Short Introduction* to the analysis of contracts. Contracts are necessary for commerce and social life generally. Hutcheson then draws a distinction which has passed into the literature of moral philosophy:

> We must distinguish from the contracts the bare declaration of our
> future intentions; which neither transfer any right to others nor bind us
> ... (*Short Introduction*, p. 178)

More controversially Hutcheson distinguishes contracts proper from
'imperfect promises' which are binding only if the promisee is worthy of
the favour to be bestowed, and does not forfeit favour by bad conduct.

The bindingness of contracts proper relates to two conditions:
the understanding and the will. Thus, minors cannot be expected to
understand contracts. Voluntary consent is the other condition for valid
contracts. One important source of invalid contracts, Hutcheson says, is
fear. There are two sorts of fear: fear that the other party will not fulfil his
side of the bargain, and fear of some evil threatened. As far as the first
sort of fear is concerned, there can be dispute as to whether the fearful
party contracted knowing that he was contracting with unjust men. But
Hutcheson is clear that contracts entered into with bad people are still
valid, because if they were not that 'would destroy all faith among men'.
He provides a detailed discussion of various cases of duress – when
the other contracting party threatens me, or when a third party does.
Hutcheson's discussion of contracts and duress here, in the subtlety and
clarity of the distinctions, compares favourably with Hume's celebrated
account of promises (*A Treatise of Human Nature*, III, II, V).

Contracts are also perceived by Hutcheson as forming the basis of
civil government. In fact, Hutcheson recognises 'three different acts
of a whole people': a contract to form a society, a decree deciding the
constitution, and a contract between the governors and the people
(*System*, p. 192). He discusses different forms of constitution and how
far the rights of governors extend (*System*, p. 195). Significantly, there is
a right of the people to rebel (*System*, p. 195).

Hutcheson's discussion of economic questions is found in several
chapters in the *System of Moral Philosophy* and the *Short Introduction
to Moral Philosophy* (see for example, pp. 170–6), but the greatest
concentration of economic discussion is in chapter XII of Book II of
the *System*. In particular, there is a discussion of value, by which Adam
Smith, who attended Hutcheson's lectures, has clearly been greatly
influenced. Hutcheson distinguishes the demand side and the supply
side as they affect value. He begins from the premise that 'The natural

ground of all value or price is some sort of use which goods afford in life; this is prerequisite to all estimation . . . prices depend on these two [factors], the demand, and the difficulty of acquiring, or cultivating for human use' (*System*, p. 198). In his discussion of supply Hutcheson argues that value is affected by such factors as the kind of labour involved, the materials used, the skill of the artist, rent, remuneration and interest. The introduction of precious metals and, later, coinage is explained by the need to have a common measure of exchange. The rest of the chapter is largely taken up with discussing the problems of the debasement of coinage.

No less an authority than Edwin Cannan has claimed in the Introduction to his edition of *The Wealth of Nations* that 'Probably it is in this chapter that the germ of *The Wealth of Nations* is to be found.'[14] This claim is certainly highly plausible and would in itself justify a study of Hutcheson's economics. But Hutcheson's economic thought also has an interest in its own right.

Notes to the Introduction

1. A. N. Prior, *Logic and the Basis of Ethics*, Oxford, Clarendon Press, 1956, p. 31.

2. Norman Kemp Smith, *The Philosophy of David Hume*, London, Macmillan, 1941, p. 13.

3. David Hume, *Enquiry Concerning Human Understanding* (1748), ed. L. A. Selby-Bigge, Oxford University Press, 1902, sect. VII, Part 1.

4. Adam Smith, *The Theory of Moral Sentiments* (6th edn 1790), Oxford, Clarendon Press, 1976, VII, iii, 3.

5. Immanuel Kant, *Critique of Practical Reason* (1788), trans. and ed. L. W. Beck, Chicago, IL, University of Chicago Press, 1949, p. 28.

6. David Fate Norton, 'Francis Hutcheson in America' in *Studies on Voltaire and the Eighteenth Century*, ed. Theodore Besterman, vol. CCIV, Geneva, Institut et musée Voltaire, 1976, pp. 1547–68.

7. N. Fiering, *Moral Philosophy at Seventeenth-Century Harvard*, Chapel Hill, NC, University of North Carolina Press, 1981, p. 199.

8. W. R. Scott, *Francis Hutcheson*, Cambridge, Cambridge University Press, 1900, p. 285.

9. James Stuart, *Historical Memoirs of the City of Armagh*, Dublin, Browne and Nolan, 1910, ch. 33.

10. Allan Ramsay, *A Dialogue on Taste* (1762), Kessinger Publishing, 2010, pp. 29ff.

11. John Locke, *Essay Concerning Human Understanding* (1690), London, Dent, 1976, II, viii, 8.

12. George Berkeley, *A Treatise Concerning the Principles of Human Knowledge* (1710), London, Dent, 1975, Introduction, sect. 3.

13. Caroline Robbins, *The Eighteenth-Century Commonwealthman,* Cambridge, MA, Harvard University Press, 1961, p. 188.

14. Edwin Cannan, Introduction, *The Wealth of Nations*, Oxford, Clarendon Press, 1896, p. xxvi.

NOTE ON THE TEXTS AND PRINCIPLES OF THE SELECTION

Hutcheson's main writings can be placed in two groups: his Dublin and his Glasgow writings. His Dublin writings were completed in a short time (1725–8), and were revised by him throughout his life. I have made my major selections from these works. They are:

Treatise I: *An Inquiry Concerning Beauty, Order, Harmony, Design*
Treatise II: *An Inquiry Concerning the Original of Our Ideas of Virtue or Moral Good*
Treatise III: *An Essay on the Nature and Conduct of the Passions and Affections*
Treatise IV: *Illustrations on the Moral Sense*

The first two were published together as *An Inquiry into the Original of Our Ideas of Beauty and Virtue* (London, 1725). My selections are from the revised 4th edition, 1738. Treatises III and IV were published together as *An Essay on the Nature and Conduct of the Passions, with Illustrations on the Moral Sense* (London and Dublin, 1728). My selections are from the 3rd edition, 1742.

In view of the importance of Hutcheson in the history of aesthetics I have added from the Dublin period *Reflections upon Laughter*, published in the *Dublin Journal* 1725–6 as a series of letters written under pseudonyms and reprinted in *Hibernicus's Letters*, 1729. My selections are from the 4th edition (Glasgow, 1750).

It is much harder to reach a decision on the writings of the Glasgow period. The *System of Moral Philosophy* was written 1733–7 but Hutcheson himself did not publish it and dismisses it as a 'confused book . . . a farrago'.* I have therefore selected from it only a token passage

---

* Letter to Mr Thomas Drennan, 15 June 1741 (Glasgow University Library MS Gen. 1018, item 8).

of moral philosophy, but larger (and important) passages on political philosophy and on economics. These are taken from the posthumous first edition, Glasgow, 1755. I have also selected extracts on jurisprudence and political philosophy from *A Short Introduction to Moral Philosophy*. This was a 'compend' of his lectures and it is probable that Hutcheson translated it into English himself. It illustrates the Stoic influence on his later thought, especially on his legal and political philosophy. I have taken selections from the first edition, Glasgow, 1747.

Since Hutcheson's thought is of interest to a range of eighteenth-century specialists I have grouped the selections in terms of subject matter rather than chronologically. In all cases the spelling has been modified and italics and initial capital letters have been reduced. Some of Hutcheson's footnotes have been omitted. Editorial footnotes are enclosed in square brackets. Three asterisks in the text indicate that material has been omitted from the original.

CHRONOLOGY OF HUTCHESON'S LIFE

Year	Age	Life
1694		8 August, birth of Francis Hutcheson at Drumalig. Lives with family at Ballyrea, two miles from Armagh
1702	8	With elder brother Hans goes to stay with Alexander Hutcheson, their grandfather, and obtains a good classical education at Saintfield Old School (a 'dissenting school')
1708	14	Attends 'dissenting academy' at Killyleagh, Co. Down

CHRONOLOGY OF HUTCHESON'S TIMES

Year	Cultural Context	Historical Events
1685	Birth of Bishop George Berkeley. Births of J. S. Bach and G. F. Handel	
1687	Isaac Newton, *Principia*	
1688		'Glorious Revolution'
1689		Accession of William III and Mary II. Highlanders win Battle of Killiecrankie
1690	John Locke, *Essay Concerning Human Understanding*	Establishment of Presbyterianism
1692	Birth of Joseph Butler, Bishop of Durham	Massacre at Glencoe of the Macdonalds by a Campbell regiment to whom they had given hospitality
1694	Birth of Voltaire	
1698		Darien expedition
1702		Accession of Queen Anne
1704		Marlborough's victory at Blenheim
1707	Birth of Thomas Fielding	Act of Union of Scotland and England
1708		Abolition of the Scottish Privy Council
1709	Bishop Berkeley, *An Essay Towards a New Theory of Vision* Birth of Samuel Johnson	Battle of Pultava – Peter the Great of Russia defeats Charles XII of Sweden

Year	Age	Life
1711	17	Death of Alexander Hutcheson (grandfather). Matriculates at Glasgow University, and studies Arts
1713	19	Begins study of Theology at Glasgow University
1717	23	Leaves Glasgow University. Tutor to the Earl of Kilmarnock. Returns to Ireland
1719	25	Licensed as a probationer in Armagh
1721 or 1722	27	Opens a 'dissenting academy' in Dublin
1722–23	28–29	Meets Lord Molesworth, a devotee of Shaftesbury, and is introduced to Edward Synge, friend of Bishop Berkeley
1724	30	James Arbuckle joins the Molesworth Circle, becomes an associate of Hutcheson and later of Swift
1725	31	Marries Miss Mary Wilson. Publication of *An Inquiry into the Original of our Ideas of Beauty and Virtue* (London). Is introduced to Archbishop King

Year	Cultural Context	Historical Events
1710	Birth of Thomas Reid Bishop Berkeley, *A Treatise Concerning the Principles of Human Knowledge*	
1711	Birth of David Hume Shaftesbury, *Characteristics of Men, Manners, Opinions, Times*. Alexander Pope, *Essay on Criticism*. Addison and Steele found the *Spectator*	Accession of Emperor Charles VI of the Holy Roman Empire
1712	Birth of Jean-Jacques Rousseau	Patronage Act: recreated lay patronage, a direct affront to the power of the Kirk Birth of Frederick the Great
1713	Death of Lord Shaftesbury Birth of Allan Ramsay, painter of Hutcheson's portrait	Treaty of Utrecht (ending war involving Western and Central Europe and American colonies)
1714	Publication of *The Fable of Bees*	Death of Queen Anne; accession of George I
1715		First Jacobite Rebellion in Scotland. Accession of Louis XV of France
1716	Death of Gottfried Leibniz	
1719		Toleration Act
1720		'South Sea Bubble'
1721	Birth of Tobias Smollett	Sir Robert Walpole Prime Minister (until 1742): Whig policy of moderation
1723	Birth of Adam Smith	
1724	Birth of Immanuel Kant Death of William Wollaston	
1725	Death of Lord Molesworth	Accession of Catherine I of Russia Treaty of Vienna between Austria and Spain

Year	Age	Life
1725–6	31–32	*Reflections upon Laughter* and *Remarks on the Fable of the Bees* published in the *Dublin Journal*
1726	32	Associates with the Vice-Regal Court of Lord Carteret, Lord Lieutenant of Ireland
1728	34	*Essay on the Nature and Conduct of the Passions, with Illustrations on the Moral Sense* (London and Dublin). Correspondence with Gilbert Burnet in the *London Journal*
1729	35	Death of father, John Hutcheson ('the best friend I have in the world'). Elected to Chair of Moral Philosophy at Glasgow University
1730	36	Takes up Chair at Glasgow University; inaugural lecture, *De Naturali Hominum Socialitate*
1733–7	39–43	Composition of *A System of Moral Philosophy*
1735	41	*Considerations on Patronage Addressed to the Gentlemen of Scotland*
1737	43	Prosecuted (unsuccessfully) by the Presbytery of Glasgow for contravening the Westminster Confession

Year	Cultural Context	Historical Events
1726	*Fifteen Sermons*, Bishop Butler (preached at Rolls Chapel) Jonathan Swift, *Gulliver's Travels*	
1727	Act abolishing medieval system of Regents and introducing modern professorial system	Death of George I; accession of George II
1728	Birth of Robert Adam, architect John Gay, *The Beggar's Opera*	
1728–9	John Balguy, *The Foundations of Moral Goodness*, Parts 1 and 2	
1729	Death of Samuel Clarke. Death of Gershom Carmichael, Professor of Moral Philosophy, Glasgow University and Hutcheson's predecessor	Treaty of Seville between Britain and Spain
1730	John and Charles Wesley found Methodism	Accession of Anne of Russia
1731	Ralph Cudworth, *Treatise Concerning Eternal and Immutable Morality*	Treaty of Vienna between Britain, Holland, Spain and Austria
1732	Birth of F. J. Haydn	
1733–4	Pope, *Essay on Man*	Outbreak of War of Polish Succession
1736	Bishop Butler, *Dissertation on the Nature of Virtue*	Law punishing witchcraft with death repealed by Westminster
1739–43	Correspondence between Hume and Hutcheson: Hume's *Treatise*	'War of Jenkins' Ear' against Spain
1740		Accession of Frederick II (the Great) of Prussia, and of Maria Theresa of Austria

Year	Age	Life
1742	48	*The Meditations of Marcus Aurelius,* translated from the Greek (in conjunction with James Moor). *Compendiaria* ('compends' of lecture material on ethics, jurisprudence and metaphysics)
1745	51	Declines offer of Chair of Moral Philosophy at Edinburgh University
1746	52	Visits Dublin, contracts fever and dies 8 August
1747		'Compends' published in English as *A Short Introduction to Moral Philosophy in Three Books, containing the Elements of Ethics and the Law of Nature*
1755		*A System of Moral Philosophy* published by his son Francis Hutcheson, MD, with a biography by William Leechman, Professor of Divinity at Glasgow University
1759		*Logicae Compendium*

Year	Cultural Context	Historical Events
1741	Handel, *Messiah*	
1741–2	Hume, *Essays Moral and Political*	
1742		Accession of Emperor Charles VII of the Holy Roman Empire
1743	Robert Foulis appointed University Printer. Election of Hutcheson's liberal colleague William Leechman to the Chair of Divinity, Glasgow University	Britain, Austria and Sardinia sign Treaty of Worms (against France)
1745		Second Jacobite Uprising
1746	James Moor elected Professor of Greek, Glasgow University	Charles Edward Stuart defeated at Culloden
1748	Charles Montesquieu, *Esprit des lois*	War of Austrian Succession ends with Peace of Aix-la-Chapelle
1750	Death of Bach	
1753	Death of Bishop Berkeley	
1754		War between French and British in America
1755	Publication of Dr Johnson's *Dictionary*	
1756	Birth of W. A. Mozart	Beginning of Seven Years' War
1759	Smith, *The Theory of Moral Sentiments*. Death of Handel	Battle of Minden British capture Quebec

PREFACE TO THE TWO INQUIRIES

(First printed 1725; reprinted here from the revised
4th edition, 1738)

AESTHETICS

TREATISE I: AN INQUIRY CONCERNING
BEAUTY, ORDER, HARMONY, DESIGN

(First printed 1725; reprinted here from the revised
4th edition, 1738)

REFLECTIONS UPON LAUGHTER

(First printed in the *Dublin Journal* 1725–6; reprinted here
from the 4th edition, 1750)

PREFACE TO THE TWO INQUIRIES

There is no part of philosophy of more importance than a just knowledge of human nature and its various powers and dispositions. Our late inquiries have been very much employed about our understanding, and the several methods of obtaining truth. We generally acknowledge that the importance of any truth is nothing else than its moment, or efficacy to make men happy, or to give them the greatest and most lasting pleasure; and wisdom denotes only a capacity of pursuing this end by the best means. It must surely then be of the greatest importance to have distinct conceptions of this end itself, as well as of the means necessary to obtain it, that we may find out which are the greatest and most lasting pleasures, and not employ our reason, after all our laborious improvements of it, in trifling pursuits. It is to be feared, indeed, that most of our studies, without this inquiry, will be of very little use to us; for they seem to have scarce any other tendency than to lead us into speculative knowledge itself. Nor are we distinctly told how it is that knowledge, or truth, is pleasant to us.

This consideration put the author of the following papers upon inquiring into the various pleasures which human nature is capable of receiving. We shall generally find in our modern philosophic writings nothing farther on this head than some bare division of them into *Sensible* and *Rational*, and some trite commonplace arguments to prove the latter more valuable than the former. Our sensible pleasures are slightly passed over and explained only by some instances of tastes, smells, sounds, or such like, which men of any tolerable reflection generally look upon as very trifling satisfactions. Our rational pleasures have had much the same kind of treatment. We are seldom taught any other notion of rational pleasure than that which we have upon reflecting on our possession, or claim to those objects which may be occasions of pleasure. Such objects we call advantageous; but advantage, or interest, cannot be distinctly conceived till we know what those pleasures are which advantageous objects are apt to excite, and what senses or powers of perception we have with respect to such objects. We may perhaps find such an inquiry of more importance in *morals*, to prove what we call the reality of virtue, or that it is the surest happiness of the agent, than one would first imagine.

In reflecting upon our *external senses*, we plainly see that our perceptions of pleasure or pain do not depend directly upon our will. Objects do not please us according as we incline they should. The presence of some objects necessarily pleases us, and the presence of others as necessarily displeases us. Nor can we by our will any otherwise procure pleasure or avoid pain than by procuring the former kind of objects and avoiding the latter. By the very frame of our nature the one is made the occasion of delight and the other of dissatisfaction.

The same observation will hold in all our other pleasures and pains. For there are many other sorts of objects which will please or displease us as necessarily, as material objects do when they operate on our organs of sense. There are few objects which are not thus constituted the necessary occasion of some pleasure or pain. Thus we find ourselves pleased with a regular form, a piece of architecture or painting, a composition of notes, a theorem, an action, an affection, a character. And we are conscious that this pleasure necessarily arises from the contemplation of the idea which is then present to our minds, with all its circumstances, although some of these ideas have nothing of what we commonly call sensible perception in them; and in those which have, the pleasure arises from some *uniformity, order, arrangement, imitation,* and not from the simple ideas of *colour* or *sound* or *mode of extension* separately considered.

These determinations to be pleased with certain complex forms the author chooses to call *senses,* distinguishing them from the powers which commonly go by that name calling our power of perceiving the *beauty* of regularity, order, harmony, an *internal sense,* and that determination to approve affections, actions, or characters of rational agents, which we call *virtuous,* he marks by the name of a *moral sense.*

His principal design is to show that human nature was not left quite indifferent in the affair of virtue, to form to itself observations concerning the advantage or disadvantage of actions, and accordingly to regulate its conduct. The weakness of our reason, and the avocations arising from the infirmities and necessities of our nature, are so great that very few men could ever have formed those long deductions of reason which show some actions to be in the whole advantageous to the agent, and their contraries pernicious. The Author of nature has much better furnished us for a virtuous conduct than some moralists seem to imagine, by almost as quick and powerful instructions as we have for the preservation of our bodies. He has given us strong affections to be the springs of each virtuous action, and made virtue a lovely form, that we might easily distinguish it from its contrary, and be made happy by the pursuit of it.

This moral sense of beauty in actions and affections may appear strange at first view. Some of our moralists themselves are offended at it in my Lord Shaftesbury, so much are they accustomed to deduce every approbation or aversion from rational views of private interest (except it be merely in the simple ideas of the external senses) and have such a horror at *innate ideas*, which they imagine this borders upon. But this moral sense has no relation to innate ideas, as will appear in the second Treatise. Our gentlemen of good taste can tell us of a great many senses, tastes, and relishes for beauty, harmony, imitation in painting and poetry; and may not we find too in mankind a relish for a beauty in characters, in manners? It will perhaps be found that the greater part of the ingenious arts are calculated to please some natural powers pretty different either from what we commonly call *reason*, or the external senses.

In the first Treatise the author perhaps in some instances has gone too far in supposing a greater agreement of mankind in their sense of beauty than experience will confirm; but all he is solicitous about is to show that there is some sense of beauty natural to men; that we find as great an agreement of men in their relishes of forms as in their external senses, which all agree to be natural; and that pleasure or pain, delight or aversion, are naturally joined to their perceptions. If the reader be convinced of this it will be no difficult matter to apprehend another superior sense, natural also to men, determining them to be pleased with actions, characters, affections. This is the moral sense which makes the subject of the second Treatise.

The proper occasions of perception by the external senses occur to us as soon as we come into the world, whence perhaps we easily look upon these senses to be natural; but the objects of the superior senses of beauty and virtue generally do not. It is probably some little time before children reflect or at least let us know that they reflect upon proportion and similitude, upon affections, characters, tempers, or come to know the external actions which are evidence of them. Hence, we imagine that their sense of beauty, and their moral sentiments of actions must be entirely owing to instruction and education; whereas it is as easy to conceive how a character, a temper, as soon as they are observed, may be constituted by nature the necessary occasion of pleasure, or an object of approbation, as a taste or a sound, though these objects present themselves to our observation sooner than the other.

*   *   *

TREATISE I:
AN INQUIRY CONCERNING BEAUTY, ORDER, HARMONY, DESIGN

Section I:
Concerning some Powers of Perception, Distinct from what is Generally Understood by Sensation

To make the following observations understood, it may be necessary to premise some definitions, and observations, either universally acknowledged, or sufficiently proved by many writers both ancient and modern, concerning our perceptions called *sensations*, and the actions of the mind consequent upon them.

I. Those ideas which are raised in the mind upon the presence of external objects, and their acting upon our bodies, are called *sensations*. We find that the mind in such cases is passive, and has not power directly to prevent the perception or idea, or to vary it at its reception, as long as we continue our bodies in a state fit to be acted upon by the external object.

II. When two perceptions are entirely different from each other, or agree in nothing but the general idea of sensation, we call the powers of receiving those different perceptions different *senses*. Thus seeing and hearing denote the different powers of receiving the ideas of colours and sounds. And although colours have great differences among themselves, as also have sounds, yet there is greater agreement among the most opposite colours, than between any colour and a sound. Hence we call all colours perceptions of the same sense. All the several senses seem to have their distinct organs, except *feeling*, which is in some degree diffused over the whole body.

III. The mind has a power of *compounding* ideas which were received separately; of *comparing* objects by means of the ideas, and of observing their *relations* and *proportions*; of *enlarging* and *diminishing* its ideas at pleasure, or in any certain *ratio* or degree; and of considering *separately* each of the simple ideas, which might perhaps have been impressed jointly in the sensation. This last operation we commonly call *abstraction*.

IV. The ideas of corporeal substances are compounded of the various simple ideas jointly impressed when they presented themselves to our senses. We define substances only by enumerating these sensible ideas; and such definitions may raise a clear enough idea of the substances in the mind of one who never immediately perceived the substance, provided he has separately received by his senses all the simple ideas which are in the composition of the complex one of the substance defined. But if there be any simple ideas which he has not received, or if he wants any of the senses necessary for the perception of them, no definition can raise any simple idea which has not been before perceived by the senses.

v. Hence it follows that when instruction, education, or prejudice of any kind raise any desire or aversion toward an object, this desire or aversion must be founded upon an opinion of some perfection, or some deficiency in those qualities for perception of which we have the proper senses. Thus if beauty be desired by one who has not the sense of sight, the desire must be raised by some apprehended regularity of figure, sweetness of voice, smoothness, or softness, or some other quality perceivable by the other senses, without relation to the ideas of colour.

VI. Many of our sensitive perceptions are pleasant, and many painful, immediately, and that without any knowledge of the cause of this pleasure or pain, or how the objects excite it, or are the occasions of it, or without seeing to what farther advantage or detriment the use of such objects might tend. Nor would the most accurate knowledge of these things vary either the pleasure or pain of the perception, however it might give a rational pleasure distinct from the sensible; or might raise a distinct joy from a prospect of farther advantage in the object, or aversion from an apprehension of evil.

VII. The simple ideas raised in different persons by the same object are probably some way different when they disagree in their approbation or dislike, and in the same person when his fancy at one time differs from what it was at another. This will appear from reflecting on those objects to which we have now an aversion, though they were formerly agreeable. And we shall generally find that there is some accidental conjunction of a disagreeable idea which always recurs with the object, as in those wines to which men acquire an aversion after they have taken them in an emetic preparation, we are conscious that the idea is altered from what it was when that wine was agreeable, by the conjunction of the ideas of loathing and sickness of the stomach. The like change of idea may be insensibly made by the change of our bodies as we advance in years, or when we are accustomed to any object, which may occasion an indifference toward meats we were fond of in our childhood, and may make some objects cease to raise the disagreeable ideas which they excited upon our first use of them. Many of our simple perceptions are disagreeable only through the too great intenseness of the quality: thus moderate light is agreeable, very strong light may be painful; moderate bitter may be pleasant, a higher degree may be offensive. A change in our organs will necessarily occasion a change in the intenseness of the perception at least, nay, sometimes will occasion a quite contrary perception: thus a warm hand shall feel that water cold which a cold hand shall feel warm.

We shall not find it perhaps so easy to account for the diversity of fancy about more complex ideas of objects including many in which we regard many ideas of different senses at once, as some perceptions of those called *primary qualities*, and some *secondary*, as explained by Mr Locke; for instance, in the different fancies about architecture, gardening, dress. Of the two former, we shall offer something in Sect. VI. As to dress, we may generally account for the diversity of fancies from a like conjunction of ideas. Thus if either from anything in nature, or from the opinion of our country or acquaintance, the fancying of glaring colours be looked upon as an evidence of levity, or of any other evil quality of mind, or if any colour or fashion be commonly used by rustics, or by men of any disagreeable profession, employment, or temper, these additional ideas may recur constantly with that of the colour or fashion, and cause a constant dislike to them in those who join the additional ideas, although the colour or form be no way disagreeable of themselves, and actually do please others who join no such ideas to them. But there appears no ground to believe such a diversity in human minds, as that the same simple idea or perception should give pleasure to one and pain to another, or to the same person at different times, not to say that it seems a contradiction that the same simple idea should do so.

VIII. The only pleasure of sense which many philosophers seem to consider is that which accompanies the simple ideas of

sensation. But there are far greater pleasures in those complex ideas
of objects, which obtain the names of *beautiful, regular, harmonious.*
Thus every one acknowledges he is more delighted with a fine face,
a just picture, than with the view of any one colour, were it as strong
and lively as possible; and more pleased with a prospect of the sun
arising among settled clouds, and colouring their edges with a starry
hemisphere, a fine landscape, a regular building, than with a clear
blue sky, a smooth sea, or a large open plain, not diversified by
woods, hills, waters, buildings. And yet even these latter appearances
are not quite simple. So in music, the pleasure of fine composition
is incomparably greater than of any one note, how sweet, full, or
swelling soever.

IX. Let it be observed that in the following papers the word *beauty*
is taken for *the idea raised in us,* and a *sense* of beauty for *our power of
receiving this idea. Harmony* also denotes *our pleasant ideas arising from
composition of sounds,* and a *good ear* (as it is generally taken) a *power of
perceiving this pleasure.* In the following sections, an attempt is made to
discover what is the immediate occasion of these pleasant ideas, or what
real quality in the objects ordinarily excites them.

x. It is of no consequence whether we call these ideas of beauty and
harmony perceptions of the external senses of seeing and hearing, or
not. I should rather choose to call our power of perceiving these ideas
an *internal sense,* were it only for the convenience of distinguishing
them from other sensations of seeing and hearing which men may
have without perception of beauty and harmony. It is plain from
experience that many men have in the common meaning the senses
of seeing and hearing perfect enough. They perceive all the *simple
ideas* separately, and have their pleasures; they distinguish them from
each other, such as one colour from another, either quite different, or
the stronger or fainter of the same colour, when they are placed beside
each other, although they may often confound their names when they
occur apart from each other, as some do the names of green and blue.
They can tell in separate notes, the higher, lower, sharper or flatter,
when separately sounded; in figures they discern the length, breadth,
wideness of each line, surface, angle; and may be as capable of hearing
and seeing at great distances as any men whatsoever. And yet perhaps
they shall find no pleasure in musical compositions, in painting,

architecture, natural landscape, or but a very weak one in comparison of what others enjoy from the same objects. This greater capacity of receiving such pleasant ideas we commonly call a *fine genius* or *taste*. In music we seem universally to acknowledge something like a distinct sense from the external one of hearing, and call it a *good ear*; and the like distinction we should probably acknowledge in other objects, had we also got distinct names to denote these *powers* of perception by.

XI. We generally imagine the brute animals endowed with the same sort of powers of perception as our external senses, and having sometimes greater acuteness in them; but we conceive few or none of them with any of these sublimer powers of perception here called *internal senses*, or at least if some of them have them, it is in a degree much inferior to ours.

There will appear another reason perhaps hereafter for calling this power of perceiving the ideas of beauty an *internal sense*, from this, that in some other affairs where our external senses are not much concerned, we discern a sort of beauty, very like, in many respects, to that observed in sensible objects, and accompanied with like pleasure. Such is that beauty perceived in theorems, or universal truths, in general causes, and in some extensive principles of action.

XII. Let one consider, first, that 'tis probable a being may have the full power of external sensation, which we enjoy, so as to perceive each colour, line, surface, as we do; yet, without the power of *comparing*, or of discerning the similitudes of proportions. Again, it may discern these also, and yet have no pleasure or delight accompanying these perceptions. The bare idea of the form is something separable from pleasure, as may appear from the different *tastes* of men about the beauty of forms, where we don't imagine that they differ in any ideas, either of the primary or secondary qualities. *Similitude, proportion, analogy* or *equality* of proportion are objects of the understanding, and must be actually known before we know the natural causes of our pleasure. But pleasure perhaps is not necessarily connected with perception of them, and may be felt where the proportion is not known or attended to, and may not be felt where the proportion is observed. Since then there are such different powers of perception, where what are commonly called *external* senses are the same, since the most accurate knowledge of what the external senses discover may often not give the pleasure of

beauty or harmony which yet one of a good taste will enjoy at once
without much knowledge, we may justly use another name for these
higher and more delightful perceptions of beauty and harmony, and
call the *power* of receiving such impressions an *internal sense*. The
difference of the perceptions seems sufficient to vindicate the use of a
different name, especially when we are told in what meaning the word
is applied.

This superior power of perception is justly called a *sense* because of its
affinity to the other senses in this, that the pleasure does not arise from
any *knowledge* of principles, proportions, causes, or of the usefulness of
the object, but strikes us at first with the idea of beauty. Nor does the
most accurate knowledge increase this pleasure of beauty, however it
may superadd a distinct rational pleasure from prospects of advantage,
or from the increase of knowledge.*

XIII. And farther, the ideas of beauty and harmony, like other
sensible ideas, are *necessarily* pleasant to us, as well as immediately so.
Neither can any resolution of our own, nor any prospect of advantage
or disadvantage, vary the beauty or deformity of an object. For as in the
external sensations, no view of interest will make an object grateful, nor
view of detriment distinct from immediate pain in the perception, make
it disagreeable to the sense. So propose the whole world as a reward,
or threaten the greatest evil, to make us approve a deformed object, or
disapprove a beautiful one: dissimulation may be procured by rewards
or threatenings, or we may in external conduct abstain from any pursuit
of the beautiful, and pursue the deformed, but our *sentiments* of the
forms, and our *perceptions*, would continue invariably the same.

XIV. Hence it plainly appears that some objects are *immediately* the
occasions of this pleasure of beauty, and that we have senses fitted for
perceiving it, and that it is distinct from that *joy* which arises upon
prospect of advantage. Nay, do not we often see convenience and use
neglected to obtain beauty, without any other prospect of advantage
in the beautiful form than the suggesting the pleasant ideas of beauty?
Now this shows us that however we may pursue beautiful objects from
self-love, with a view to obtain the pleasures of beauty, as in architecture,
gardening, and many other affairs, yet there must be a *sense* of

* See Art. VI.

beauty, antecedent to prospects even of this advantage, without which
sense these objects would not be thus advantageous, nor excite in us this
pleasure which constitutes them advantageous. Our sense of beauty from
objects, by which they are constituted good to us, is very distinct from
our desire of them when they are thus constituted. Our desire of beauty
may be counterbalanced by rewards or threatenings, but never our *sense*
of it, even as fear of death may make us desire a bitter potion, or neglect
those meats which the sense of taste would recommend as pleasant, but
cannot make that potion agreeable to the *sense*, or meat disagreeable to
it, which was not so antecedently to this prospect. The same holds true
of the sense of beauty and harmony; that the pursuit of such objects is
frequently neglected, from prospects of advantage, aversion to labour,
or any other motive of interest does not prove that we have no *sense*
of beauty, but only that our desire of it may be counter-balanced by a
stronger desire. So gold outweighing silver is never adduced as proof
that the latter is void of gravity.

xv. Had we no such sense of beauty and harmony, houses, gardens,
dress, equipage might have been recommended to us as convenient,
fruitful, warm, easy, but never as *beautiful*. And in faces I see nothing
which could please us but liveliness of colour and smoothness of
surface. And yet nothing is more certain than that all these objects
are recommended under quite different views on many occasions.
'Tis true, what chiefly pleases in the countenance are the indications
of moral dispositions; and yet, were we by the longest acquaintance
fully convinced of the best moral dispositions in any person, with that
countenance we now think deformed, this would never hinder our
immediate dislike of the form, or our liking other forms more. And
custom, education, or example could never give us perceptions distinct
from those of the senses which we had the use of before, or recommend
objects under another conception than grateful to them.* But of the
influence of custom, education, example, upon the sense of beauty, we
shall treat below.†

xvi. Beauty in corporeal forms is either *original* or *comparative*; or, if
any like the terms better, *absolute* or *relative*. Only let it be observed that
by absolute or original beauty is not understood any quality supposed

* See Art. VI.
† See Sect. VII.

to be in the object which should of itself be beautiful, without relation to any mind which perceives it. For beauty, like other names of sensible ideas, properly denotes the *perception* of some mind; so *cold, hot, sweet, bitter,* denote the sensations in our minds, to which perhaps there is no resemblance in the objects which excite these ideas in us, however we generally imagine otherwise. The ideas of beauty and harmony, being excited upon our perception of some primary quality, and having relation to figure and time, may indeed have a nearer resemblance to objects than these sensations, which seem not so much any pictures of objects as modifications of the perceiving mind; and yet, were there no mind with a sense of beauty to contemplate objects, I see not how they could be called beautiful. We therefore by absolute beauty* understand only that beauty which we perceive in objects without comparison to anything external, of which the object is supposed an imitation or picture, such as that beauty perceived from the works of nature, artificial forms, figures. Comparative or relative beauty is that which we perceive in objects commonly considered as *imitations* or *resemblances* of something else. These two kinds of beauty employ the three following sections.

Section II:
Of Original or Absolute Beauty

I. Since it is certain that we have *ideas* of beauty and harmony, let us examine what *quality* in objects excites these ideas, or is the occasion of them. And let it be here observed that our inquiry is only about the qualities which are beautiful to *men*, or about the foundation of their sense of beauty. For as was above hinted, beauty has always relation to the sense of some mind; and when we afterwards show how generally the objects which occur to us are beautiful, we mean that such objects are agreeable to the sense of men, for there are many objects which seem no way beautiful to men, and yet other animals seem delighted with

---

* This division of beauty is taken from the different foundations of pleasure to our sense of it, rather than from the objects themselves; for most of the following instances of relative beauty have also absolute beauty, and many of the instances of absolute beauty have also relative beauty in some respect or other. But we may distinctly consider these two fountains of pleasure, uniformity in the object itself, and resemblance to some original.

them: they may have senses otherwise constituted than those of men, and may have the ideas of beauty excited by objects of a quite different form. We see animals fitted for every place, and what to men appears rude and shapeless, or loathsome, may be to them a paradise.

II. That we may more distinctly discover the general foundation or occasion of the ideas of beauty among men, it will be necessary to consider it first in its simpler kinds, such as occurs to us in regular figures; and we may perhaps find that the same foundation extends to all the more complex species of it.

III. The figures which excite in us the ideas of beauty seem to be those in which there is *uniformity amidst variety*. There are many conceptions of objects which are agreeable upon other accounts, such as *grandeur*, *novelty*, *sanctity*, and some others, which shall be mentioned hereafter.* But what we call beautiful in objects, to speak in the mathematical style, seems to be in compound ratio of uniformity and variety: so that where the uniformity of bodies is equal, the beauty is as the variety; and where the variety is equal, the beauty is as the uniformity. This may seem probable, and hold pretty generally.

First, the variety increases the beauty in equal uniformity. The beauty of an equilateral triangle is less than that of the square, which is less than that of a pentagon, and this again is surpassed by the hexagon. When indeed the number of sides is much increased, the proportion of them to the radius, or diameter of the figure, or of the circle to which regular polygons have an obvious relation, is so much lost to our observation, that the beauty does not always increase with the number of sides, and the want of parallelism in the sides of heptagons, and other figures of odd numbers, may also diminish their beauty. So in solids, the icosahedron surpasses the dodecahedron, and this the octahedron, which is still more beautiful than the cube, and this again surpasses the regular pyramid. The obvious ground of this is greater variety with equal uniformity.

The greater uniformity increases the beauty amidst equal variety in these instances: an equilateral triangle, or even an isosceles, surpasses the scalenum; a square surpasses the rhombus or lozenge, and this again the rhomboides, which is still more beautiful than the trapezium, or any

* See Sect. VI, Art. XI.

figure with irregular curved sides. So the regular solids surpass all other solids of equal number of plane surfaces. And the same is observable not only in the five perfectly regular solids, but in all those which have any considerable uniformity, as cylinders, prisms, pyramids, obelisks, which please every eye more than any rude figures, where there is no unity or resemblance among the parts.

Instances of the compound ratio we have in comparing circles or spheres with ellipses or spheroids not very eccentric, and in comparing the compound solids, the exoctahedron [hexoctahedron], and icosidodecahedron, with the perfectly regular ones of which they are compounded; and we shall find that the want of that most perfect uniformity observable in the latter is compensated by the greater variety in the former, so that the beauty is nearly equal.

IV. These observations would probably hold true for the most part, and might be confirmed by the judgment of children in the simpler figures, where the variety is not too great for their comprehension. And however uncertain some of the particular aforesaid instances may seem, yet this is perpetually to be observed, that children are fond of all regular figures in their little diversions, although they be no more convenient or useful for them than the figures of our common pebbles. We see how early they discover a taste or sense of beauty in desiring to see buildings, regular gardens, or even representations of them in pictures of any kind.

v. The same foundation we have for our sense of beauty in the works of nature. In every part of the world which we call beautiful there is a surprising uniformity amidst an almost infinite variety.

* * *

VIII. Again, as to the beauty of animals, either in their inward structure, which we come to the knowledge of by experience and long observation, or their outward form, we shall find surprising uniformity among all the species which are known to us, in the structure of those parts upon which life depends more immediately. And how amazing is the unity of mechanism when we shall find an almost infinite diversity of motions, all their actions in walking, running, flying, swimming; all their serious efforts for self-preservation, all their freakish contortions when they are gay and sportful, in all their various limbs, performed by one simple contrivance of a contracting muscle, applied with inconceivable diversities to answer all these ends. Various engines might have obtained the same ends; but then there had been less uniformity, and the beauty of our animal systems, and of particular animals, had been much less, when this surprising unity of mechanism had been removed from them.

IX. Among animals of the same species unity is very obvious, and this resemblance is the very ground of our ranking them in such classes or species, notwithstanding the great diversities in bulk, colour, shape, which are observed even in those called of the same species. And then in each individual, how universal is that beauty which arises from the exact resemblance of all the external double members to each other, which seems the universal intention of nature, when no accident prevents it! We see the want of this resemblance never fails to pass for an imperfection, and want of beauty, though no other inconvenience ensues, as when the eyes are not exactly like, or one arm or leg is a little shorter or smaller than its fellow.

As to that most powerful beauty in countenances, airs, gestures, motions, we shall show in the second Treatise* that it arises from some imagined indication of morally good dispositions of the mind. In motion there is also a natural beauty, when at fixed periods like gestures and steps are regularly repeated, suiting the time and air of music, which is observed in regular dancing.

X. There is a farther beauty in animals, arising from a certain proportion of the various parts to each other, which still pleases the sense of spectators, though they cannot calculate it with the accuracy of a statuary. The statuary knows what proportion of each part of the face to the whole face is most agreeable, and can tell us the same of the proportion of the face to the body, or any parts of it, and between the diameters and lengths of each limb. When this proportion of the head to the body is remarkably altered, we shall have a giant or a dwarf; and hence it is that either the one or the other may be represented to us even in miniature, without relation to any external object, by observing how the body surpasses the proportion it should have to the head in giants, and falls below it in dwarfs. There is a farther beauty arising from that figure which is a natural indication of

* Treat. II, Sect. VI, Art. III.

strength; but this may be passed over, because our approbation of this shape flows from an opinion of advantage, and not from the form itself.

The beauty arising from mechanism apparently adapted to the necessities and advantages of any animal, which pleases us even though there be no advantage to ourselves ensuing from it, will be considered under the head of *Relative Beauty*, or *Design*.*

* * *

XIII. Under *original beauty* we may include *harmony*, or *beauty of sound*, if that expression can be allowed, because harmony is not usually conceived as an imitation of anything else. Harmony often raises pleasure in those who know not what is the occasion of it; and yet the foundation of this pleasure is known to be a sort of uniformity. When the several vibrations of one note regularly coincide with the vibrations of another they make an agreeable composition; and such notes are called *concords*. Thus the vibrations of any one note coincide in time with two vibrations of its octave; and two vibrations of any note coincide with three of its fifth, and so on in the rest of the concords. Now no composition can be harmonious in which the notes are not, for the most part, disposed according to these natural proportions. Besides which, a due regard must be had to the *key*, which governs the whole, and to the *time* and *humour* in which the composition is begun, a frequent and inartificial change of any of which will produce the greatest and most unnatural discord. This will appear by observing the dissonance which would arise from tacking parts of different tunes together as one, although both were separately agreeable. A like uniformity is also observable among the *basses*, *tenors*, *trebles* of the same tune.

There is indeed observable, in the best compositions, a mysterious effect of discords; they often give as great a pleasure as continued harmony, whether by refreshing the ear with variety, or by awakening the attention, and enlivening the relish for the succeeding harmony of concords, as shades enliven and beautify pictures, or by some other means not yet known. Certain it is, however, that they have their place, and some good

---

* Treat. I, Sect. IV, Art. VII.

effect in our best compositions. Some other powers of music may be considered hereafter.*

xiv. But in all these instances of beauty† let it be observed that the pleasure is communicated to those who never reflected on this general foundation, and that all here alleged is this, that the pleasant sensation arises only from objects in which there is *uniformity amidst variety*. We may have the sensation without knowing what is the occasion of it, as a man's taste may suggest ideas of sweets, acids, bitters, though he be ignorant of the forms of the small bodies, or their motions, which excite these perceptions in him.

Section III:
Of the Beauty of Theorems

i. The beauty of *theorems*, or universal truths demonstrated, deserves a distinct consideration, being of a nature pretty different from the former kinds of beauty; and yet there is none in which we shall see such an amazing variety with uniformity, and hence arises a very great pleasure distinct from prospects of any farther advantage.

ii. For in one theorem we may find included, with the most exact agreement, an infinite multitude of particular truths, nay, often a multitude of infinities, so that although the necessity of forming abstract ideas and universal theorems arises perhaps from the limitation of our minds which cannot admit an infinite multitude of singular ideas or judgments at once, yet this power gives us an evidence of the largeness of the human capacity above our imagination. Thus, for instance, the 47th Proposition of the 1st Book of Euclid's *Elements* contains an infinite multitude of truths concerning the infinite possible sizes of right-angled triangles, as you make the area greater or less; and in each of these sizes you may find an infinite multitude of dissimilar triangles, as you vary the proportion of the base to the perpendicular, all which infinites agree in the general theorem. In algebraic and fluxional calculations we shall find a like

* See Sect. IV, Art. VII.

† There is nothing singular in applying the word *beauty* to sounds. The ancients observe the peculiar dignity of the sense of seeing and hearing, that in their objects we discern the καλὸν [beauty], which we don't ascribe to the objects of the other senses.

variety of particular truths included in general theorems, not only
in general equations applicable to all kinds of quantity, but in more
particular investigations of areas and tangents, in which one manner
of operation shall discover theorems applicable to many orders
of species of curves, to the infinite sizes of each species, and to the
infinite points of the infinite individuals of each size.

* * *

IV. Again, let us take a metaphysical axiom, such as this. *Every
whole is greater than its part*, and we shall find no beauty in the
contemplation. For though this proposition contains many infinities
of particular truths, yet the unity is inconsiderable, since they all
agree only in a vague undetermined conception of *whole* and *part*,
and in an indefinite excess of the former above the latter, which is
sometimes great and sometimes small. So, should we hear that the
cylinder is greater than the inscribed sphere, and this again greater
than the cone of the same altitude and diameter of the base, we shall
find no pleasure in this knowledge of a general relation of greater and
less, without any precise difference or proportion. But when we see
the universal exact agreement of all possible sizes of such systems of
solids, that they preserve to each other the constant ratio of 3, 2, 1,
how beautiful is the theorem, and how are we ravished with its first
discovery!

We may likewise observe that easy or obvious propositions, even
where the unity is sufficiently distinct, and determinate, do not please us
so much as those which, being less obvious, give us some surprise in the
discovery. Thus we find little pleasure in discovering that *A line bisecting
the vertical angle of an isosceles triangle, bisects the base*, or the reverse; or
that *Equilateral triangles are equiangular*. These truths we almost know
intuitively, without demonstration. They are like common goods, or
those which men have long possessed, which do not give such sensible
joys as much smaller new additions may give us. But let none hence
imagine that the sole pleasure of theorems is from surprise; for the same
novelty of a single experiment does not please us much, nor ought we to
conclude from the greater pleasure accompanying a new or unexpected
advantage, that surprise, or novelty is the only pleasure of life, or the
only ground of delight in truth. Another kind of surprise in certain

theorems increases our pleasure above that we have in theorems of greater extent; when we discover a general truth which upon some confused notion we had reputed false, as that *Asymptotes always approaching should never meet the curve*. This is like the joy of unexpected advantage where we dreaded evil. But still the unity of many particulars in the general theorem is necessary to give pleasure in any theorem.

v. There is another beauty in propositions when one theorem contains a great multitude of corollaries easily deducible from it. Thus there are some leading or fundamental properties upon which a long series of theorems can be naturally built. Such a theorem is the 35th of the 1st Book of Euclid, from which the whole art of measuring right-lined areas is deduced by resolution into triangles which are the halves of so many parallelograms, and these are each respectively equal to so many rectangles of the base into the perpendicular altitude. The 47th of the 1st Book is another of like beauty, and so are many others in higher parts of geometry. In the search of nature there is the like beauty in the knowledge of some great principles or universal forces from which innumerable effects do flow. Such is *gravitation* in Sir Isaac Newton's scheme. What is the aim of our ingenious geometers? A continual enlargement of theorems, or making them extensive, showing how what was formerly known of one figure extends to many others, to figures very unlike the former in appearance.

It is easy to see how men are charmed with the beauty of such knowledge, besides its usefulness, and how this sets them upon deducing the properties of each figure from one genesis, and demonstrating the mechanic forces from one theorem of the composition of motion, even after they have sufficient knowledge and certainty in all these truths from distinct independent demonstrations. And this pleasure we enjoy even when we have no prospect of obtaining any other advantage from such manner of deduction than the immediate pleasure of contemplating the beauty; nor could love of fame excite us to such regular methods of deduction, were we not conscious that mankind are pleased with them immediately, by this *internal sense* of their beauty.

It is no less easy to see into what absurd attempts men have been led by this sense of beauty, and an affectation of obtaining it in the other sciences as well as the mathematics. 'Twas this probably which set Descartes on that hopeful project of deducing all human knowledge from one proposition, viz. *Cogito, ergo sum*; while others pleaded that *Impossibile est idem simul esse & non esse* had much fairer pretensions to the style and title of *Principium humanae Cognitionis absolute primum.* Mr Leibniz had an equal affection for his favourite principle of a *sufficient reason* for everything in nature, and boasts of the wonders he had wrought in the intellectual world by its assistance. If we look into particular sciences we see the inconveniences of this love of uniformity. How awkwardly does Pufendorf deduce the several duties of men to God, themselves, and their neighbours from his single fundamental principle of *sociableness to the whole race of mankind*? This observation is a strong proof that men perceive the beauty of uniformity in the sciences, since they are led into unnatural deductions by pursuing it too far.

*   *   *

VII. As to the works of art, were we to run through the various artificial contrivances or structures, we should constantly find the foundation of the beauty which appears in them to be some kind of uniformity or unity of proportion among the parts, and of each part to the whole. As there is a great diversity of proportions possible, and different kinds of uniformity, so there is room enough for that diversity of fancies observable in architecture, gardening, and such like arts in different nations: they all have uniformity, though the parts in one may differ from those in another. The Chinese or Persian buildings are not like the Grecian and Roman, and yet the former has its uniformity of the various parts to each other, and to the whole, as well as the latter. In that kind of architecture which the Europeans call *regular*, the uniformity of parts is very obvious, the several parts are regular figures, and either equal or similar at least in the same range: the pedestals are parallelopipedons or square prisms; the pillars, cylinders nearly; the arches circular, and all those in the same row equal; there is the same proportion everywhere observed in the same range between the diameters of pillars and their heights, their capitals, the diameters of arches, the heights of the pedestals, the projections of the cornice, and all the ornaments in each of our five orders. And though other countries do not follow the Grecian or Roman proportions, yet there is even among them a proportion retained, a uniformity and resemblance of corresponding figures; and every deviation in one part from that proportion which is observed in the rest of the building is displeasing to every eye, and destroys or diminishes at least the beauty of the whole.

VIII. The same might be observed through all other works of art, even to the meanest utensil, the beauty of every one of which we shall always find to have the same foundation of *uniformity amidst variety*, without which they appear mean, irregular, and deformed.

Section IV:
Of Relative or Comparative Beauty

I. If the preceeding thoughts concerning the foundation of *absolute beauty* be just, we may easily understand wherein *relative beauty* consists. All beauty is relative to the sense of some mind perceiving it; but what we call *relative* is that which is apprehended in any object commonly considered as an *imitation* of some original. And this beauty is founded on a conformity, or a kind of unity between the original and the copy. The original may be either some object in nature, or some established idea; for if there be any known idea as a standard, and rules to fix this image or idea by, we may make a beautiful imitation. Thus a statuary, painter, or poet may please with an Hercules, if his piece retains that grandeur, and those marks of strength and courage which we imagine in that hero.

And farther, to obtain comparative beauty alone, it is not necessary that there be any beauty in the original. The imitation of absolute beauty may indeed in the whole make a more lively piece, and yet an exact imitation shall still be beautiful, though the original were entirely void of it. Thus the deformities of old age in a picture, the rudest rocks or mountains in a landscape, if well represented, shall have abundant beauty, though perhaps not so great as if the original were absolutely beautiful, and as well represented. Nay, perhaps the novelty may make us prefer the representation of irregularity.

II. The same observation holds true in the descriptions of the poets either of natural objects or persons; and this relative beauty is what they should principally endeavour to obtain, as the peculiar beauty

of their works. By the *Moratae Fabulae*, or the ἤϑη of Aristotle.* We
are not to understand virtuous manners, but a just representation of
manners or characters as they are in nature, and that the actions and
sentiments be suited to the characters of the persons to whom they are
ascribed in epic and dramatic poetry. Perhaps very good reasons may
be suggested from the nature of our passions to prove that a poet should
not draw his characters perfectly virtuous. These characters indeed
abstractly considered might give more pleasure, and have more beauty
than the imperfect ones which occur in life with a mixture of good and
evil; but it may suffice at present to suggest against this choice that we
have more lively ideas of imperfect men with all their passions, than of
morally perfect heroes such as really never occur to our observation,
and of which consequently we cannot judge exactly as to their
agreement with the copy. And farther, through consciousness of our
own state we are more nearly touched and affected by the imperfect
characters, since in them we see represented, in the persons of others,
the contrasts of inclinations, and the struggles between the passions
of self-love and those of honour and virtue which we often feel in our
own breasts. This is the perfection of beauty for which Homer is justly
admired, as well as for the variety of his characters.

  III. Many other beauties of poetry may be reduced under this class
of *relative beauty*. The *probability* is absolutely necessary to make us
imagine *resemblance*. It is by resemblance that *similitudes*, *metaphors*,
and *allegories* are made beautiful, whether either the subject or the thing
compared to it have beauty or not; the beauty indeed is greater when
both have some original beauty or dignity as well as resemblance, and
this is the foundation of the rule of studying *decency* in metaphors and
similes as well as likeness. The *measures* and *cadence* are instances of
harmony, and come under the head of absolute beauty.

  IV. We may here observe a strange proneness in our minds to make
perpetual comparisons of all things which occur to our observation,
even of those which are very different from each other. There are certain
resemblances in the motions of all animals upon like passions, which
easily found a comparison; but this does not serve to entertain our
fancy. Inanimate objects have often such positions as resemble those

---

* [*Poetics* vi, ed.]

of the human body in various circumstances. These airs or gestures of the body are indications of certain dispositions in the mind, so that our very passions and affections, as well as other circumstances, obtain a resemblance to natural inanimate objects. Thus a tempest at sea is often an emblem of wrath; a plant or tree drooping under the rain of a person in sorrow; a poppy bending its stalk, or a flower withering when cut by the plough resembles the death of a blooming hero; an aged oak in the mountains shall represent an old empire; a flame seizing a wood shall represent a war. In short, everything in nature, by our strange inclination to resemblance, shall be brought to represent other things, even the most remote, especially the passions and circumstances of human nature in which we are more nearly concerned; and to confirm this and furnish instances of it one need only look into Homer or Virgil. A fruitful fancy would find in a grove, or a wood an emblem for every character in a commonwealth, and every turn of temper or station in life.

v. Concerning that kind of comparative beauty which has a necessary relation to some established idea, we may observe that some works of art acquire a distinct beauty by their correspondence to some universally supposed intention in the artificers, or the persons who employed him. And to obtain this beauty sometimes they do not form their works so as to attain the highest perfection of original beauty separately considered, because a composition of this relative beauty, along with some degree of the original kind, may give more pleasure than a more perfect original beauty separately. Thus we see that strict regularity in laying out of gardens in parterres, vistas, parallel walks, is often neglected to obtain an imitation of nature even in some of its wildness. And we are more pleased with this imitation, especially when the scene is large and spacious, than with the more confined exactness of regular works. So likewise in the monuments erected in honour of deceased heroes, although a cylinder, or prism, or regular solid may have more original beauty than a very acute pyramid or obelisk, yet the latter pleases more by answering better to supposed intentions of stability and being conspicuous. For the same reason, cubes or square prisms are generally chosen for the pedestals of statues, and not any of the more beautiful solids, which do not seem so secure from rolling. This may be the reason too why columns or pillars look best when made a little taper from the middle, or a third from the bottom, that they may not seem top-heavy and in danger of falling.

VI. The like reason may influence artists in many other instances to depart from the rules of original beauty as above laid down. And yet this is no argument against our sense of beauty being founded, as was above explained, on uniformity amidst variety, but only an evidence that our sense of beauty of the original kind may be varied and overbalanced by another kind of beauty.

VII. This beauty arising from correspondence to intention would open to curious observers a new scene of beauty in the works of nature, by considering how the mechanism of the various parts known to us seems adapted to the perfection of that part, and yet in subordination to the good of some system or whole. We generally suppose the good of the greatest whole, or of all beings, to have been the intention of the Author of nature, and cannot avoid being pleased when we see any part of this design executed in the systems we are acquainted with. The observations already made on this subject are in everyone's hand, in the treatise of our late improvers of *mechanical philosophy*. We shall only observe here that everyone has a certain pleasure in seeing any design well executed by curious mechanism, even when his own advantage is no way concerned, and also in discovering the design to which any complex machine is adapted, when he has perhaps had a general knowledge of the machine before, without seeing its correspondence or aptness to execute any design.

The arguments by which we prove reason and design in any cause from the beauty of the effects are so frequently used in some of the highest subjects that it may be necessary to inquire a little more particularly into them, to see how far they will hold, and with what degree of evidence.

Section V:
Concerning our Reasonings about Design and Wisdom in the Cause, from the Beauty or Regularity of Effects

I. There seems to be no necessary connection of our pleasing ideas of beauty with the uniformity or regularity of the objects, from the nature of things, antecedent to some constitution of the Author of our nature, which has made such forms pleasant to us. Other minds may be so framed as to receive no pleasure from uniformity, and we actually find that the same regular forms seem not equally to please all the animals known to us, as shall probably appear hereafter. Therefore let us make what is the most unfavourable supposition to the present argument, viz. that the constitution of our sense so as to approve uniformity is merely arbitrary in the Author of our nature, and that there are an infinity of tastes or relishes of beauty possible, so that it would be impossible to throw together fifty or a hundred pebbles which should not make an agreeable habitation for some animal or other, and appear beautiful to it. And then it is plain that from the perception of beauty in any one effect we should have no reason to conclude design in the cause; for a sense might be so constituted as to be pleased with such irregularity as may be the effect of an undirected force. But then, as there are an infinity of forms possible into which any system may be reduced, an infinity of places in which animals may be situated, and an infinity of relishes or senses in these animals is supposed possible, that in the immense spaces any one animal should by chance be placed in a system agreeable to its taste must be improbable as infinite to one at least. And much more unreasonable is it to expect from chance that a multitude of animals agreeing in their sense of beauty should obtain agreeable places.

II. There is also the same probability that in any one system of matter an undirected force will produce a regular form as any one given irregular one. But still the irregular forms into which any system may be ranged surpass in multitude the regular as infinite does unity; for what holds in one small system will hold in a thousand, a million, a universe, with more advantage, viz. that the irregular forms possible infinitely surpass the regular. For instance, the area of an inch square is capable of an infinity of regular forms, the equilateral triangle, the square, the pentagon, hexagon, heptagon, etc.; but for each one regular form there are an infinity of irregular, as an infinity of scalena for the one equilateral triangle, an infinity of trapezia for the one square, of irregular pentagons for the one regular, and so on. And therefore supposing any one system agitated by undesigned force, it is infinitely more probable that it will resolve itself into an irregular form than a regular. Thus, that a system of six parts upon agitation shall not obtain the form of a regular hexagon is at least infinite to unity; and the more complex we make the system, the greater is the hazard, from a very obvious reason.

We see this confirmed by our constant experience, that regularity never arises from any undesigned force of ours; and from this we conclude that wherever there is any regularity in the disposition of a system capable of many other dispositions, there must have been design in the cause; and the force of this evidence increases according to the multiplicity of parts employed.

But this conclusion is too rash unless some farther proof be introduced, and what leads us into it is this. Men who have a sense of beauty in regularity are led generally in all their arrangements of bodies to study some kind of regularity, and seldom ever design irregularity: hence we judge the same of other beings too, viz. that they study regularity, and presume upon intention in the cause wherever we see it, making irregularity always a presumption of want of design, whereas if other agents have different senses of beauty, or if they have no sense of it at all, irregularity may as well be designed as regularity. And then let it be observed that in this case there is just the same reason to conclude design in the cause from any one irregular effect as from a regular one. For since there are an infinity of other forms possible as well as this irregular one produced, and since to such a being void of a sense of beauty, all forms are as to its own relish indifferent, and all agitated matter meeting must make some form or other, and all forms, upon supposition that the force is applied by an agent void of a sense of beauty, would equally prove design, it is plain that no one form proves it more than another, or can prove it at all, except from a general metaphysical consideration, that there is no proper agent without design and intention, and that every effect flows from the intention of some cause.

* * *

VII. May we not then justly count it altogether absurd, and next to an absolute strict impossibility, that all the powers of undirected force should ever effect such a complex machine as the most imperfect plant, or the meanest animal, even in one instance? For the improbability just increases as the complication of mechanism in these natural bodies surpasses that simple combination above mentioned.

VIII. Let it be here observed that the preceding reasoning from the frequency of regular bodies of one form in the universe, and from the combinations of various bodies, is entirely independent on any perception of beauty, and would equally prove design in the cause although there were no being which perceived beauty in any form whatsoever; for it is, in short, this: *that the recurring of any effect oftener than the laws of hazard determine, gives presumption of design; and, that combinations which no undesigned force could give us reason to expect must necessarily prove the same; and, that with superior probability, as the multitude of cases in which the contrary might happen, surpasses all the cases in which this could happen* – which appears to be in the simplest cases at least as infinite does to unity. And the frequency of similar irregular forms, or exact combinations of them, is an equal argument of design in the cause, since the similarity, or exact combinations of irregular forms, are as little to be expected from all the powers of undirected force as any sort whatsoever.

* * *

XVII. Hitherto the proof amounts only to *design* or *intention* barely, in opposition to *blind force* or *chance*; and we see the proof of this is independent on the arbitrary constitution of our internal sense of beauty. Beauty is often supposed an argument of more than design, to wit, wisdom and prudence in the cause. Let us inquire also into this.

Wisdom denotes *the pursuing of the best ends by the best means*; and therefore before we can from any effect prove the cause to be wise we must know what is best to the cause or agent. Among men who have pleasure in contemplating uniformity, the beauty of effects is an argument of wisdom, because this is good to them; but the same argument would not hold as to a being void of this sense of beauty. And therefore the beauty apparent to us in nature will not of itself prove wisdom in the cause, unless this cause, or Author of nature, be supposed benevolent; and then indeed the happiness of mankind is desirable or good to the Supreme Cause, and that form which pleases us is an argument of his wisdom. And the strength of this argument is always in proportion to the degree of beauty produced in nature, and exposed to the view of any rational agent, since upon supposition of a benevolent Deity all apparent beauty produced is an evidence of the execution of a benevolent design to give them the pleasures of beauty.

But what more immediately proves wisdom is this: when we see any machine with a great complication of parts actually obtaining an end we justly conclude that since this could not have been the effect of chance, it must have been intended for that end, which is obtained by it. And then the ends or intentions, being in part known, the complication of organs, and their nice disposition adapted to this end, is an evidence of a comprehensive large understanding in the cause, according to the multiplicity of parts, and the appositeness of their structure, even when we do not know the intention of the whole.

xix. There is another kind of beauty from which we conclude wisdom in the cause, as well as design, *when we see many useful or beautiful effects flowing from one general cause.* There is a very good reason for this conclusion among men. Interest must lead beings of limited powers, who are incapable of a great diversity of operations, and distracted by them, to choose this frugal economy of their forces, and to look upon such management as an evidence of wisdom in other beings like themselves. Nor is this speculative reason all which influences them, for even beside this consideration of interest they are determined by a sense of beauty where that reason does not hold, as when we are judging of the productions of other agents about whose economy we are not solicitous. Thus, who does not approve of it as a perfection in clock-work that three or four motions of the hour, minute, and second hands, and monthly plate, should arise from one spring or weight, rather than from three, or four springs, or weights, in a very compound machine, which should perform the same effects, and answer all the same purposes with equal exactness? Now the foundation of this beauty plainly appears to be a uniformity, or unity of cause amidst diversity of effects.

xx. We shall hereafter* offer some reasons why the Author of nature

* See Sect. VIII.

may choose to operate in this manner by general laws and universal extensive causes, although the reason just now mentioned does not hold with an almighty being. This is certain, that we have some of the most delightful instances of universal causes in the works of nature, and that the most studious men in these subjects are so delighted with the observation of them that they always look upon them as evidences of wisdom in the administration of nature, from a sense of beauty.

Section VI:
Of the Universality of the Sense of Beauty Among Men

I. We before insinuated that all beauty has a relation to some perceiving power. And, consequently, since we know not how great a variety of senses there may be among animals, there is no form in nature concerning which we can pronounce that it has no beauty; for it may still please some perceiving power. But our *Inquiry* is confined to men; and before we examine the *universality* of this sense of beauty, or their agreement in approving uniformity, it may be proper to consider whether, as the other senses which give us pleasure do also give us pain, so this sense of beauty does make some objects disagreeable to us, and the occasion of pain.

That many objects give no pleasure to our sense is obvious: many are certainly void of beauty. But then there is no form which seems necessarily disagreeable of itself, when we dread no other evil from it, and compare it with nothing better of the kind. Many objects are naturally displeasing, and distasteful to our external senses, as well as others pleasing and agreeable, as smells, tastes, and some separate sounds; but as to our sense of beauty, no composition of objects which give not unpleasant simple ideas, seem positively unpleasant or painful of itself, had we never observed anything better of the kind. Deformity is only the absence of beauty, or deficiency in the beauty expected in any species. Thus bad music pleases rustics who never heard any better, and the finest ear is not offended with tuning of instruments if it be not too tedious, where no harmony is expected; and yet much smaller dissonancy shall offend amidst the performance, where harmony is expected. A rude heap of stones is no way offensive to one who shall be displeased with irregularity in architecture, where beauty was expected.

And had there been a species of that form which we now call ugly or deformed, and had we never seen or expected greater beauty, we should have received no disgust from it, although the pleasure would not have been so great in this form as in those we now admire. Our sense of beauty seems designed to give us positive pleasure, but not positive pain or disgust, any farther than what arises from disappointment.

II. There are indeed many faces which at first view are apt to raise dislike; but this is generally not from any deformity which of itself is positively displeasing, but either from want of expected beauty, or much more from their carrying some natural indications of morally bad dispositions, which we all acquire a faculty of discerning in countenances, airs, and gestures. That this is not occasioned by any form positively disgusting will appear from this, that if upon long acquaintance we are sure of finding sweetness of temper, humanity, and cheerfulness, although the bodily form continues, it shall give us no disgust or displeasure; whereas if anything were naturally disagreeable, or the occasion of pain, or positive distaste, it would always continue so, even although the aversion we might have toward it were counterbalanced by other considerations. There are horrors raised by some objects, which are only the effect of fear of ourselves, or compassion towards others, when either reason, or some foolish association of ideas, makes us apprehend danger, and not the effect of anything in the form itself; for we find that most of those objects which excite horror at first, when experience or reason has removed the fear, may become the occasions of pleasure, as ravenous beasts, a tempestuous sea, a craggy precipice, a dark shady valley.

III. We shall see hereafter* that associations of ideas make objects pleasant and delightful which are not naturally apt to give any such pleasures; and the same way, the casual conjunctions of ideas may give a disgust where there is nothing disagreeable in the form itself. And this is the occasion of many fantastic aversions to figures of some animals, and to some other forms. Thus swine, serpents of all kinds, and some insects really beautiful enough, are beheld with aversion by many people who have got some accidental ideas associated to them. And for distastes of this kind, no other account can be given.

* See below, Arts XII, XIII, of this section.

IV. But as to the universal agreement of mankind in their sense of beauty from uniformity amidst variety, we must consult experience. And as we allow all men reason, since all men are capable of understanding simple arguments, though few are capable of complex demonstrations, so in this case it must be sufficient to prove this sense of beauty universal if all men are better pleased with uniformity in the simpler instances than the contrary, even when there is no advantage observed attending it; and likewise if all men, according as their capacity enlarges, so as to receive and compare more complex ideas, have a greater delight in uniformity, and are pleased with its more complex kinds, both original and relative.

Now let us consider if ever any person was void of this sense in the simpler instances. Few trials have been made in the simplest instances of harmony, because as soon as we find an ear incapable of relishing complex compositions, such as our tunes are, no farther pains are employed about such. But in figures, did ever any man make choice of a trapezium, or any irregular curve, for the ichnography or plan of his house, without necessity, or some great motive of convenience? Or to make the opposite walls not parallel, or unequal in height? Were ever trapeziums, irregular polygons or curves, chosen for the forms of doors or windows, though these figures might have answered the uses as well, and would have often saved a great part of the time, labour, and expense to workmen which is now employed in suiting the stones and timber to the regular forms? Among all the fantastic modes of dress, none was ever quite void of uniformity, if it were only in the resemblance of the two sides of the same robe, and in some general aptitude to the human form. The pictish painting had always relative beauty, by resemblance to other objects, and often those objects were originally beautiful. However justly we might here apply Horace's censure of impertinent descriptions of poetry:

*Sed non erat his locus**

But never were any so extravagant as to affect such figures as are made by the casual spilling of liquid colours. Who was ever pleased with an inequality of heights in windows of the same range, or dissimilar shapes

---

* Horace, *De Arte Poetica*, line 19. ['For such things there is a place, but not just now.' Trans. H. R. Fairclough.]

of them? With unequal legs or arms, eyes or cheeks in a mistress? It must however be acknowledged that interest may often counterbalance our sense of beauty in this affair as well as in others, and superior good qualities may make us overlook such imperfections.

v. Nay farther, it may perhaps appear that regularity and uniformity are so copiously diffused through the universe, and we are so readily determined to pursue this as the foundation of beauty in works of art, that there is scarcely anything ever fancied as beautiful where there is not really something of this uniformity and regularity. We are indeed often mistaken in imagining that there is the greatest possible beauty, where it is but very imperfect; but still it is some degree of beauty which pleases, although there may be higher degrees which we do not observe; and our sense acts with full regularity when we are pleased, although we are kept by a false prejudice from pursuing objects which would please us more.

A Goth, for instance, is mistaken when from education he imagines the architecture of his country to be the most perfect; and a conjunction of some hostile ideas may make him have an aversion to Roman buildings, and study to demolish them, as some of our reformers did the popish buildings, not being able to separate the ideas of the superstitious worship from the forms of the buildings where it was practised. And yet it is still real beauty which pleases the Goth, founded upon uniformity amidst variety. For the Gothic pillars are uniform to each other, not only in their sections, which are lozenge-formed, but also in their heights and ornaments. Their arches are not one uniform curve, but yet they are segments of similar curves, and generally equal in the same ranges. The very Indian buildings have some kind of uniformity, and many of the Eastern nations, though they differ much from us, yet have great regularity in their manner, as well as the Romans in theirs. Our Indian screens, which wonderfully supply our imaginations with ideas of deformity, in which nature is very churlish and sparing, do want indeed all the beauty arising from proportions of parts and conformity to nature; and yet they cannot divest themselves of all beauty and uniformity in the separate parts. And this diversifying the human body into various contortions may give some wild pleasure from variety, since some uniformity to the human shape is still retained.

VI. There is one sort of beauty which might perhaps have been better mentioned before, but will not be impertinent here, because the taste or relish of it is universal in all nations, and with the young as well as the old, and that is the beauty of history. Everyone knows how dull a study it is to read over a collection of gazettes, which shall perhaps relate all the same events with the historian. The superior pleasure then of history must arise, like that of poetry, from the manners: when we see a character well drawn wherein we find the secret causes of a great diversity of seemingly inconsistent actions; or an interest of state laid open, or an artful view nicely unfolded, the execution of which influences very different and opposite actions as the circumstances may alter. Now this reduces the whole to an unity of design at least; and this may be observed in the very fables which entertain children, otherwise we cannot make them relish them.

VII. What has been said will probably be assented to if we always remember in our inquiries into the universality of the sense of beauty that there may be real beauty where there is not the greatest, and that there are an infinity of different forms which may all have some unity, and yet differ from each other. So that men may have different fancies of beauty, and yet uniformity be the universal foundation of our approbation of any form whatsoever as beautiful. And we shall find that it is so in architecture, gardening, dress, equipage, and furniture of houses, even among the most uncultivated nations, where uniformity still pleases, without any other advantage than the pleasure of the contemplation of it.

VIII. It will deserve our consideration on this subject how, in like cases, we form very different judgments concerning the *internal* and *external senses*. Nothing is more ordinary among those, who, after Mr Locke, have rejected *innate ideas*, than to allege that all our relish for beauty and order is either from prospect of advantage, custom, or education, for no other reason but the *variety* of fancies in the world; and from this they conclude that our fancies do not arise from any *natural power of perception*, or *sense*. And yet all allow our *external senses* to be *natural*, and that the pleasures or pains of their sensations, however they may be increased or diminished by custom or education, and counterbalanced by interest, yet are really antecedent to custom, habit, education, or prospect of interest. Now it is certain that there is at least as great a variety of fancies about their objects as the objects of beauty. Nay, it is much more difficult, and perhaps impossible, to bring the fancies or relishes of the external senses to any general foundation at all, or to find any rule for the agreeable or disagreeable; and yet we allow that these are *natural* powers of perception.

IX. The reason of this different judgment can be no other than this: that we have got distinct names for the external senses, and none, or very few, for the internal, and by this are led, as in many other cases, to look upon the former as some way more fixed and real and natural than the latter. The *sense* of harmony has got its name, viz. a *good ear*; and we are generally brought to acknowledge this *natural* power of *perception*, or *a sense* some way distinct from hearing. Now it is certain that there is as necessary a perception of *beauty* upon the presence of regular objects, as of *harmony* upon hearing certain sounds.

X. But let it be observed here once for all that an *internal sense* no more presupposes an *innate idea*, or principle of knowledge, than the *external*. Both are *natural* powers of *perception*, or determinations of the mind to receive necessarily certain ideas from the presence of objects. The *internal sense* is *a passive power of receiving ideas of beauty from all objects in which there is uniformity amidst variety*. Nor does there seem anything more difficult in this matter than that the mind should be always determined to receive the idea of *sweet* when particles of such a form enter the pores of the tongue, or to have the idea of *sound* upon any quick undulation of the air. The one seems to have as little connection with its idea as the other; and the same power could with equal ease constitute the former the occasion of ideas as the latter.

XI. The *association of ideas** above hinted at is one great cause of the apparent diversity of fancies in the sense of beauty, as well as in the external senses, and often makes men have an aversion to objects of beauty, and a liking to others void of it, but under different conceptions than those of beauty or deformity. And here it may not be improper to give some instances of some of these associations. The beauty of trees, their cool shades, and their aptness to conceal from observation have made groves and woods the usual retreat to those who love solitude,

---

* See above, Art. III of this section.

especially to the religious, the pensive, the melancholy, and the amorous. And do not we find that we have so joined the ideas of these dispositions of mind with those external objects that they always recur to us along with them? The cunning of the heathen priests might make such obscure places the scene of the fictitious appearances of their deities; and hence we join ideas of something divine to them. We know the like effect in the ideas of our churches, from the perpetual use of them only in religious exercises. The faint light in Gothic buildings has had the same association of a very foreign idea which our poet shows in his epithet,

A dim religious light.*

* * *

XII. There is also another charm in music to various persons, which is distinct from harmony and is occasioned by its raising agreeable passions. The human voice is obviously varied by all the stronger passions: now when our ear discerns any resemblance between the air of a tune, whether sung or played upon an instrument, either in its time, or modulation, or any other circumstance, to the sound of the human voice in any passion, we shall be touched by it in a very sensible manner, and have melancholy, joy, gravity, thoughtfulness excited in us by a sort of *sympathy* or *contagion*. The same connection is observable between the very air of a tune and the words expressing any passion which we have heard it fitted to, so that they shall both recur to us together, though but one of them affects our senses.

Now in such a diversity of pleasing or displeasing ideas which may be joined with forms of bodies, or tunes, when men are of such different dispositions, and prone to such a variety of passions, it is no wonder that they should often disagree in their fancies of objects, even although their sense of beauty and harmony were perfectly uniform; because many other ideas may either please or displease, according to persons' tempers and past circumstances. We know how agreeable a very wild country may be to any person who has spent the cheerful days of his youth in it, and how disagreeable very beautiful places may be if they were the scenes of his misery. And this may help us in

* Milton, *Il Penseroso*.

many cases to account for the diversities of fancy, without denying the uniformity of our internal sense of beauty.

XIII. *Grandeur* and *Novelty* are two ideas different from *Beauty*, which often recommend objects to us. The reason of this is foreign to the present subject. See *Spectator* No 412.*

Section VII:
Of the Power of Custom, Education, and Example,
as to our Internal Senses

I. Custom, Education, and Example are so often alleged in this affair, as the occasion of our relish for beautiful objects, and for our approbation of, or delight in a certain conduct in life in a moral species, that it is necessary to examine these three particularly, to make it appear that there is a natural power of perception, or sense of beauty in objects, antecedent to all custom, education, or example.

* * *

II. . . . [H]ad we no natural sense of beauty from uniformity, custom could never have made us imagine any beauty in objects; if we had no ear, custom could never have given us pleasures of harmony. When we have these natural senses antecedently, custom may make us capable of extending our views farther and of receiving more complex ideas of beauty in bodies, or harmony in sounds, by increasing our attention and quickness of perception. But however custom may increase our power of receiving or comparing complex ideas, yet it seems rather to weaken than strengthen the ideas of beauty, or the impressions of pleasure from regular objects, else how is it possible that any person could go into the open air on a sunny day, or clear evening, without the most extravagant raptures, such as Milton† represents our ancestor in upon his first creation? For such any person would fall into upon the first representation of such a scene.

Custom in like manner may make it easier for any person to discern the use of a complex machine and approve it as advantageous; but he would never have imagined it beautiful had he no natural sense of beauty. Custom may make us quicker in apprehending the truth of

* [See Introduction, p. xxiv fn.]
† See *Paradise Lost*, Book 8.

complex theorems, but we all find the pleasure or beauty of theorems as strong at first as ever. Custom makes us more capable of retaining and comparing complex ideas, so as to discuss more complicated uniformity which escapes the observation of novices in any art; but all this presupposes a natural sense of beauty in uniformity. For had there been nothing in forms which constituted the necessary occasion of pleasure to our senses, no repetition of indifferent ideas as to pleasure or pain, beauty or deformity, could ever have made them grow pleasing or displeasing.

III. The effect of education is this, that thereby we receive many speculative opinions which are sometimes true and sometimes false, and are often led to believe that objects may be naturally apt to give pleasure or pain to our external senses which in reality have no such qualities. And farther, by education there are some strong associations of ideas without any reason, by mere accident sometimes, as well as by design, which it is very hard for us ever after to break asunder. Thus aversions are raised to darkness, and to many kinds of meat, and to certain innocent actions. Approbations without ground are raised in like manner. But in all these instances, education never makes us apprehend any qualities in objects which we have not naturally senses capable of perceiving. We know what sickness of the stomach is, and may without ground believe that very healthful meats will raise this; we by our sight and smell receive disagreeable ideas of the food of swine, and their styes, and perhaps cannot prevent the recurring of these ideas at table. But never were men naturally blind prejudiced against objects as of a disagreeable colour, or in favour of others as of a beautiful colour. They perhaps hear men dispraise one colour, and may imagine this colour to be some quite different sensible quality of the other senses, but that is all. And the same way, a man naturally void of taste could by no education receive the ideas of taste, or be prejudiced in favour of meats as delicious. So had we no natural sense of beauty and harmony we could never be prejudiced in favour of objects or sounds as beautiful or harmonious. Education may make an unattentive Goth imagine that his countrymen have attained the perfection of architecture, and an aversion to their enemies the Romans may have joined some disagreeable ideas to their very buildings, and excited them to their demolition; but he had never formed these prejudices had he been void of a sense of beauty. Did ever blind men debate whether purple or scarlet were the finer colour, or could any education prejudice them in favour of either as colours?

Thus education and custom may influence our internal senses, where they are antecedently, by enlarging the capacity of our minds to retain and compare the parts of complex compositions; and then if the finest objects are presented to us we grow conscious of a pleasure far superior to what common performances excite. But all this presupposes our sense of beauty to be natural. Instruction in anatomy, observation of nature and those airs of the countenance, or passion, may enable us to know where there is a just imitation. But why should an exact imitation please upon observation if we had not naturally a sense of beauty in it, more than the observing the situation of fifty or a hundred pebbles thrown at random? And should we observe them ever so often, we should never dream of their growing beautiful.

IV. There is something worth our observation as to the manner of rooting out the prejudices of education, not quite foreign to the present purpose. When the prejudice arises from association of ideas without any natural connection, we must frequently force ourselves to bear representations of those objects, or the use of them when separated from the disagreeable idea; and this may at last disjoin the unreasonable association, especially if we can join new agreeable ideas to them. Thus opinions of superstition are best removed by pleasant conversation of persons we esteem for their virtue, or by observing that they despise such opinions. But when the prejudice arises from an apprehension or opinion of natural evil as the attendant or consequent of any object or action, if the evil be apprehended to be the constant and immediate attendant, a few trials without receiving any damage will remove the prejudice, as in that against meats. But where the evil is not represented as the perpetual concomitant, but as what may possibly or probably at some time or other accompany the use of the object, there must be frequent reasoning with ourselves, or a long series of trials without any detriment, to remove the prejudice. Such is the case of our fear of spirits in the dark and in church-yards. And when the evil is represented as the consequence perhaps a long time after, or in a future state, it is then hardest of all to remove the prejudice; and this is only to be effected by slow processes of reason, because in this case there can be no trials made. And this is the case of superstitious prejudices against actions apprehended as offensive to the Deity; and hence it is that they are so hard to root out.

v. Example seems to operate in this manner. We are conscious that we act very much for pleasure or private good, and are thereby led to imagine that others do so too: hence we conclude there must be some perfection in the objects which we see others pursue, and evil in those which we observe them constantly shunning. Or the example of others may serve to us as so many trials to remove the apprehension of evil in objects to which we had an aversion. But all this is done upon an apprehension of qualities perceivable by the senses which we have; for no example will induce the blind or deaf to pursue objects as coloured or sonorous, nor could example any more engage us to pursue objects as beautiful or harmonious, had we no natural sense of beauty or harmony.

Example may make us conclude without examination that our countrymen have obtained the perfection of beauty in their works, or that there is less beauty in the orders of architecture or painting used in other nations, and so content ourselves with very imperfect forms. And fear of contempt as void of taste or genius often makes us join in approving the performances of the reputed masters in our country, and restrains those who have naturally a fine genius or the internal sense very acute, from studying to obtain the greatest perfection. It makes also those of a bad taste pretend to a livelier perception of beauty than in reality they have. But all this presupposes some natural power of receiving ideas of beauty and harmony. Nor can example effect anything farther unless it be to lead men to pursue objects by implicit faith for some perfection which the pursuer is conscious he does not know or which perhaps is some very different quality from the idea perceived by those of a good taste in such affairs.

Section VIII:
Of the Importance of the Internal Senses in Life, and the Final Causes of Them

I. The busy part of mankind may look upon these things as airy dreams of an inflamed imagination which a wise man should despise who rationally pursues more solid possessions independent on fancy; but a little reflection will convince us that the gratifications of our internal senses are as natural, real, and satisfying enjoyments as any sensible pleasure whatsoever, and that they are the chief ends for which we commonly pursue wealth or power. For how is wealth or power advantageous? How do they make us happy, or prove good to us? No otherwise than as they supply gratifications to our senses or faculties of perceiving pleasure. Now, are these senses or faculties only the external ones? No. Everybody sees that a small portion of wealth or power will supply more pleasures of the external senses than we can enjoy. We know that scarcity often heightens these perceptions more than abundance, which cloys the appetite which is necessary to all pleasure in enjoyment; and hence the poet's advice is perfectly just:

> *Tu pulmentaria quaere*
> *Sudando**

In short, the only use of a great fortune above a very small one except in good offices and moral pleasures must be to supply us with the pleasures of beauty, order and harmony.

* * *

II. As to the *final causes* of this internal sense, we need not inquire whether, to an almighty and all-knowing Being, there be any real excellence in regular forms, in acting by general laws, in knowing by general theorems. We seem scarce capable of answering such questions anyway; nor need we inquire whether other animals may not discern uniformity and regularity in objects which escape our observation, and may not perhaps have their senses constituted so as to perceive beauty from the same foundation which we do, in objects which our senses are

---

* Horace, *Satires*, Bk II, Sat. ii, v. 20. ['So you earn your sauce with hard exercise.' Trans. H. R. Fairclough.]

not fit to examine or compare. We shall confine ourselves to a subject where we have some certain foundation to go upon and only inquire if we can find any reasons worthy of the great Author of nature for making such a connection between regular objects and the pleasure which accompanies our perceptions of them; or, what reasons might possibly influence him to create the world as it at present is as far as we can observe, everywhere full of regularity and uniformity.

Let it be here observed that as far as we know concerning any of the great bodies of the universe, we see forms and motions really beautiful to our senses; and if we were placed in any planet, the apparent courses would still be regular and uniform, and consequently beautiful to us. Now this gives us no small ground to imagine that if the senses of their inhabitants are in the same manner adapted to their habitations and the objects occurring to their view as ours are here, their senses must be upon the same general foundation with ours.

* * *

Now from the whole we may conclude that supposing the Deity so kind as to connect sensible pleasure with certain actions or contemplations beside the rational advantage perceivable in them, there is a great moral necessity from his goodness that the internal sense of men should be constituted as it is at present so as to make uniformity amidst variety the occasion of pleasure. For were it not so, but on the contrary, if irregular objects, particular truths and operations pleased us, beside the endless toil this would involve us in, there must arise a perpetual dissatisfaction in all rational agents with themselves, since reason and interest would lead us to simple general causes while a contrary sense of beauty would make us disapprove them. Universal theorems would appear to our understanding the best means of increasing our knowledge of what might be useful, while a contrary sense would set us on the search after particular truths. Thought and reflection would recommend objects with uniformity amidst variety, and yet this perverse instinct would involve us in labyrinths of confusion and dissimilitude. And hence we see how suitable it is to the sagacious bounty which we suppose in the Deity to constitute our internal senses in the manner in which they are, by which pleasure is joined to the contemplation of those objects which a finite mind can best imprint and retain the ideas of with the least distraction; to those actions which are most efficacious and fruitful in useful effect; and to those theorems which most enlarge our minds.

III. As to the other question, What reason might influence the Deity, whom no diversity of operation could distract or weary, to choose to operate by simplest means and general laws, and to diffuse uniformity, proportion, and similitude through all the parts of nature which we can observe? perhaps there may be some real excellence in this manner of operation, and in these forms, which we know not. But this we may probably say, that since the divine goodness, for the reasons above mentioned, has constituted our sense of beauty as it is at present, the same goodness might have determined the Great Architect to adorn this stupendous theatre in a manner agreeable to the spectators, and that part which is exposed to the observation of men so as to be pleasant to them, especially if we suppose that he designed to discover himself to them as wise and good, as well as powerful; for thus he has given them greater evidences through the whole earth of his art, wisdom, design, and bounty, than they can possibly have for the reason, counsel, and good-will of their fellow creatures, with whom they converse, with full persuasion of these qualities in them, about their common affairs.

As to the operations of the Deity by general laws, there is still a farther reason from a sense superior to these already considered, even that of virtue, or the beauty of action, which is the foundation of our greatest happiness. For were there no general laws fixed to the course of nature there could be no prudence or design in men, no rational expectation of effects from causes, no schemes of action projected, or any regular execution. If, then, according to the frame of our nature, our greatest happiness must depend upon our actions, as it may perhaps be made appear it does, the universe must be governed not by particular wills but by general laws upon which we can found our expectations and project our schemes of action. Nay farther, though general laws did ordinarily obtain, yet if the Deity usually stopped their effects whenever it was necessary to prevent any particular evils, this would effectually and justly supersede all human prudence and care about actions, since a superior mind did thus relieve men from their charge.

REFLECTIONS UPON LAUGHTER

Advertisement

The following papers were originally published in the *Dublin Journal* by the late Mr Arbuckle. Concerning the merit of them, that ingenious author, at the close of his work, expresses himself in the following manner. 'The learned and ingenious author of the *Inquiry into the Original of Our Ideas of Beauty and Virtue* will therefore, I hope, excuse me if, to do justice to myself, I am obliged to name him for the three papers upon laughter, which are written in so curious and new a strain of thinking: and also for the forty-fifth, forty-sixth, and forty-seventh papers, containing so many judicious remarks on that pernicious book, *The Fable of the Bees*.'

I

*... Rapias in jus malis ridentem alienis**
TO HIBERNICUS

There is scarce anything that concerns human nature, which does not deserve to be inquired into. I send you some thoughts upon a very uncommon subject, laughter, which you may publish, if you think they can be of any use, to help us to understand what so often happens in our own minds, and to know the use for which it is designed in the constitution of our nature.

Aristotle, in his *Art of Poetry*, has very justly explained the nature of one species of laughter, viz. the Ridiculing of Persons, the occasion or object of which he tells us is: Ἁμάϛημα τι κὶ αἶχς ἀνώδυννον κὶ οὐ 'some mistake, or some turpitude, without grievous pain, and not very

---

* [Horace, *Satires*, Bk II, Sat. iii, v. 72. 'When you drag him into court he will laugh at your expense.' Trans. H. R. Fairclough.]

pernicious or destructive.'* But this he never intended as a general account of all sorts of laughter.

But Mr Hobbes, who very much owes his character of philosopher to his assuming positive solemn airs, which he uses most when he is going to assert some palpable absurdity, or some ill-natured nonsense, assures us that 'Laughter is nothing else but sudden glory, arising from some sudden conception of some eminency in ourselves, by comparison with the infirmity of others, or with our own formerly: for men laugh at the follies of themselves past, when they come suddenly to remembrance, except they bring with them any present dishonour.'†

This notion the authors of the *Spectator*, No. 47, have adopted from Mr Hobbes. That bold author having carried on his inquiries, in a singular manner, without regard to authorities, and having fallen into a way of speaking which was much more intelligible than that of the Schoolmen, soon became agreeable to many free wits of his age. His grand view was to deduce all human actions from self-love: by some bad fortune he has overlooked everything which is generous or kind in mankind, and represents men in that light in which a thorough knave or coward beholds them, suspecting all friendship, love, or social affection, of hypocrisy, or selfish design or fear.

The learned world has often been told that Pufendorf had strongly imbibed Hobbes's first principles, although he draws much better consequences from them; and this last author, as he is certainly much preferable to the generality of the Schoolmen, in distinct intelligible reasoning, has been made the grand instructor in morals to all who have of late given themselves to that study. Hence it is that the old notions of natural affections, and kind instincts, the *sensus communis*, the *decorum*, and *honestum*, are almost banished out of our books of morals. We must never hear of them in any of our lectures for fear of innate ideas: all must be interest, and some selfish view; laughter itself must be a joy from the same spring.

If Mr Hobbes's notion be just, then, first, there can be no laughter on any occasion where we make no comparison of ourselves to others, or of our present state to a worse state, or where we do not observe some superiority to ourselves above some other thing: and again, it must

---

* [Aristotle, *Poetics*, ch. V.]

† [*Human Nature*, ch. IX. Cf. *Leviathan*, Part I, ch. VI.]

follow, that every sudden appearance of superiority over another must excite laughter, when we attend to it. If both these conclusions be false, the notion from whence they are drawn must be so too.

First then, that laughter often arises without any imagined superiority of ourselves, may appear from one great fund of pleasantry, the parody, and burlesque allusion, which move laughter in those who may have the highest veneration for the writing alluded to, and also admire the wit of the person who makes the allusion. Thus many a profound admirer of the machinery in Homer and Virgil has laughed heartily at the interposition of Pallas, in *Hudibras*, to save the bold Talgol from the knight's pistol, presented to the outside of his skull:

> But Pallas came in shape of rust,
> And 'twixt the spring and hammer thrust
> Her Gorgon shield, which made the cock
> Stand stiff, as 'twere transform'd to stock.*

And few, who read, this, imagine themselves superior either to Homer or Butler; we indeed generally imagine ourselves superior in sense to the valorous knight, but not in this point, of firing pistols. And pray, would any mortal have laughed, had the poet told, in a simple unadorned manner, that his knight attempted to shoot Talgol, but his pistol was so rusty that it would not give fire? And yet this would have given us the same ground of sudden glory from our superiority over the doughty knight.

Again, to what do we compare ourselves or imagine ourselves superior, when we laugh at this fantastical imitation of the poetical imagery, and similitudes of the morning?

> The sun, long since, had in the lap
> Of Thetis taken out his nap;
> And like a lobster boil'd, the morn
> From black to red began to turn.†

Many an orthodox Scotch Presbyterian, which sect few accuse of disregard for the holy scriptures, has been put to it to preserve his gravity, upon hearing the application of Scripture made by his countryman Dr Pitcairn, as he observed a crowd in the streets about a mason, who had fallen along with his scaffold, and was overwhelmed with the ruins of

---

* [*Hudibras*, I, ii, 781.]
† [*Hudibras*, II, ii, 29.]

the chimney which he had been building, and which fell immediately
after the fall of the poor mason: 'Blessed are the dead which die in
the Lord, for they rest from their labours, and their works follow
them.' And yet few imagine themselves superior either to the apostle
or the doctor. Their superiority to the poor mason, I am sure, could
never have raised such laughter, for this occurred to them before the
doctor's consolation. In this case no opinion of superiority could have
occasioned the laughter, unless we say that people imagined themselves
superior to the doctor in religion: but an imagined superiority to a
doctor in religion is not a matter so rare as to raise sudden joy; and
with people who value religion, the impiety of another is no matter of
laughter.

It is said* that when men of wit make us laugh, it is by representing
some oddness or infirmity in themselves, or others. Thus allusions
made on trifling occasions, to the most solemn figured speeches of great
writers, contain such an obvious impropriety, that we imagine ourselves
incapable of such mistakes as the alluder seemingly falls into; so that
in this case too there is an imagined superiority. But in answer to this,
we may observe, that we often laugh at such allusions, when we are
conscious that the person who raises the laugh knows abundantly the
justest propriety of speaking, and knows, at present, the oddness and
impropriety of his own allusion as well as any in company; nay, laughs
at it himself. We often admire his wit in such allusions, and study to
imitate him in it, as far as we can. Now, what sudden sense of glory, or
joy in our superiority, can arise from observing a quality in another,
which we study to imitate, I cannot imagine. I doubt if men compared
themselves with the alluder, whom they study to imitate, they would
rather often grow grave or sorrowful.

Nay, farther, this is so far from truth, that imagined superiority moves
our laughter, that one would imagine from some instances the very
contrary: for if laughter arose from our imagined superiority, then, the
more that any object appeared inferior to us, the greater would be the
jest; and the nearer anyone came to an equality with us, or resemblance
of our actions, the less we should be moved with laughter. But we see,
on the contrary, that some ingenuity in dogs and monkeys, which comes

---

* See the *Spectator*. [See Introduction, p. xxiv fn.]

near to some of our own arts, very often makes us merry; whereas their duller actions, in which they are much below us, are no matter of jest at all. Whence the author in the *Spectator* drew his observation, that the actions of beasts, which move our laughter, bear a resemblance to a human blunder, I confess I cannot guess; I fear the very contrary is true, that their imitation of our grave, wise actions would be fittest to raise mirth in the observer.

The second part of the argument, that opinion of superiority suddenly incited in us does not move to laughter, seems the most obvious thing imaginable. If we observe an object in pain while we are at ease, we are in greater danger of weeping than laughing; and yet here is occasion for Hobbes's sudden joy. It must be a very merry state in which a fine gentleman is, when well dressed, in his coach, he passes our streets, where he will see so many ragged beggars, and porters, and chairmen sweating at their labour, on every side of him. It is a great pity that we had not an infirmary or lazar-house to retire to in cloudy weather, to get an afternoon of laughter at these inferior objects: Strange! – that none of our Hobbists banish all canary birds and squirrels, and lap-dogs, and pugs, and cats out of their houses, and substitute in their places asses, and owls, and snails, and oysters, to be merry upon. From these they might have higher joys of superiority, than from those with whom we now please ourselves. Pride, or an high opinion of ourselves, must be entirely inconsistent with gravity; emptiness must always make men solemn in their behaviour; and conscious virtue and great abilities must always be upon the sneer. An orthodox believer, who is very sure that he is in the true way to salvation, must always be merry upon heretics, to whom he is so much superior in his own opinion; and no other passion but mirth should arise upon hearing of their heterodoxy. In general, all men of true sense, and reflection, and integrity, of great capacity for business, and penetration into the tempers and interests of men, must be the merriest little grigs imaginable; Democritus must be the sole leader of all the philosophers; and perpetual laughter must succeed into the place of the long beard,

> ... To be the grace
> Both of our wisdom and our face.*

* [*Hudibras*, I, i, 241.]

It is pretty strange that the authors whom we mentioned above have never distinguished between the words laughter and ridicule; this last is but one particular species of the former, when we are laughing at the follies of others; and in this species there may be some pretence to allege that some imagined superiority may occasion it. But then there are innumerable instances of laughter where no person is ridiculed; nor does he who laughs compare himself to anything whatsoever. Thus how often do we laugh at some out-of-the-way description of natural objects, to which we never compare our state at all. I fancy few have ever read the City Shower* without a strong disposition to laughter, and instead of imagining any superiority, are very sensible of a turn of wit in the author which they despair of imitating: thus what relation to our affairs has that simile of *Hudibras*,

> Instead of trumpet and of drum,
> Which makes the warrior's stomach come,
> And whets mens valour sharp, like beer
> By thunder turn'd to vinegar.†

The laughter is not here raised against either valour or martial music, but merely by the wild resemblance of a mean event.

And then farther, even in ridicule itself there must be something else than bare opinion to raise it, as may appear from this, that if anyone would relate in the simplest manner these very weaknesses of others, their extravagant passions, their absurd opinions, upon which the man of wit would rally, should we hear the best vouchers of all the facts alleged, we shall not be disposed to laughter by bare narration. Or should one do a real important injury to another, by taking advantage of his weakness, or by some pernicious fraud let us see another's simplicity, this is no matter of laughter: and yet these important cheats do really discover our superiority over the person cheated, more than the trifling impostures of our humourists. The opinion of our superiority may raise a sedate joy in our minds, very different from laughter; but such a thought seldom arises in our minds in the hurry of a cheerful conversation among friends, where there is often an high mutual esteem. But we go to our closets often to spin out some fine conjectures about the principles of our

---

* [*A Description of a City Shower* is the name of a poem by Jonathan Swift published in the *Tatler* in 1710. It parodies the style of Virgil's *Georgics* and makes fun of city life as portrayed by Augustan poets.]
† [*Hudibras*, I, ii, 107.]

actions, which no mortal is conscious of in himself during the action; thus the same authors above-mentioned tell us that the desire which we have to see tragical representations is because of the secret pleasure we find in thinking ourselves secure from such evils; we know from what sect this notion was derived.

> Quibus ipse malis liber es, quia cernere suave.
>
> Lucretius*

This pleasure must indeed be a secret one, so very secret, that many a kind compassionate heart was never conscious of it, but felt itself in a continual state of horror and sorrow; our desiring such sights flows from a kind instinct of nature, a secret bond between us and our fellow-creatures.

> Naturae imperio gemimus cum funus adultae
> Virginis occurrit, vel terra clauditur infans.
> . . . Quis enim bonus . . .
> Ulla aliena sibi credat mala.
>
> Juvenal†

II
TO THE AUTHOR OF THE DUBLIN JOURNAL

> Humano capiti cervicem pictor equinam
> Jungere si velit, et varias inducere plumas,
> Undique conlatis membris, ut turpiter atrum
> Desinat in piscem mulier formosa superne;
> Spectatum admissi risum teneatis amici?
>
> Horace‡

SIR,

In my former letter, I attempted to show that Mr Hobbes's account of laughter was not just. I shall now endeavour to discover some other

---

* [*De Rerum Natura*, Bk I, line 4: 'because to perceive what ills you are free from yourself is pleasant'. Trans. W. H. D. Rouse.]

† [*Satires*, XV.138: 'It is at Nature's behest that we weep when we meet the bier of a full-grown maiden, or when the earth closes over a babe . . . For what good man . . . believes that any human woes concern him not?' Trans. G. G. Ramsay.]

‡ [*De Arte Poetica*, 1: 'If a painter chose to join a human head to the neck of a horse, and to spread feathers of many a hue over limbs picked up now here now there, so that what at top is a lovely woman ends below in a black and ugly fish, could you, my friend, if favoured with a private view, refrain from laughing?' Trans. H. R. Fairclough.]

ground of that sensation, action, passion, or affection, I know not which of them a philosopher would call it.

The ingenious Mr Addison, in his treatise of the pleasures of the imagination, has justly observed many sublimer sensations than those commonly mentioned among philosophers: he observes, particularly, that we receive sensations of pleasure from those objects which are great, new, or beautiful; and, on the contrary, that objects which are more narrow and confined, or deformed and irregular, give us disagreeable ideas. It is unquestionable that we have a great number of perceptions which can scarcely reduce to any of the five senses, as they are commonly explained; such as either the ideas of grandeur, dignity, decency, beauty, harmony; or, on the other hand, of meanness, baseness, indecency, deformity; and that we apply these ideas not only to material objects, but to characters, abilities, actions.

It may be farther observed, that by some strange associations of ideas made in our infancy, we have frequently some of these ideas recurring along with a great many objects, with which they have no other connection than what custom and education, or frequent allusions, give them, or at most, some very distant resemblance. The very affections of our minds are ascribed to inanimate objects; and some animals, perfect enough in their own kind, are made constant emblems of some vices or meanness: whereas other kinds are made emblems of the contrary qualities. For instances of these associations, partly from nature, partly from custom, we may take the following ones: sanctity in our churches, magnificence in public buildings, affection between the oak and ivy, the elm and vine; hospitality in a shade, a pleasant sensation of grandeur in the sky, the sea, and mountains, distinct from a bare apprehension or image of their extension; solemnity and horror in shady woods. An ass is the common emblem of stupidity and sloth, a swine of selfish luxury; an eagle of a great genius; a lion of intrepidity; an ant or bee of low industry, and prudent economy. Some inanimate objects have in like manner some accessary ideas of meanness, either for some natural reason, or oftener by mere chance and custom.

Now, the same ingenious author observes, in the *Spectator*, Vol. I, No 62, that what we call a great genius, such as becomes a heroic poet, gives us pleasure by filling the mind with great conceptions; and therefore they bring most of their similitudes and metaphors from objects of dignity and grandeur, where the resemblance is generally very obvious. This is not usually called wit, but something nobler. What we call grave wit consists in bringing such resembling ideas together, as one could scarce have imagined had so exact a relation to each other; or when the resemblance is carried on through many more particulars than we could have at first expected: and this therefore gives the pleasure of surprise. In this serious wit, though we are not solicitous about the grandeur of the images, we must still beware of bringing in ideas of baseness or deformity, unless we are studying to represent an object as base and deformed. Now this sort of wit is seldom apt to move laughter, more than heroic poetry.

That then which seems generally the cause of laughter is the bringing together of images which have contrary additional ideas, as well as some resemblance in the principal idea: this contrast between ideas of grandeur, dignity, sanctity, perfection, and ideas of meanness, baseness, profanity, seems to be the very spirit of burlesque: and the greatest part of our raillery and jest is founded upon it.

We also find ourselves moved to laughter by an overstraining of wit, by bringing resemblances from subjects of a quite different kind from the subject to which they are compared. When we see, instead of the easiness, and natural resemblance, which constitutes true wit, a forced straining of a likeness, our laughter is apt to arise; as also, when the only resemblance is not in the idea, but in the sound of the words. And this is the matter of laughter in the pun.

Let us see if this thought may not be confirmed in many instances. If any writing has obtained an high character for grandeur, sanctity, inspiration, or sublimity of thoughts, and boldness of images, the application of any known sentence of such writings to low, vulgar, or base subjects, never fails to divert the audience, and set them a laughing. This fund of laughter the ancients had by allusions to Homer: of this the lives of some of the philosophers in Diogenes Laertius supply abundance of instances. Our late burlesque writers derive a great part of their pleasantry from their introducing, on the most trifling occasions, allusions to some of the bold schemes, or figures, or sentences, of the great poets, upon the most solemn subjects. *Hudibras* and *Don Quixote* will supply one with instances of this in almost every page. It were to be wished that the boldness of our age had never carried their ludicrous allusions to yet more venerable writings. We know that allusions to the phrases of holy writ have obtained to some gentlemen a character of wit, and often furnish laughter to their hearers, when their imaginations have been too barren to give any other entertainment. But I appeal to the religious themselves, if these allusions are not apt to move laughter, unless a more strong affection of the mind, a religious horror at the profanity of such allusions, prevents their allowing themselves the liberty of laughing at them. Now in this affair I fancy anyone will acknowledge that an opinion of superiority is not at all the occasion of the laughter.

Again, any little accident to which we have joined the idea of meanness, befalling a person of great gravity, ability, dignity, is a matter of laughter, for the very same reason: thus the strange contortions of the body in a fall, the dirtying of a decent dress, the natural functions which we study to conceal from sight, are matter of laughter when they occur to observation in persons of whom we have high ideas. Nay, the very human form has the ideas of dignity so generally joined with it, that even in ordinary persons such mean accidents are matter of jest; but still the jest is increased by the dignity, gravity, or modesty of the person, which shows that it is this contrast, or opposition of ideas of dignity and meanness, which is the occasion of laughter.

We generally imagine in mankind some degree of wisdom above other animals, and have high ideas of them on this account. If then along with our notion of wisdom in our fellows, there occurs any instance of gross inadvertence, or great mistake, this is a great cause of laughter. Our countrymen are very subject to little trips of this kind, and furnish often some diversion to their neighbours, not only by mistakes in their speech, but in actions. Yet even this kind of laughter cannot well be said to arise from our sense of superiority. This alone may give a sedate joy, but not be a matter of laughter, since we shall find the same kind of laughter arising in us, where this opinion of superiority does not attend it: for if the most ingenious person in the world, whom the whole company esteems, should through inadvertent hearing, or any other mistake, answer quite from the purpose, the whole audience may laugh heartily, without the least abatement of their good opinion. Thus we know some very ingenious men have not in the least suffered in their characters by an extemporary pun, which raises the laugh very readily; whereas a premeditated pun, which diminishes our opinion of a writer, will seldom raise any laughter.

Again, the more violent passions, as fear, anger, sorrow, compassion, are generally looked upon as something great and solemn; the beholding of these passions in another strikes a man with gravity. Now if these passions are artfully, or accidentally, raised upon a small or fictitious occasion, they move the laughter of those who imagine the occasions to be small and contemptible, or who are conscious of the fraud: this is the occasion of the laugh in biting, as they call such deceptions.

According to this scheme, there must necessarily arise a great diversity in men's sentiments of the ridiculous in actions or characters, according as their ideas of dignity and wisdom are various. A truly wise man, who places the dignity of human nature in good affections and suitable actions, may be apt to laugh at those who employ their most solemn and strong affections about what, to the wise man, appears perhaps very useless or mean. The same solemnity of behaviour and keenness of passion, about a place or ceremony, which ordinary people only employ about the absolute necessaries of life, may make them laugh at their betters. When a gentleman of pleasure, who thinks that good fellowship and gallantry are the only valuable enjoyments of life, observes men, with great solemnity and earnestness, heaping up money, without using it, or incumbering themselves with purchases and mortgages, which the gay gentleman, with his paternal revenues, thinks very silly affairs, he may make himself very merry upon them: and the frugal man, in his turn, makes the same jest of the man of pleasure. The successful gamester, whom no disaster forces to lay aside the trifling ideas of an amusement in his play, may laugh to see the serious looks and passions of the gravest business arising in the loser, amidst the ideas of a recreation. There is indeed in these last cases an opinion of superiority in the laughter; but this is not the proper occasion of his laughter; otherwise I see not how we should ever meet with a composed countenance anywhere. Men have their different relishes of life, most people prefer their own taste to that of others; but this moves no laughter, unless, in representing the pursuits of others, they do join together some whimsical image of the opposite ideas.

In the more polite nations, there are certain modes of dress, behaviour, ceremony, generally received by all the better sort, as they are commonly called: to these modes, ideas of decency, grandeur, and dignity are generally joined. Hence men are fond of imitating the mode; and if in any polite assembly, a contrary dress, behaviour, or ceremony appear, to which we have joined in our country the contrary ideas of meanness, rusticity, sullenness, a laugh does ordinarily arise, or a disposition to it, in those who have not the thorough good breeding, or reflection, to restrain themselves, or break through these customary associations.

And hence we may see, that what is counted ridiculous in one age or nation, may not be so in another. We are apt to laugh at Homer, when he compares Ajax unwillingly retreating to an ass driven out of a cornfield; or when he compares him to a boar; or Ulysses tossing all night without sleep through anxiety to a pudding frying on the coals. Those three similes have got low mean ideas joined to them with us, which it is very probable they had not in Greece in Homer's days; nay, as to one of them, the boar, it is well known that in some countries of Europe, where they have wild boars for hunting, even in our times, they have not these low sordid ideas joined to that animal, which we have in these kingdoms, who never see them but in their dirty styes, or on dunghills. This may teach us how impermanent a great many jests are, which are made upon the style of some other ancient writings, in ages when manners were very different from ours, though perhaps fully as rational, and every way as human and just.

III

TO THE AUTHOR OF THE DUBLIN JOURNAL

. . . Ridiculum acri
Fortius et melius magnas plerumque secat res*

SIR,

To treat this subject of laughter gravely may subject the author to a censure like to that which Longinus makes upon a prior treatise of the Sublime, because wrote in a manner very unsuitable to the subject. But yet it may be worth our pains to consider the effects of laughter, and the ends for which it was implanted in our nature, that thence we may know the proper use of it: which may be done in the following observations.

First, we may observe, that laughter, like many other dispositions of our mind, is necessarily pleasant to us, when it begins in the natural manner, from one perception in the mind of something ludicrous, and does not take its rise unnaturally from external motions in the body. Everyone is conscious that a state of laughter is an easy and agreeable state, that the recurring or suggestion of ludicrous images tends to dispel fretfulness, anxiety, or sorrow, and to reduce the mind to an easy, happy state; as on the other hand, an easy and happy state is that in which we are most lively and acute in perceiving the ludicrous in objects. Anything that gives us pleasure puts us also in a fitness for laughter, when something ridiculous occurs; and ridiculous objects, occurring to a soured temper, will be apt to recover it to easiness. The implanting then a sense of the ridiculous, in our nature, was giving us an avenue to pleasure, and an easy remedy for discontent and sorrow.

Again, laughter, like other associations, is very contagious: our whole frame is so sociable, that one merry countenance may diffuse cheerfulness to many; nor are they all fools who are apt to laugh before they know the jest, however curiosity in wise men may restrain it, that their attention may be kept awake.

We are disposed by laughter to a good opinion of the person who raises it, if neither ourselves nor our friends are made the

---

* [Horace, *Satires*, Bk I, Sat. x, vv. 14–15: 'Jesting oft cuts hard knots more forcefully and effectively than gravity.' Trans. H. R. Fairclough.]

butt. Laughter is none of the smallest bonds to common friendships, though it be of less consequence in great heroic friendships.

If an object, action, or event, be truly great in every respect, it will have no natural relation or resemblance to anything mean or base; and consequently no mean idea can be joined to it with any natural resemblance. If we make some forced remote jests upon such subjects, they can never be pleasing to a man of sense and reflection, but raise contempt of the ridiculer, as void of just sense of those things which are truly great. As to any great and truly sublime sentiments, we may perhaps find that, by a playing upon words, they may be applied to a trifling or mean action, or object; but this application will not diminish our high idea of the great sentiment. He must be of a poor trifling temper who would lose his relish of the grandeur and beauty of that noble sentence of the holy writ, mentioned in the former paper, from the doctor's application of it. *Virgil Travesty** may often come into an ingenious man's head, when he reads the original, and make him uneasy with impertinent interruptions, but will never diminish his admiration of Virgil. Who dislikes that line in Homer, by which Diogenes the Cynic answered his neighbour at an execution, who was inquiring into the cause of the criminal's damnation, which had been the counterfeiting of the ancient purple?

Ἔλλαβε ποςφύςεϑ Οανάϑ ῳ μοίεα χεαταιπ[†]

Let any of our wits try their mettle in ridiculing the opinion of a good and wise mind governing the whole universe; let them try to ridicule integrity and honesty, gratitude, generosity, or the love of one's country, accompanied with wisdom. All their art will never diminish the admiration which we must have for such dispositions, wherever we observe them pure and unmixed with any low views, or any folly in the exercise of them.

When in any object there is a mixture of what is truly great, along with something weak or mean, ridicule may, with a weak mind which cannot separate the great from the mean, bring the whole into disesteem, or make the whole appear weak or contemptible: but with a person of just discernment and reflec-

---

* [Paul Scarron, *Le virgile travesti*.]

† [Homer, *Iliad*, V.83: 'and down over his eyes came dark death and mighty fate'. Trans. A. T. Murray.]

tion it will have no other effect but to separate what is great from what is not so.

When any object either good or evil is aggravated and increased by the violence of our passions, or an enthusiastic admiration, or fear, the application of ridicule is the readiest way to bring down our high imaginations to a conformity to the real moment or importance of the affair. Ridicule gives our minds as it were a bend to the contrary side; so that upon reflection they may be more capable of settling in a just conformity to nature.

Laughter is received in a different manner by the person ridiculed, according as he who uses the ridicule evidences good-nature, friendship, and esteem of the person whom he laughs at, or the contrary.

The enormous crime or grievous calamity of another is not itself a subject which can be naturally turned into ridicule: the former raises horror in us, and hatred, and the latter pity. When laughter arises on such occasions, it is not excited by the guilt or the misery. To observe the contortions of the human body in the air, upon the blowing up of an enemy's ship, may raise laughter in those who do not reflect on the agony and distress of the sufferers; but the reflecting on this distress could never move laughter of itself. So some fantastic circumstances accompanying a crime may raise laughter; but a piece of cruel barbarity, or treacherous villainy, of itself, must raise very contrary passions. A jest is not ordinary in an impeachment of a criminal, or an investive oration: it rather diminishes than increases the abhorrence in the audience, and may justly raise contempt of the orator for an unnatural affectation of wit. Jesting is still more unnatural in discourses designed to move compassion toward the distressed. A forced unnatural ridicule on either of these occasions, must be apt to raise, in the guilty or the miserable, hatred against the laughter; since it must be supposed to show from hatred in him toward the object of his ridicule, or from want of all compassion. The guilty will take laughter to be a triumph over him as contemptible; the miserable will interpret it as hardness of heart, and insensibility of the calamities of another. This is the natural effect of joining to either of these objects mean ludicrous ideas.

If smaller faults, such as are not inconsistent with a character in the main amiable, be set in a ridiculous light, the guilty are apt to be made sensible of their folly, more than by a bare grave admonition. In many of our faults, occasioned by too great violence of some passion, we get such enthusiastic apprehensions of some objects, as lead us to justify our conduct: the joining of opposite ideas or images allays this enthusiasm; and, if this be done with good nature, it may be the least offensive, and most effectual, reproof.

Ridicule upon the smallest faults, when it does not appear to flow from kindness, is apt to be extremely provoking, since the applying of mean ideas to our conduct discovers contempt of us in the ridiculer, and that he designs to make us contemptible to others.

Ridicule applied to those qualities or circumstances in one of our companions, which neither he nor the ridiculer thinks dishonourable, is agreeable to everyone; the butt himself is as well pleased as any in company.

Ridicule upon any small misfortune or injury, which we have received with sorrow or keen resentment, when it is applied by a third person, with appearance of good-nature, is exceeding useful to abate our concern or resentment, and to reconcile us to the person who injured us, if he does not persist in his injury.

From this consideration of the effects of laughter it may be easy to see for what cause, or end, a sense of the ridiculous was implanted in human nature, and how it ought to be managed.

It is plainly of considerable moment in human society. It is often a great occasion of pleasure, and enlivens our conversation exceedingly, when it is conducted by good-nature. It spreads a pleasantry of temper over multitudes at once; and one merry easy mind may by this means diffuse a like disposition over all who are in company. There is nothing of which we are more communicative than of a good jest: and many a man, who is incapable of obliging us otherwise, can oblige us by his mirth, and really insinuate himself into our kind affections, and good wishes.

But this is not all the use of laughter. It is well-known that our passions of every kind lead us into wild enthusiastic apprehensions of their several objects. When any object seems great in comparison of ourselves, our minds are apt to run into a perfect veneration: when an object appears formidable, a weak mind will run into a panic, an unreasonable, impotent horror. Now in both these cases, by our sense of the ridiculous, we are made capable of relief from any pleasant, ingenious well-wisher, by more effectual means, than the most solemn, sedate reasoning. Nothing is so properly applied to the false grandeur, either of good or evil, as ridicule: nothing will sooner prevent our excessive admiration of mixed grandeur, or hinder our being led by that, which is, perhaps, really great in such an object, to imitate also and approve what is really mean.

I question not but the jest of Elijah upon the false deity, whom his countrymen had set up, had been very effectual to rectify their notions of the divine nature, as we find that like jests have been very seasonable in other nations. Baal, no doubt, had been represented as a great personage of unconquerable power; but how ridiculous does the image appear, when the prophet sets before them, at once, the poor ideas which must arise from such a limitation of nature as could be represented by their statues, and the high ideas of omniscience, and omnipotence, with which the people declared themselves possessed by their invocation: 'Cry aloud, either he is talking, or pursuing, or he is on a journey, or he is asleep.'

This engine of ridicule, no doubt, may be abused, and have a bad effect upon a weak mind; but with men of any reflection, there is little fear that it will ever be very pernicious. An attempt of ridicule before such men, upon a subject every way great, is sure to return upon the author of it. One might dare the boldest wit in company with men of sense, to make a jest upon a completely great action, or character. Let him try the story of Scipio and his fair captive, upon the taking of Cartagena, or the old story of Pylades and Orestes; I fancy he would sooner appear in a fool's coat himself, than he could put either of these characters in such a dress. The only danger is in objects of a mixed nature before people of little judgment, who, by jests upon the weak side, are sometimes led into neglect, or contempt, of that which is truly valuable in any character, institution, or office. And this may show us the impertinence, and pernicious tendency of general undistinguished jests upon any character, or office, which has been too much overrated. But, that ridicule may be abused, does not prove it useless, or unnecessary, more than a like possibility of abuse would prove all our senses and passions impertinent or hurtful. Ridicule, like other edged tools, may do good in a wise man's hands, though fools may cut their fingers with it, or be injurious to an unwary bystander.

The rules to avoid abuse of this kind of ridicule are, first, either never to attempt ridicule upon what is every way great, whether it be any great being, character, or sentiments; or, if our wit must sometimes run into allusions, on low occasions, to the expressions of great sentiments, let it not be in weak company, who have not a just discernment of true grandeur. And, secondly, concerning objects of a mixed nature, partly great, and partly mean, let us never turn the meanness into ridicule without acknowledging what is truly great, and paying a just veneration to it. In this sort of jesting we ought to be cautious of our company.

> *Discit enim citius, meminitque libentius illud,*
> *Quod quis deridet, quam quod probat et veneratur.*
>
> Horace*

Another valuable purpose of ridicule is with relation to smaller vices, which are often more effectually corrected by ridicule, than by grave admonition. Men have been laughed out of faults which a sermon could not reform: nay, there are many little indecencies which are improper to be mentioned in such solemn discourses. Now ridicule, with contempt or ill-nature, is indeed always irritating and offensive; but we may, by testifying a just esteem for the good qualities of the person ridiculed, and our concern for his interests, let him see that our ridicule of his weakness flows from love to him, and then we may hope for a good effect. This then is another necessary rule, that along with our ridicule of smaller faults we should always join evidences of good-nature and esteem.

As to jests upon imperfections, which one cannot amend, I cannot see of what use they can be: men of sense cannot relish such jests; foolish trifling minds may by them be led to despise the truest merit, which is not exempted from the casual misfortunes of our moral state. If these imperfections occur along with a vicious character, against which people should be alarmed and cautioned, it is below a wise man to raise aversions to bad men from their necessary infirmities, when they have a juster handle from their vicious dispositions.

I shall conclude this essay with the words of father Malebranche,

---

* [*Epistles*, II.i.262: 'For men more quickly learn and more gladly recall what they deride than what they approve and esteem.' Trans. H. R. Fairclough.]

upon the last subject of laughter, the smaller misfortunes of others. That author amidst all his visions shows sometimes as fine sense as any of his neighbours.

'There is nothing more admirably contrived than those natural correspondences observable between the inclination of men's minds and the motions of their bodies . . . All this secret chainwork is a miracle, which can never sufficiently be admired or understood. Upon sense of some surprising evil, which appears too strong for one to overcome with his own strength, he raises, suppose, a loud cry: this cry, forced out by the disposition of our machine, pierces the ears of those who are near, and makes them understand it, let them be of what nation or quality soever; for it is the cry of all nations, and all conditions, as indeed it ought to be. It raises a commotion in their brain . . . and makes them run to give succour without so much as knowing it. It soon obliges their will to desire, and their understanding to contrive, provided that it was just and according to the rules of society. For an indiscreet cry-out made upon no occasion, or out of an idle fear, produces, in the assistants, indignation or laughter instead of pity . . . That indiscreet cry naturally produces aversion, and desire of revenging the affront offered to nature, if he that made it without cause, did it wilfully: but it ought only to produce the passion of derision, mingled with some compassion, without aversion or desire of revenge, if it were a fright, that is, a false appearance of a pressing exigency which caused the clamour. For scoff or ridicule is necessary to reassure and correct the man as fearful; and compassion to succour him as weak. It is impossible to conceive anything better ordered.'*

I am, Sir,
Your very humble servant,
PHILOMEIDES.

* [Nicolas Malebranche, *De la recherche de la vérité*, Bk IV, ch. 13.]

MORAL PHILOSOPHY

TREATISE II: AN INQUIRY CONCERNING THE ORIGINAL OF OUR IDEAS OF VIRTUE OR MORAL GOOD

(First printed 1725; reprinted here from the revised
4th edition, 1738)

TREATISE III: AN ESSAY ON THE NATURE AND CONDUCT OF THE PASSIONS AND AFFECTIONS

(First printed 1728; reprinted here from the 3rd edition, 1742)

TREATISE IV: ILLUSTRATIONS ON THE MORAL SENSE

(First printed 1728; reprinted here from the 3rd edition, 1742)

A SYSTEM OF MORAL PHILOSOPHY

(Book I, Chapter 4, 'Concerning the Moral Sense', first printed
posthumously, 1755)

TREATISE II:
AN INQUIRY CONCERNING THE ORIGINAL OF OUR IDEAS OF VIRTUE OR MORAL GOOD

Introduction

The word *moral goodness*, in this treatise, denotes our idea of some quality apprehended in actions, which procures approbation, attended with desire of the agent's happiness. *Moral evil* denotes our idea of a contrary quality, which excites condemnation or dislike. Approbation and condemnation are probably simple ideas, which cannot be farther explained. We must be contented with these imperfect descriptions, until we discover whether we really have such ideas, and what general foundation there is in nature for this difference of actions, as morally good or evil.

These descriptions seem to contain an universally acknowledged difference of *moral good* and *evil*, from *natural*. All men who speak of moral good, acknowledge that it procures approbation and good-will toward those we apprehend possessed of it; whereas natural good does not. In this matter men must consult their own breasts. How differently are they affected toward these they suppose possessed of honesty, faith, generosity, kindness; and those who are possessed of the natural goods, such as houses, lands, gardens, vineyards, health, strength, sagacity? We shall find that we necessarily love and approve the possessors of the former; but the possession of the latter procures no approbation or good-will at all toward the possessor, but often contrary affections of envy and hatred. In the same manner, whatever quality we apprehend to be morally evil, raises our dislike toward the person in whom we observe it, such as treachery, cruelty, ingratitude; whereas we heartily love, esteem, and pity many who are exposed to natural evils, such as pain, poverty, hunger, sickness, death.

Now the first question on this subject is, 'Whence arise these different ideas of actions?'

Because we shall afterwards frequently use the words *interest*, *advantage*, *natural good*, it is necessary here to fix their ideas. The pleasure in our sensible perceptions of any kind, gives us our first idea of *natural good* or *happiness*; and then all objects which are apt to excite this pleasure are called *immediately good*. Those objects which may procure others immediately pleasant, are called *advantageous*; and we pursue both kinds from a view of *interest*, or from *self-love*.

Our *sense* of pleasure is antecedent to advantage or interest, and is the foundation of it. We do not perceive pleasure in objects, because it is our interest to do so; but objects or actions are advantageous, and are pursued or undertaken from interest, because we receive pleasure from them. Our perception of pleasure is necessary, and nothing is advantageous or naturally good to us, but what is apt to raise pleasure mediately, or immediately. Such objects as we know either from experience of sense, or reason, to be immediately or mediately advantageous, or apt to minister pleasure, we are said to pursue from *self-interest*, when our intention is only to enjoy this pleasure, which they have the power of exciting. Thus meats, drink, harmony, fine prospects, painting, statues, are perceived by our senses to be immediately good; and our reason shows riches and power to be mediately so, that is, apt to furnish us with objects of immediate pleasure: and both kinds of these natural goods are pursued from interest, or self-love.

Now the greatest part of our latter moralists establish it as undeniable, 'that all moral qualities have necessarily some relation to the *law* of a *superior*, of sufficient power to make us happy or miserable'; and since all laws operate only by sanctions of rewards, or punishments, which determine us to obedience by motives of *self-interest*, they suppose, 'that it is thus that laws do constitute some actions *mediately good*, or *advantageous*, and others the same way *disadvantageous*'. They say indeed, 'that a benevolent legislator constitutes no actions advantageous to the agent by law, but such as in their own nature tend to the natural good of the *whole*, or, at least, are not inconsistent with it; and that therefore we approve the virtue of others, because it has some small tendency to our happiness, either from its own nature, or from this general consideration, that obedience to a benevolent legislator is in general advantageous to the whole, and to us in particular; and that for the contrary reasons alone, we disapprove the vice of others, that is, the prohibited action, as tending to our particular detriment in some degree.' And then they maintain, 'that we are determined to obedience to laws, or deterred from disobedience, merely by motives of self-interest, to obtain either the natural good arising from the commanded action, or the rewards promised by the sanction; or to avoid the natural evil consequences of disobedience, or at least the penalties of the law.'

Some other moralists suppose 'an *immediate natural good* in the actions called virtuous; that is, that we are determined to perceive some *beauty* in the actions of others, and to love the agent, even without reflecting upon any advantage which can any way redound to us from the action; that we have also a secret sense of pleasure arising from reflection upon such of our own actions as we call virtuous, even when we expect no other advantage from them.' But they allege at the same time, 'that we are excited to perform these actions, even as we pursue, or purchase pictures, statues, landscapes, from *self-interest*, to obtain this pleasure which arises from reflection upon the action, or some other future advantage.' The design of the following sections is to inquire into this matter; and perhaps the reasons to be offered may prove,

I. 'That some actions have to men an *immediate goodness*; or, that by a *superior sense*, which I call a *moral one*, we *approve* the actions of others, and perceive them to be their perfection and dignity, and are determined to love the agent; a like perception we have in reflecting on such actions of our own, without any view of natural advantage from them.'

II. It may perhaps also appear, 'that the *affection*, *desire*, or *intention*, which gains approbation to the actions flowing from it, is not an intention to obtain even this pleasant self-approbation; much less the future rewards from sanctions of laws, or any other natural good, which may be the consequence of the virtuous action; but an entirely different principle of action from self-love, or desire of private good.'

Section I:

Of the Moral Sense by which we Perceive Virtue and Vice, and Approve or Disapprove them in Others

I. That the perceptions of *moral good* and *evil*, are perfectly different from those of *natural good* or *advantage*, every one must convince himself, by reflecting upon the different manner in which he finds himself affected when these objects occur to him. Had we no sense of good distinct from the advantage or interest arising from the external senses, and the perceptions of beauty and harmony; the sensations and affections toward a fruitful field, or commodious habitation, would be much the same with what we have toward a generous friend, or any noble character; for both are or may be advantageous to us: and we should no more admire any action, or love any person in a distant country, or age, whose influence could not extend to us, than we love the mountains of Peru, while we are unconcerned in the Spanish trade. We should have the same sentiments and affections toward inanimate beings, which we have toward rational agents, which yet everyone knows to be false. Upon comparison, we say, 'Why should we approve or love inanimate beings? They have no intention of good to us, or to any other person; their nature makes them fit for our uses, which they neither know nor study to serve. But it is not so with rational agents: they study the interest, and desire the happiness of other beings with whom they converse.'

We are all then conscious of the difference between that *approbation* or perception of *moral excellence*, which *benevolence* excites toward the person in whom we observe it, and that opinion of *natural goodness*, which only raises *desire* of possession toward the good object. Now 'what should make this difference, if all approbation, or sense of good be from prospect of advantage? Do not inanimate objects promote our advantage as well as benevolent persons, who do us offices of kindness and friendship? should we not then have the same endearing approbation of both? or only the same cold opinion of advantage in both?' The reason why it is not so, must be this, 'that we have a distinct perception of *beauty* or *excellence* in the kind affections of rational agents; whence we are determined to admire and love such characters and persons.'

Suppose we reap the same advantage from two men, one of whom serves us from an ultimate desire of our happiness, or good-will toward us; the other from views of self-interest, or by constraint: both are in this case equally beneficial or advantageous to us, and yet we shall have quite different sentiments of them. We must then certainly have other perceptions of moral actions, than those of advantage: and that power of receiving these perceptions may be called a *moral sense,* since the definition agrees to it, viz. a determination of the mind, to receive any idea from the presence of an object which occurs to us, independent on our will.*

This perhaps will be equally evident from our ideas of evil, done to us designedly by a rational agent. Our senses of natural good and evil would make us receive, with equal serenity and composure, an assault, a buffet, an affront from a neighbour, a cheat from a partner, or trustee, as we would an equal damage from the fall of a beam, a tile, or a tempest; and we should have the same affections and sentiments on both occasions. Villainy, treachery, cruelty, would be as meekly resented as a blast, or mildew, or an overflowing stream. But I fancy every one is very differently affected on these occasions, though there may be equal natural evil in both. Nay, actions no way detrimental may occasion the strongest anger and indignation, if they evidence only impotent hatred or contempt. And, on the other hand, the intervention of moral ideas may prevent our condemnation of the agent, or bad moral apprehension of that action, which causes to us the greatest natural evil. Thus the opinion of justice in any sentence, will prevent all ideas of moral evil in the execution, or hatred toward the magistrate, who is the immediate cause of our greatest sufferings.

II. In our sentiments of actions which affect ourselves, there is indeed a mixture of the ideas of natural and moral good, which require some attention to separate them. But when we reflect upon the actions which affect other persons only, we may observe the moral ideas unmixed with those of natural good or evil. For let it be here observed, that those senses by which we perceive pleasure in natural objects, whence they are constituted advantageous, could never raise in us any desire of *public good,* but only of what was good to ourselves in particular. Nor could they ever make us approve an action merely because of its

* See the Preface [p. 4].

promoting the happiness of others. And yet, as soon as any action is represented to us as flowing from love, humanity, gratitude, compassion, a study of the good of others, and an ultimate desire of their happiness, although it were in the most distant part of the world, or in some past age, we feel joy within us, admire the lovely action, and praise its author. And on the contrary, every action represented as flowing from ill-will, desire of the misery of others without view to any prevalent good to the public, or ingratitude, raises abhorrence and aversion.

It is true indeed, that the actions we approve in others, are generally imagined to tend to the natural good of mankind, or of some parts of it. But whence this secret chain between each person and mankind? How is my interest connected with the most distant parts of it? And yet I must admire actions which show good-will toward them, and love the author. Whence this love, compassion, indignation and hatred toward even feigned characters, in the most distant ages, and nations, according as they appear kind, faithful, compassionate, or of the opposite dispositions, toward their imaginary contemporaries? If there is no moral sense, which makes benevolent actions appear beautiful; if all approbation be from the interest of the approver,

What's Hecuba to us, or we to Hecuba?*

III. Some refined explainers of self-love may tell us, 'that we approve or condemn characters, according as we apprehend we should have been supported, or injured by them, had we lived in their days'. But how obvious is the answer, if we only observe, that had we no sense of moral good in humanity, mercy, faithfulness, why should not self-love, and our sense of natural good engage us always to the victorious side, and make us admire and love the successful tyrant, or traitor? Why do not we love Sinon or Pyrrhus, in the Aeneid? for, had we been Greeks, these two would have been very advantageous characters. Why are we affected with the fortunes of Priamus, Polites, Coroebus or Aeneas? Would not the parsimony of a miser be as advantageous to his heir, as the generosity of a worthy man is to his friend? And cannot we as easily imagine ourselves heirs to misers, as the favourites of heroes? Why don't we then approve both alike? It is plain we have some secret sense which

* Tragedy of Hamlet.

determines our approbation without regard to self-interest; otherwise we should always favour the fortunate side without regard to virtue, and suppose ourselves engaged with that party.

As Mr Hobbes explains all the sensations of pity by our fear of the like evils, when by imagination we place ourselves in the case of the sufferers,* so others explain all approbation and condemnation of actions in distant ages or nations, by a like effort of imagination: we place ourselves in the case of others, and then discern an imaginary private advantage or disadvantage in these actions. But as his account of pity will never explain how the sensation increases, according to the apprehended worth of the sufferer, or according to the affection we formerly had to him; since the sufferings of any stranger may suggest the same possibility of our suffering the like: so this explication will never account for our high approbation of brave unsuccessful attempts, which we see prove detrimental both to the agent, and to those for whose service they were intended; here there is no private advantage to be imagined. Nor will it account for our abhorrence of such injuries as we are incapable of suffering. Sure, when a man abhors the attempts of the young Tarquin, he does not imagine that he has changed his sex like Caeneus. And then, when one corrects his imagination, by remembering his own situation, and circumstances, we find the moral approbation and condemnation continues as lively as it was before, though the imagination of advantage is gone.

* * *

VI. A late witty author† says, 'that the leaders of mankind do not really admire such actions as those of Regulus, or Decius, but only observe, that men of such dispositions are very useful for the defence of any State; and therefore by panegyrics, and statues, they encourage such tempers in others, as the most tractable and useful.' Here first let us consider, if a traitor, who would sell his own country to us, may not often be as advantageous to us, as an hero who defends us: and yet we can love the treason, and hate the traitor. We can at the same time praise a gallant enemy, who is very pernicious to us. Is there nothing in all this but an opinion of advantage?

---

* [Cf. Hobbes, *Human Nature*, ch. IX.]

† See the *Fable of the Bees*, pages 34, 36, 3rd edition.

Again, upon this scheme what could a statue or panegyric effect? – Men love praise. – They will do the actions which they observe to be praised. – Praise, with men who have no other idea of good but self-interest, is the opinion which a nation or party have of a man as useful to them. – Regulus, or Cato, or Decius, had no advantage by the actions which profited their country, and therefore they themselves could not admire them, however the persons who reaped the advantage might praise such actions. – Regulus or Cato could not possibly praise or love another hero for a virtuous action; for this would not gain them the advantage of honour; and their own actions they must have looked upon as the hard terms on which honour was to be purchased, without any thing amiable in them, which they could contemplate or reflect upon with pleasure. Nay, what should excite a Cato or a Decius to desire praise, if it is only the cold opinion of others that they were useful to the State, without any perception of excellence in such conduct? – Now how unlike is this to what the least observation would teach a man concerning such characters?

But says he,* 'These wondrous cunning governors made men believe, by their statues and panegyrics, that there was public spirit, and that this was in itself excellent; and hence men are led to admire it in others, and to imitate it in themselves, forgetting the pursuit of their own advantage.' So easy a matter it seems to him, to quit judging of others by what we feel in ourselves! – for a person who is wholly selfish, to imagine others to be public-spirited! – for one who has no ideas of good but in his own advantage, to be led by the persuasions of others, into a conception of goodness in what is avowedly detrimental to himself, and profitable to others; nay, so entirely, as not to approve the action thoroughly, but so far as he was conscious that it proceeded from a disinterested study of the good of others! – Yet this it seems statues and panegyrics can accomplish!

Nil intra est oleam, nil extra est in nuce duri!†

*   *   *

_____

* See the same author in the same place.
† [Hor. Ep. I, Lib. 2, v. 31. 'The olive has no hardness within, the nut has none without!' Trans. H. R. Fairclough.]

VII. If what is said makes it appear, that we have some other amiable idea of actions than that of advantageous to ourselves, we may conclude, 'that this perception of moral good is not derived from custom, education, example, or study.' These give us no new ideas: they might make us see private advantage in actions whose usefulness did not at first appear; or give us opinions of some tendency of actions to our detriment, by some nice deductions of reason, or by a rash prejudice, when upon the first view of the action we should have observed no such thing: but they never could have made us apprehend actions as amiable or odious, without any consideration of our own advantage.

VIII. It remains then, 'that as the Author of nature has determined us to receive, by our external senses, pleasant or disagreeable ideas of objects, according as they are useful or hurtful to our bodies; and to receive from uniform objects the pleasures of beauty and harmony, to excite us to the pursuit of knowledge, and to reward us for it; or to be an argument to us of his goodness, as the uniformity itself proves his existence, whether we had a sense of beauty in uniformity or not; in the same manner he has given us a *moral sense*, to direct our actions, and to give us still nobler pleasures: so that while we are only intending the good of others, we undesignedly promote our own greatest private good.'

We are not to imagine, that this moral sense, more than the other senses, supposes any innate ideas, knowledge, or practical proposition: we mean by it only a determination of our minds to receive the simple ideas of approbation or condemnation, from actions observed, antecedent to any opinions of advantage or loss to redound to ourselves from them; even as we are pleased with a regular form, or an harmonious composition, without having any knowledge of mathematics, or seeing any advantage in that form or composition, different from the immediate pleasure.

That we may discern more distinctly the difference between moral perceptions and others, let us consider, when we taste a pleasant fruit, we are conscious of pleasure; when another tastes it, we only conclude or form an opinion that he enjoys pleasure; and, abstracting from some previous good-will or anger, his enjoying this pleasure is to us a matter wholly indifferent, raising no new sentiment or affection. But when we are under the influence of a virtuous temper, and thereby engaged in virtuous actions, we are not always conscious of any pleasure, nor are we only pursuing private pleasures, as will appear hereafter: it is only by *reflex acts* upon our temper and conduct, that virtue never fails to give pleasure. When also we judge the temper of another to be virtuous, we do not necessarily imagine him *then* to enjoy pleasure, though we know *reflection* will give it to him: and farther, our apprehension of his virtuous temper raises sentiments of approbation, esteem or admiration, and the affection of good-will toward him. The quality approved by our moral sense is conceived to reside in the person approved, and to be a perfection and dignity in him: approbation of another's virtue is not conceived as making the approver happy, or virtuous, or worthy, though it is attended with some small pleasure. Virtue is then called *amiable* or *lovely*, from its raising good-will or love in spectators toward the agent; and not from the agent's perceiving the virtuous temper to be advantageous to him, or desiring to obtain it under that view. A virtuous temper is called *good* or *beatific*, not that it is always attended with pleasure in the agent; much less that some small pleasure attends the contemplation of it in the approver: but from this, that every spectator is persuaded that the reflex acts of the virtuous agent upon his own temper will give him the highest pleasures. The admired quality is conceived as the perfection of the agent, and such a one as is distinct from the pleasure either in the agent or the approver; though it is a sure source of pleasure to the agent. The perception of the approver, though attended with pleasure, plainly represents something quite distinct from this pleasure; even as the perception of external forms is attended with pleasure, and yet represents something distinct from this pleasure. This may prevent many cavils upon this subject.

Section II:
Concerning the Immediate Motive to Virtuous Actions

The *motives* of human actions, or their immediate causes, would be best understood after considering the passions and affections; but here we shall only consider the springs of the actions which we call *virtuous,* as far as it is necessary to settle the general foundation of the moral sense.

I. Every action, which we apprehend as either *morally good* or *evil*, is always supposed to flow from some *affection* toward sensitive natures; and whatever we call *virtue* or *vice*, is either some such *affection*, or some *action* consequent upon it. Or it may perhaps be enough to make an action or omission, appear vicious, if it argues the want of such affection toward rational agents, as we expect in characters counted morally good. All the actions counted *religious* in any country, are supposed, by those who count them so, to flow from some affections toward the Deity; and whatever we call *social virtue*, we still suppose to flow from affections toward our fellow-creatures: for in this all seem to agree, 'that the external motions, when accompanied with no affections toward God or man, or evidencing no want of the *expected* affections toward either, can have no moral good or evil in them.'

Ask, for instance, the most abstemious hermit, if *temperance* of itself would be morally good, supposing it showed no obedience toward the Deity, made us no fitter for devotion, or the service of mankind, or the search after truth, than *luxury*; and he will easily grant, that it would be no moral good, though still it might be naturally good or advantageous to health: and mere *courage* or contempt of danger, if we conceive it to have no regard to the defence of the innocent, or repairing of wrongs or self-interest, would only entitle its possessor to bedlam. When such sort of courage is sometimes admired, it is upon some secret apprehension of a good intention in the use of it, or as a natural ability capable of an useful application. *Prudence*, if it was only employed in promoting private interest, is never imagined to be a *virtue*: and *justice*, or observing a strict equality, if it has no regard to the good of mankind, the preservation of rights, and securing peace, is a quality properer for its ordinary *gestamen*, a beam and scales, than for a rational agent. So that these four qualities, commonly called *cardinal virtues*, obtain that name, because they are dispositions universally necessary to promote *public good*, and denote *affections* toward *rational agents*; otherwise there would appear no *virtue* in them.

II. Now, if it can be made appear, that none of these affections which we approve as virtuous, are either self-love, or desire of private interest; since all virtue is either some such affections, or actions consequent upon them; it must necessarily follow, 'that virtue springs from some other affection than self-love, or desire of private advantage. And where self-interest excites to the same action, the approbation is given only to the disinterested principle.'

The affections which are of most importance in morals, are commonly included under the names *love* and *hatred*. Now in discoursing of *love*,
we need not be cautioned not to include that love between the sexes,
which, when no other affections accompany it, is only desire of pleasure, and is never counted a virtue. *Love* toward rational agents, is subdivided into love of *complacence* or *esteem*, and love of *benevolence*: and
hatred is subdivided into hatred of *displicence* or *contempt*, and hatred
of *malice*. *Complacence* denotes approbation of any person by our moral
sense; and is rather a perception than an affection; though the affection
of good-will is ordinarily subsequent to it. *Benevolence* is the desire of
the happiness of another. Their opposites are called *dislike* and *malice*.
Concerning each of these separately we shall consider, 'whether they
can be influenced by motives of self-interest'.

Complacence, esteem, or good-liking, at first view appears to be
disinterested, and so *displicence* or dislike; and are entirely excited by
some moral qualities, good or evil, apprehended to be in the objects;
which qualities the very frame of our nature determines us to approve
or disapprove, according to the moral sense above explained.* Propose
to a man all the rewards in the world, or threaten all the punishments,
to engage him to esteem and complacence toward a person entirely
unknown, or if known, apprehended to be cruel, treacherous,
ungrateful; you may procure external obsequiousness, or good offices,
or dissimulation; but real esteem no price can purchase. And the same is
obvious as to contempt, which no motive of advantage can prevent. On
the contrary, represent a character as generous, kind, faithful, humane,
though in the most distant parts of the world, and we cannot avoid
esteem and complacence. A bribe may possibly make us attempt to ruin
such a man, or some strong motive of advantage may excite us to oppose
his interest; but it can never make us disapprove him, while we retain
the same opinion of his temper and intentions. Nay, when we consult
our own hearts, we shall find, that we can scarce ever persuade ourselves
to attempt any mischief against such persons, from any motive of
advantage; nor execute it without the strongest reluctance and remorse,
until we have blinded ourselves into a false opinion about his temper.

* See Sect. I.

III. As to the love of *benevolence*, the very name excludes self-interest. We never call that man *benevolent*, who is in fact useful to others, but at the same time only intends his own interest, without any ultimate desire of the good of others. If there be any real good-will or kindness at all, it must be disinterested; for the most useful action imaginable loses all appearance of benevolence, as soon as we discern that it only flowed from self-love, or interest. Thus, never were any human actions more advantageous, than the inventions of fire, and iron; but if these were casual, or if the inventor only intended his own interest in them, there is nothing which can be called *benevolent* in them. Wherever then benevolence is supposed, there it is imagined disinterested, and designed for the good of others. To raise benevolence, no more is required than calmly to consider any sensitive nature not pernicious to others. Gratitude arises from benefits conferred from good-will on ourselves, or those we love; complacence is a perception of the moral sense. Gratitude includes some complacence, and complacence still raises a stronger good-will than that we have toward indifferent characters, where there is no opposition of interests.

But it must be here observed, that as all men have *self-love*, as well as *benevolence*, these two principles may jointly excite a man to the same action; and then they are to be considered as two forces impelling the same body to motion; sometimes they conspire, sometimes are indifferent to each other, and sometimes are in some degree opposite. Thus, if a man have such strong benevolence, as would have produced an action without any views of self-interest; that such a man has also in view private advantage, along with public good, as the effect of his action, does no way diminish the benevolence of the action. When he would not have produced so much public good, had it not been for prospect of self-interest, then the effect of self-love is to be deducted, and his benevolence is proportioned to the remainder of good, which pure benevolence would have produced. When a man's benevolence is hurtful to himself, then self-love is opposite to benevolence, and the benevolence is proportioned to the sum of the good produced, added to the resistance of self-love surmounted by it. In most cases it is impossible for men to know how far their fellows are influenced by the one or other of these principles; but yet the general truth is sufficiently certain, that this is the way in which the benevolence of actions is to be computed.

IV. There are two ways in which some may deduce benevolence from self-love, the one supposing that 'we voluntarily bring this affection upon ourselves, whenever we have an opinion that it will be for our interest to have this affection, either as it may be immediately pleasant, or may afford pleasant reflection afterwards by our moral sense, or as it may tend to procure some external reward from God or man.' The other scheme alleges no such power in us of raising desire or affection of any kind by our choice or volition; but 'supposes our minds determined by the frame of their nature to desire whatever is apprehended as the means of any private happiness; and that the observation of the happiness of other persons, in many cases is made the necessary occasion of pleasure to the observer, as their misery is the occasion of his uneasiness: and in consequence of this connection, as soon as we have observed it, we begin to desire the happiness of others as the means of obtaining this happiness to ourselves, which we expect from the contemplation of others in a happy state. They allege it to be impossible to desire either the happiness of another, or any event whatsoever, without conceiving it as the means of some happiness or pleasure to ourselves; but own at the same time, that desire is not raised in us directly by any volition, but arises necessarily upon our apprehending any object or event to be conducive to our happiness.'

That the former scheme is not just, may appear from this general consideration, that 'neither benevolence nor any other affection or desire can be directly raised by volition.' If they could, then we could be bribed into any affection whatsoever toward any object, even the most improper: we might raise jealousy, fear, anger, love, toward any sort of persons indifferently by an hire, even as we engage men to external actions, or to the dissimulation of passions; but this every person will by his own reflection find to be impossible. The prospect of any advantage to arise to us from having any affection, may indeed turn our attention to those qualities in the object, which are naturally constituted the necessary causes or occasions of the advantageous affection; and if we find such qualities in the object, the affection will certainly arise. Thus indirectly the prospect of advantage may tend to raise any affection; but if these qualities be not found or apprehended in the object, no volition of ours, nor desire, will ever raise any affection in us.

But more particularly, that desire of the good of others, which we approve as virtuous, cannot be alleged to be voluntarily raised from prospect of any pleasure accompanying the affection itself: for it is plain that our benevolence is not always accompanied with pleasure; nay, it is often attended with pain, when the object is in distress. Desire in general is rather uneasy than pleasant. It is true, indeed, all the passions and affections justify themselves; while they continue, (as Malebranche expresses it) we generally approve our being thus affected on this occasion, as an innocent disposition, or a just one, and condemn a person who would be otherwise affected on the like occasion. So the sorrowful, the angry, the jealous, the compassionate, approve their several passions on the apprehended occasion; but we should not therefore conclude, that sorrow, anger, jealousy or pity are pleasant, or chosen for their concomitant pleasure. The case is plainly thus: the frame of our nature on the occasions which move these passions, determines us to be thus affected, and to approve our affection at least as innocent. Uneasiness generally attends our desires of any kind; and this sensation tends to fix our attention, and to continue the desire. But the desire does not terminate upon the removal of the pain accompanying the desire, but upon some other event: the concomitant pain is what we seldom reflect upon, unless when it is very violent. Nor does any desire or affection terminate upon the pleasure which may accompany the affection; much less is it raised by an act of our will, with a view to obtain this pleasure.

The same reflection will show, that we do not by an act of our will raise in ourselves that benevolence which we approve as virtuous, with a view to obtain future pleasures of self-approbation by our moral sense. Could we raise affections in this manner, we should be engaged to any affection by the prospect of an interest equivalent to this of self-approbation, such as wealth or sensual pleasure, which with many tempers are more powerful; and yet we universally own, that *that* disposition to do good offices to others, which is raised by these motives, is not virtuous: how can we then imagine, that the virtuous benevolence is brought upon us by a motive equally *selfish*?

* * *

v. The other scheme is more plausible: that benevolence is not raised by any volition upon prospect of advantage; but that we desire the happiness of others, as conceiving it necessary to procure some pleasant sensations which we expect to feel upon seeing others happy; and that for like reason we have aversion to their misery. This connection between the happiness of others and our pleasure, say they, is chiefly felt among friends, parents and children, and eminently virtuous characters. But this benevolence flows as directly from self-love as any other desire.

To show that this scheme is not true in fact, let us consider, that if in our benevolence we only desired the happiness of others as the means of this pleasure to ourselves, whence is it that no man approves the desire of the happiness of others as a means of procuring wealth or sensual pleasure to ourselves? If a person had wagered concerning the future happiness of a man of such veracity, that he would sincerely confess whether he were happy or not; would this wagerer's desire of the happiness of another, in order to win the wager, be approved as virtuous? If not, wherein does this desire differ from the former? except that in one case there is one pleasant sensation expected, and in the other case other sensations: for by increasing or diminishing the sum wagered, the interest in this case may be made either greater or less than that in the other.

Reflecting on our own minds again will best discover the truth. Many have never thought upon this connection: nor do we ordinarily intend the obtaining of any such pleasure when we do generous offices. We all often feel delight upon seeing others happy, but during our pursuit of their happiness we have no intention of obtaining this delight. We often feel the pain of compassion; but were our sole ultimate intention or desire the freeing ourselves from this pain, would the Deity offer to us either wholly to blot out all memory of the person in distress, to take away this connection, so that we should be easy during the misery of our friend on the one hand, or on the other would relieve him from his misery, we should be as ready to choose the former way as the latter; since either of them would free us from our pain, which upon this scheme is the sole end proposed by the compassionate person. – Don't we find in ourselves that our desire does not terminate upon the removal of our own pain? Were this our sole intention, we would run away, shut our eyes, or divert our thoughts from the miserable object, as the readiest way of removing our pain: this we seldom do, nay, we crowd about such objects, and voluntarily expose ourselves to this pain, unless calm reflection upon our inability to relieve the miserable, countermand our inclination, or some selfish affection, as fear of danger, overpower it.

To make this yet clearer, suppose that the Deity should declare to a good man that he should be suddenly annihilated, but at the instant of his exit it should be left to his choice whether his friend, his children, or his country should be made happy or miserable for the future, when he himself could have no sense of either pleasure or pain from their state. Pray would he be any more indifferent about their state now, that he neither hoped or feared any thing to himself from it, than he was in any prior period of his life? Nay, is it not a pretty common opinion among us, that after our decease we know nothing of what befalls those who survive us? How comes it then that we do not lose, at the approach of death, all concern for our families, friends, or country? Can there be any instance given of our desiring any thing only as the means of private good, as violently when we know that we shall not enjoy this good many minutes, as if we expected the possession of this good for many years? Is this the way we compute the value of annuities?

How the disinterested desire of the good of others should seem inconceivable, it is hard to account: perhaps it is owing to the attempts of some great men to give definitions of simple ideas. – Desire, say they, is uneasiness, or uneasy sensation upon the absence of any good. – Whereas desire is as distinct from uneasiness, as volition is from sensation. Don't they themselves often speak of our desiring to remove uneasiness? Desire then is different from uneasiness, however a sense of uneasiness accompanies it, as extension does the idea of colour, which yet is a very distinct idea. Now wherein lies the impossibility of desiring the happiness of another without conceiving it as the means of obtaining any thing farther, even as we desire our own happiness without farther view? If any allege, that we desire our own happiness as the means of removing the uneasiness we feel in the absence of happiness, then at least the desire of removing our own uneasiness is an ultimate desire: and why may we not have other ultimate desires?

'But can any being be concerned about the absence of an event which gives it no uneasiness?' Perhaps superior natures desire without uneasy sensation. But what if we cannot? We may be uneasy while a desired event is in suspense, and yet not desire this event only as the means of removing this uneasiness: nay, if we did not desire the event without view to this uneasiness, we should never have brought the uneasiness upon ourselves by desiring it. So likewise we may feel delight upon the existence of a desired event, when yet we did not desire the event only as the means of obtaining this delight; even as we often receive delight from events which we had an aversion to.

* * *

VII. As to malice, *human nature* seems scarce capable of malicious disinterested hatred, or a sedate ultimate desire of the misery of others, when we imagine them no way pernicious to us, or opposite to our interest: and for that hatred which makes us oppose those whose interests are opposite to ours, it is only the effect of self-love, and not of disinterested malice. A sudden passion may give us wrong representations of our fellow-creatures, and for a little time represent them as absolutely evil; and during this imagination perhaps we may give some evidences of disinterested malice: but as soon as we reflect upon human nature, and form just conceptions, this unnatural passion is allayed, and only self-love remains, which may make us, from self-interest, oppose our adversaries.

* * *

x. Having removed these false springs of virtuous actions, let us next establish the true one, viz. some determination of our nature to study the good of others; or some instinct, antecedent to all reason from interest, which influences us to the love of others; even as the moral sense, above explained,* determines us to approve the actions which flow from this love in ourselves or others. This *disinterested affection*, may appear strange to men impressed with notions of *self-love*, as the *sole* spring of action, from the pulpit, the schools, the systems, and conversations regulated by them: but let us consider it in its strongest and simplest kinds; and when we see the possibility of it in these instances, we may easily discover its universal extent.

An honest *farmer* will tell you, that he studies the preservation and happiness of his children, and loves them without any design of good

* See Sect. I.

to himself. But say some of our *philosophers*, 'The happiness of their children gives parents pleasure, and their misery gives them pain; and therefore to obtain the former, and avoid the latter, they study, from *self-love*, the good of their children.' Suppose several merchants joined in partnership of their whole effects; one of them is employed abroad in managing the stock of the company; his prosperity occasions gain to all, and his losses give them pain for their share in the loss: is this then the same kind of affection with that of parents to their children? Is there the same tender, personal regard? I fancy no parent will say so. In this case of merchants there is a plain conjunction of interest; but whence the conjunction of interest between the parent and child? Do the child's sensations give pleasure or pain to the parent? Is the parent hungry, thirsty, sick, when his children are so? No; but *his* naturally implanted desire of their good, and aversion to their misery, makes him be affected with joy or sorrow from their pleasures or pains. This desire then is antecedent to the conjunction of interest, and the cause of it, not the effect: it then must be *disinterested*. 'No; say others, children are parts of ourselves, and in loving them we but love ourselves in them.' A very good answer! Let us carry it as far as it will go. How are they parts of ourselves? Not as a leg or an arm: we are not conscious of their sensations. 'But their bodies were formed from parts of ours.' So is a fly, or a maggot, which may breed in any discharged blood or humour: very dear insects surely! there must be something else then which makes children parts of ourselves; and what is this but that affection, which NATURE determines us to have toward them? This love makes them parts of ourselves, and therefore does not flow from their being so before. This is indeed a good metaphor; and wherever we find a determination among several rational agents to mutual love, let each individual be looked upon as a part of a great whole, or system, and concern himself in the public good of it.

Another author thinks all this is easily deducible from self-love. 'Children are not only made of our bodies, but resemble us in body and mind; they are rational agents as we are, and we only love our own likeness in them.' Very good all this. What is *likeness*? It is not *individual sameness*; it is only being included under one general or specifical idea. Thus there is likeness between us and other men's children, thus any man is like any other, in some respects: a man is also like an angel, and in some respects like a brute. Is there then a natural disposition in every man to *love his like*, to wish well not only to his individual self, but to any other like rational or sensitive being? and this disposition strongest, where there is the greatest likeness in the more noble qualities? If all this is called by the name *self-love*; be it so: the highest mystic needs no more disinterested principle; it is not confined to the individual, but terminates ultimately on the good of others, and may extend to all; since each one some way resembles each other. Nothing can be better than this self-love, nothing more generous.

* * *

Section III:
The Sense of Virtue, and the Various Opinions about it, reducible to one General Foundation. The Manner of Computing the Morality of Actions

I. If we examine all the actions which are counted *amiable* anywhere, and inquire into the grounds upon which they are *approved*, we shall find that in the opinion of the person who approves them, they generally appear as *benevolent*, or flowing from *good-will to others*, and a study of their happiness, whether the approver be one of the persons beloved, or profited, or not; so that all those kind affections which incline us to make others happy, and all actions supposed to flow from such affections, appear *morally good*, if, while they are benevolent towards some persons, they be not pernicious to others. Nor shall we find any thing amiable in any action whatsoever, where there is no benevolence imagined; nor in any disposition, or capacity, which is not supposed applicable to, and designed for, benevolent purposes. Nay, as was before observed,* the actions which in fact are exceedingly useful, shall appear void of moral beauty, if we know they proceeded from no kind intentions towards others; and yet an unsuccessful attempt of kindness, or of promoting public good, shall appear as amiable as the most successful, if it flowed from as strong benevolence.

* * *

* See Sect. II, Art. III, par.1.

IV. Contraries may illustrate each other; let us therefore observe the general foundation of our sense of *moral evil* more particularly. *Disinterested malice*, or ultimate desire of the misery of others, is the highest pitch of what we count vicious; and every action appears evil, which is imagined to flow from any degree of this affection. Perhaps a violent passion may hurry men into it for a few moments, and our rash angry sentiments of our enemies, may represent them as having such odious dispositions; but it is very probable, from the reasons offered above,* that there is no such degree of wickedness in human nature, as, in cold blood, to desire the misery of others, when it is conceived no way useful to our interests.

* * *

The ordinary spring of vice then among men, must be a mistaken self-love, made so violent, as to overcome benevolence; or such strong appetites, or passions either selfish, or toward some narrow systems, as overcome our regard to public good; or affections arising from false, and rashly-formed opinions of mankind; which we run into through the weakness of our benevolence. When men, who had good opinions of each other, happen to have contrary interests, they are apt to have their good opinions of each other abated, by imagining a designed opposition from malice; without this, they can scarcely hate one another. Thus two candidates for the same office wish each other dead, because that is an ordinary way by which men make room for each other; but if there remains any reflection on each other's virtue, as there sometimes may in benevolent tempers, then their opposition may be without hatred; and if another better post, where there is no competition, were bestowed on one of them, the other shall rejoice at it.

v. Actions which flow solely from self-love, and yet evidence no want of benevolence, having no hurtful effects upon others, seem of a middle nature, neither virtuous nor vicious, and neither raise the love or hatred of the observer. Our reason can indeed discover certain bounds, within which we may not only act from self-love, consistently with the good of the whole; but every mortal's acting thus within these bounds for his own good, is absolutely necessary for the good of the whole; and the

* See Sect. II, Art. VII.

want of such self-love would be universally pernicious. Hence, he who pursues his own private good, with an intention also to concur with that constitution which tends to the good of the whole; and much more he who promotes his own good, with a direct view of making himself more capable of serving God, or doing good to mankind; acts not only innocently, but also honourably, and virtuously: for in both these cases, benevolence concurs with self-love to excite him to the action. And thus a *neglect* of our own good may be morally evil, and argue a want of benevolence toward the whole. But when self-love breaks over the bounds above-mentioned, and leads us into actions detrimental to others, and to the whole; or makes us insensible of the generous kind affections; then it appears vicious, and is disapproved. So also, when upon any small injuries, or sudden resentment, or any weak superstitious suggestions, our benevolence becomes so faint, as to let us entertain odious conceptions of men, or any part of them, without just ground, as if they were wholly evil, or malicious, or as if they were a worse sort of beings than they really are; these conceptions must lead us into malevolent affections, or at least weaken our good ones, and make us really vicious.

VI. *Benevolence* is a word fit enough in general, to denote the internal spring of virtue, as Bishop Cumberland always uses it. But to understand this more distinctly, it is highly necessary to observe, that under this name are included very different dispositions of the soul. Sometimes it denotes a calm, extensive affection, or good-will toward all beings capable of happiness or misery: sometimes, 2. a calm deliberate affection of the soul toward the happiness of certain smaller systems or individuals; such as patriotism, or love of a country, friendship, parental affection, as it is in persons of wisdom and self-government: or, 3. the several kind particular passions of love, pity, sympathy, congratulation. This distinction between the calm motions of the will, affections, dispositions, or instincts of the soul, and the several turbulent passions, is elsewhere more fully considered.*

Now though all these different dispositions come under the general character of benevolent, yet as they are in nature different, so they have very different degrees of moral beauty. The first sort is above

---

* See Treatise III, Sect. II, Art. II., and Treatise IV, Sect. VI, Art IV.

all amiable and excellent: it is perhaps the sole moral perfection of some superior natures; and the more this prevails and rules in any human mind, the more amiable the person appears, even when it not only checks and limits our lower appetites, but when it controls our kind particular passions, or counteracts them. The second sort of benevolence is more amiable than the third, when it is sufficiently strong to influence our conduct: and the third sort, though of a lesser moral dignity, is also beautiful, when it is no way opposite to these more noble principles. And when it is opposite, though it does not justify such actions as are really detrimental to greater systems, yet it is a strong extenuating circumstance, and much alleviates the moral deformity. We are all sensible of this, when any person from friendship, parental affection, or pity, has done something hurtful to larger societies.

VII. Here we must also observe, that every moral agent justly considers himself as a *part* of this rational system, which may be useful to the *whole*; so that he may be, in part, an object of his own universal *benevolence*. Nay farther, as was hinted above, he may see, that the preservation of the system requires everyone to be innocently solicitous about himself. Hence he may conclude, that an action which brings *greater evil* to the agent, than *good* to others, however it may evidence the strength of some particular kind attachment, or of a virtuous disposition in the agent, yet it must be founded upon a mistaken opinion of its tendency to public good; so that a man who reasoned justly, and considered the whole, would not be led into it, by the calm extensive benevolence, how strong soever it were; nor would he recommend it to the practice of others; however he might acknowledge, that the detriment arising to the agent from a kind action, did evidence a strong virtuous disposition. Nay farther, if any good was proposed to the pursuit of an agent, and he had a competitor in every respect *only equal* to himself; the *highest* universal *benevolence* possible would not lead a wise man to prefer another to himself, were there no ties of gratitude, or some other external circumstance, to move him to yield to his competitor. A man surely of the *strongest benevolence*, may justly treat himself as he would do a third person, who was a competitor of *equal merit* with the other; and as his preferring one to another, in such a case, would argue no weakness of *benevolence*; so no more would he evidence it by preferring himself to a man of only *equal abilities*.

* * *

VIII . . . In comparing the moral qualities of actions, in order to regulate our election among various actions proposed, or to find which of them has the greatest moral excellency, we are led by our moral sense of virtue to judge thus; that in *equal degrees* of happiness, expected to proceed from the action, the virtue is in proportion to the *number* of persons to whom the happiness shall extend (and here the *dignity*, or *moral importance* of persons, may compensate numbers); and in equal *numbers*, the virtue is as the *quantity* of the happiness, or natural good; or that the virtue is in a compound ratio of the *quantity* of good, and *number* of enjoyers. In the same manner, the moral evil, or vice, is as the degree of misery, and number of sufferers; so that *that action* is *best*, which procures the *greatest happiness* for the *greatest numbers*,* and *that worst*, which, in *like manner*, occasions *misery*.

Again, when the consequences of actions are of a mixed nature, partly advantageous, and partly pernicious; *that action is good*, whose *good* effects preponderate the *evil* by being useful to many, and pernicious to few; and *that evil*, which is otherwise. Here also the moral importance of characters, or dignity of persons may compensate numbers; as may also the degrees of happiness or misery: for to procure an inconsiderable good to many, but an immense evil to few, may be evil; and an immense good to few, may preponderate a small evil to many.

But the consequences which affect the morality of actions, are not only the direct and natural effects of the actions themselves; but also all those events which otherwise would not have happened. For many actions which have no immediate or natural evil effects, nay, which actually produce good effects, may be evil; if a man foresees, that the evil consequences, which will probably flow from the folly of others, upon his doing of such actions, are so great as to over-balance all the good produced by those actions, or all the evils which would flow from the omission of them: and in such cases the *probability* is to be computed on both sides. Thus, if an action of mine will

* [Hutcheson seems to have been the first to use this famous slogan.]

probably, through the mistake or corruption of others, be made a precedent in unlike cases, to very evil actions; or when my action, though good in itself, will probably provoke men to very evil actions, upon some mistaken notion of their right; any of these considerations foreseen by me, may make such an action of mine evil, whenever the evils which will probably be occasioned by the action, are greater than the evils occasioned by the omission.

And this is the reason, that many laws prohibit actions in general, even when some particular instances of those actions would be very useful; because an universal allowance of them, considering the mistakes men would probably fall into, would be more pernicious than an universal prohibition; nor could there be any more special boundaries fixed between the right and wrong cases. In such cases, it is the duty of persons to comply with the generally useful constitution; or if in some very important instances, the violation of the law would be of less evil consequence, than obedience to it, they must patiently resolve to undergo those penalties, which the State has, for valuable ends to the whole, appointed: and this disobedience will have nothing criminal in it.

* * *

XI. To find a *universal rule* to compute the morality of any actions, with all their circumstances, when we judge of the actions done by ourselves, or by others, we must observe the following propositions or axioms.

1. The moral *importance* of any agent, or the quantity of public good he produces, is in a compound proportion of his *benevolence* and *abilities*.* For it is plain that his good offices depend upon these two jointly. In like manner, the quantity of private good which any agent obtains for himself, is in a like compound proportion of his *selfish principles*, and his *abilities*. We speak here only of the external goods of this world, which one pursues from some selfish principles. For as to internal goods of the mind, these are most effectually obtained by the exercise of other affections than those called *selfish*, even those which carry the agent beyond himself toward the good of others.

* [There is a much more elaborate version of this mathematical approach to morality in the first and second editions.]

2. In comparing the virtues of different agents, when the abilities are equal, the *moments* of public good are proportioned to the goodness of the temper, or the *benevolence*; and when the *tempers* are equal, the quantities of good are as the *abilities*.

3. The virtue then or goodness of temper is directly as the *moment of good*, when other circumstances are equal, and inversely as the abilities. That is to say, where the abilities are greatest, there is less virtue evidenced in any given moment of good produced.

4. But as the natural consequences of our actions are various, some good to ourselves, and evil to the public; and others evil to ourselves, and good to the public; or either useful both to ourselves and others, or pernicious to both; the entire spring of good actions is not always *benevolence alone*; or of evil, *malice alone* (nay, sedate malice is rarely found); but in most actions we must look upon *self-love* as another force, sometimes conspiring with benevolence, and assisting it, when we are excited by views of private interest, as well as public good; and sometimes opposing benevolence, when the good action is any way difficult or painful in the performance, or detrimental in its consequences to the agent.

These selfish motives shall be hereafter* more fully explained; here we may in general denote them by the word *interest*: which when it concurs with benevolence, in any action capable of increase or diminution, must produce a greater quantity of good, than benevolence alone in the same abilities; and therefore when the moment of good, in an action partly intended for the good of the agent, is but equal to the moment of good in the action of another agent, influenced only by benevolence, the former is less virtuous; and in this case the interest must be deducted to find the true effect of the benevolence or virtue. In the same manner, when interest is opposite to benevolence, and yet is surmounted by it; this interest must be added to the moment, to increase the virtue of the action, or the strength of the benevolence. By *interest*, in this last case, is understood all the advantage which the agent might have obtained by omitting the action, which is a negative motive to it; and this, when subtracted, becomes positive.

But here we must observe, that no advantage, not *intended*, although

* See Sect. V.

casually, or naturally, redounding to us from the action, does at all affect its morality to make it less amiable: nor does any difficulty or evil unforeseen, or not resolved upon, make a kind action more virtuous; since in such cases self-love neither assists nor opposes benevolence. Nay, self-interest then only diminishes the benevolence, when without this view of interest the action would not have been undertaken, or so much good would not have been produced by the agent; and it extenuates the vice of an evil action, only when without this interest the action would not have been done by the agent, or so much evil have been produced by him.

The fourth axiom only explains the external marks by which men must judge, who do not see into each other's hearts; for it may really happen in many cases, that men may have benevolence sufficient to surmount any difficulty, and yet they may meet with none at all: and in that case, it is certain there is as much virtue in the agent, though he does not give such proof of it to his fellow-creatures, as if he had surmounted difficulties in his kind actions. And this too must be the case with the Deity, to whom nothing is difficult.

Since then, in judging of the goodness of temper in any agent, the abilities must come into computation, as is above-mentioned, and none can act beyond their natural abilities; that must be the perfection of virtue, where the moment of good produced equals the ability, or when the being acts to the utmost of his power for the public good; and hence the perfection of virtue, in this case, is as unity. And this may show us the only foundation for the boasting of the Stoics, 'that a creature supposed innocent, by pursuing virtue with his utmost power, may in virtue equal the gods.' For in their case, if the ability be *infinite*, unless the good to be produced in the whole, be so too, the virtue is not *absolutely perfect*; and the quotient can never surmount unity.

XII. In the same manner we may compute the degree of depravity of any temper, directly as the moment of evil effected, and inversely as the abilities. The springs of vicious actions however are seldom any real ultimate intention of mischief, and never ultimate deliberate malice; but only sudden anger, self-love, some selfish passion or appetite, some kind attachments to parties, or particular kind passions.

The motives of interest may sometimes strongly co-operate with a depraved temper, or may oppose it, in the same manner that they co-operate with or oppose a good temper. When they co-operate, they diminish the moral evil; when they oppose, they may argue the depravity of temper to be greater, which is able to surmount such motives of interest.

But we must observe, that not only *innocence* is expected from all mortals, but they are presumed, from their *nature*, in some measure inclined to *public good*;* so that a bare absence of this desire is enough to make an agent be reputed evil: nor is a direct intention of *public evil* necessary to make an action evil; it is enough that it flows from *self-love*, with a plain neglect of the good of others, or an insensibility of their misery, which we either *actually* foresee, or have a probable *presumption* of.

It is true indeed, that that public evil which I neither certainly foresee, nor have actual presumptions of, as the consequence of my action, does not make my *present action* criminal or odious; even although I might have foreseen this evil by a serious examination of my own actions; because such actions do not, at present, evidence either malice, or want of benevolence. But then it is also certain, that my *prior negligence*, in not examining the tendency of my actions, is a plain evidence of the want of that degree of good affections which is necessary to a virtuous character; and consequently the guilt properly lies in this neglect, rather than in an action which really flows from a good intention. *Human laws* however, which cannot examine the intentions, or secret knowledge of the agent, must judge in gross of the action itself; presupposing all that knowledge as actually attained, which we are obliged to attain.

In like manner, no good effect, which I did not actually foresee and intend, makes my action *morally good*; however *human laws* or *governors*, who cannot search into men's intentions, or know their secret designs, justly reward actions which tend to the public good, although the agent was engaged to those actions only by selfish views; and consequently had no virtuous disposition influencing him to them.

The difference in degree of guilt between *crimes of ignorance*, when the ignorance is vincible, and faulty, as to the natural tendency of the action; and *crimes of malice*, or direct evil intention; consists in this, that the former, by a *prior neglect*, argues a want of the due degree of

* See Treatise IV, Sect. VI.

benevolence, or *right affection*; the latter evidences direct *evil affections*, which are vastly more odious.

XIII. From the former reasonings we may form almost a demonstrative conclusion, 'that we have a sense of *goodness* and *moral beauty* in actions, distinct from *advantage*'; for had we no other foundation of approbation of actions, but the *advantage* which might arise to us from them, if they were done toward ourselves, we should make no account of the *abilities* of the agent, but would barely esteem them according to their *moment*. The abilities come in only to show the degree of *benevolence*, which supposes benevolence necessarily amiable. Who was ever the better pleased with a barren rocky farm, or an inconvenient house, by being told that the poor farm gave as great increase as it could; or that the house accommodated its possessor as well as it could? And yet in our sentiments of actions, whose *moment* is very inconsiderable, it shall wonderfully increase the *beauty* to allege, 'that it was all the poor agent could do for the public, or his friend.'

* * *

Section IV:
All Mankind Agree in this General Foundation of their Approbation of Moral Actions. The Ground of the different Opinions about Morals

I. To show how far mankind agree in that which we have made the *universal foundation* of this *moral sense, viz. benevolence*, we have observed already, that when we are asked the reason of our approbation of any action, we universally allege its *usefulness* to the *public*, and not to the *actor* himself.

* * *

II. And farther, we may observe, that no action of any other person was ever approved by us, but upon some apprehension, well or ill-grounded, of some really good moral quality. If we observe the sentiments of men concerning actions, we shall find, that it is always some really amiable and benevolent appearance which engages their approbation. We may perhaps commit mistakes, in judging that actions tend to the public good, which do not; or be so inadvertent, that while our attention is fixed on some *partial good effects*, we may quite overlook many *evil consequences* which counterbalance the good. Our reason may be very deficient in its office, by giving us partial representations of the tendency of actions; but it is still some apparent species of benevolence which commands our approbation.

* * *

The matter is plainly this: Men are often mistaken in the tendency of actions either to public, or private good: Nay, sometimes violent passions, while they last, will make them approve very bad actions by their moral sense, and conceive very pernicious ones to the agent, to be advantageous: But this proves only, 'That sometimes there may be some more violent motive to action, than a sense of moral good; or that men by passion may become blind even to their own interest.'

But to prove that men are void of a moral sense, we should find some instances of cruel, malicious actions, done without any motive of interest, real or apparent; and approved without any opinion of tendency to public good, or flowing from good-will.

* * *

III. From what has been said, we may easily account for the *vast diversity of moral principles*, in various nations and ages; and the grounds of this diversity are these:

1st. Different opinions of happiness, or natural good, and of the most effectual means to advance it. Thus in one country, where there prevails a courageous disposition, where liberty is counted a great good, and war an inconsiderable evil, all insurrections in defence of privileges will have the appearance of moral good to our sense, because of their appearing benevolent; and yet the same sense of moral good in benevolence, shall in another country, where the spirits of men are more abject and timorous, where civil war appears the greatest natural evil, and liberty no great purchase, make the same actions appear odious. So in Sparta, where thro' contempt of wealth the security of possessions was not much regarded, but the thing chiefly desired, as naturally good to the State, was to abound in a hardy shifting youth; theft, if dexterously performed, was so little odious, that it received the countenance of a law to give it impunity.

*   *   *

Men have reason given them, to judge of the tendencies of their actions, that they may not stupidly follow the first appearance of public good; but it is still some appearance of good which they pursue. And it is strange, that reason is universally allowed to men, notwithstanding all the stupid ridiculous opinions received in many places; and yet absurd practices, founded upon those very opinions, shall seem an argument against any moral sense, altho' the bad conduct is not owing to any irregularity in the moral sense, but to a wrong judgment or opinion. If putting the aged to death, with all its consequences, really tends to the public good, and the lesser misery of the aged, it is, no doubt, justifiable; nay, perhaps the aged choose it, in hopes of a future state. If a deformed or weak race could never, by ingenuity and art, make themselves useful to mankind, but should grow an absolutely unsupportable burden, so as to involve a whole State in misery, it is just to put them to death. This all allow to be just, in the case of an over-loaded boat in a storm. And as for killing of their children, when parents are sufficiently stocked, it is perhaps practised, and allowed from self-love; but I can scarce think it passes for a good action anywhere.

*   *   *

iv. The next ground for diversity in sentiments, is the diversity of systems, to which men, from foolish opinions, confine their benevolence. We intimated above, that it is regular and beautiful, to have stronger benevolence towards the morally good parts of mankind, who are useful to the whole, than towards the useless or pernicious. Now, if men receive a low or base opinion of any body, or sect of men; if they imagine them bent on the destruction of the more valuable parts, or but useless burdens on the earth; benevolence itself will lead them to neglect the interests of such, and to suppress them. This is the reason why, among nations who have high notions of virtue, every action toward an enemy may pass for just; why Romans and

Greeks could approve of making those they called barbarians slaves.

*   *   *

v. The last ground of diversity which occurs, are the false opinions of the will or laws of the Deity. To obey these we are determined from gratitude, and a sense of right imagined in the Deity, to dispose at pleasure the fortunes of his creatures. This is so abundantly known to have produced follies, superstitions, murders, devastations of kingdoms, from a sense of virtue and duty, that it is needless to mention particular instances. Only we may observe, 'that all those follies, or barbarities, rather confirm than destroy the opinion of a moral sense'; since the Deity is believed to have a right to dispose of his creatures; and gratitude to him, if he be conceived good, must move us to obedience to his will; if he be not conceived good, self-love may overcome our moral sense of the action which we undertake to avoid his fury.

As for the vices which commonly proceed from love of pleasure, or any violent passion, since generally the agent is soon sensible of their evil, and that sometimes amidst the heat of action, they only prove, 'that this moral sense and benevolence may be overcome by the more importunate solicitations of other desires.'

vi. Before we leave this subject, it is necessary to remove one of the strongest objections against what has been said so often, viz. 'That this *sense* is *natural*, and independent of *custom* and *education*.' The objection is this, 'That we shall find some actions always attended with the strongest abhorrence, even at first view, in some whole nations, in which there appears nothing contrary to benevolence; and that the same actions shall in another nation be counted innocent, or honourable. Thus incest, among Christians, is abhorred at first appearance as much as murder; even by those who do not know or reflect upon any necessary tendency of it to the detriment of mankind. Now we generally allow, that what is from nature in one nation, would be so in all. This abhorrence therefore cannot be from nature, since in Greece, the marrying of half-sisters was counted honourable; and among the Persian Magi, the marrying of mothers. Say they then, may not all our approbation or dislike of actions arise the same way from custom and education?'

The answer to this may be easily found from what is already said. Had we no moral sense natural to us, we should only look upon incest as hurtful to ourselves, and shun it, and never disapprove other incestuous persons, more than we do a broken merchant; so that still this abhorrence supposes a sense of moral good. And farther, it is true, that many who abhor incest do not know, or reflect upon the natural tendency of some sorts of incest to the public detriment; but wherever it is hated, it is apprehended as offensive to the Deity, and that it exposes the person concerned to his just vengeance. Now it is universally acknowledged to be the grossest ingratitude and baseness, in any creature, to counteract the will of the Deity, to whom it is under such obligations. This then is plainly a moral evil quality apprehended in incest, and reducible to the general foundation of malice, or want of benevolence. Nay farther, where this opinion 'that incest is offensive to the Deity', prevails, incest must have another direct contrariety to benevolence; since we must apprehend the incestuous, as exposing an associate, who should be dear to him by the ties of nature, to the lowest state of misery and baseness, infamy and punishment. But in those countries where no such opinion prevails of the Deity's abhorring or prohibiting incest; if no obvious natural evils attend it, it may be looked upon as innocent. And farther, as men who have the sense of tasting, may, by company and education, have prejudices against meats they never tasted, as unsavoury; so may men who have a moral sense, acquire an opinion by implicit faith, of the moral evil of actions, altho' they do not themselves discern in them any tendency to natural evil; imagining that others do; or, by education, they may have some ideas associated, which raise an abhorrence without reason. But without a *moral sense* we could receive no prejudice against actions, under any other view than as naturally disadvantageous to ourselves.

VII. The universality of this moral sense, and that it is antecedent to instruction, may appear from observing the sentiments of children, upon hearing stories with which they are commonly entertained as soon as they understand language. They always passionately interest themselves on that side where *kindness* and *humanity* are found; and detest the cruel, the covetous, the selfish, or the treacherous. How strongly do we see their passions of joy, sorrow, love, and indignation, moved by these moral representations, even tho' there have been no pains taken to give them ideas of a Deity, of laws, of a future state, or of the more intricate tendency of the *universal good* to that of each *individual.*

Section V:

A Farther Confirmation, that We have Practical Dispositions to Virtue Implanted in our Nature; with a farther Explication of our Benevolent Instincts of various Kinds, with the Additional Motives of Interest, viz. Honour, Shame and Pity

I. We have already endeavoured to prove, 'that there is a *universal determination* to *benevolence* in mankind, even toward the most distant parts of the species': but we are not to imagine, that all benevolent affections are of one kind, or alike strong. There are nearer and stronger kinds of benevolence, when the objects stand in some nearer relations to ourselves, which have obtained distinct names; such as *natural affection, gratitude, esteem.*

One species of *natural affection,* viz. that in parents towards their children, has been considered already,* we shall only observe farther, that there is the same kind of affection among collateral relations, though in a weaker degree; which is universally observable, where no opposition of interest produces contrary actions, or counter-balances the power of this natural affection.

*   *   *

II. But nothing will give us a juster idea of the wise order in which human nature is formed for universal love, and mutual good offices, than considering that strong attraction of benevolence, which we call *gratitude.* Every one knows that beneficence toward ourselves makes a much deeper impression upon us, and raises gratitude, or a stronger love toward the benefactor, than equal beneficence toward a third person. Now because of the great numbers of mankind, their distant habitations, and the incapacity of any one to be remarkably useful to great multitudes; that our benevolence might not be quite distracted with a multiplicity of objects, whose equal virtues would equally

---

* See above, Sect. II, Art. X, par. 2, 3.

recommend them to our regard; or become useless, by being equally extended to multitudes, whose interests we could not understand, nor be capable of promoting, having no intercourse of offices with them; *nature* has so well ordered it, that as our attention is more raised by those good offices which are done to ourselves or our friends, so they cause a stronger sense of approbation in us, and produce a stronger benevolence toward the authors of them. This we call *gratitude*. And thus a foundation is laid for joyful associations in all kinds of business, and virtuous friendships.

By this constitution also the benefactor is more encouraged in his beneficence, and better secured of an increase of happiness by grateful returns, than if his virtue were only to be honoured by the colder general sentiments of persons unconcerned, who could not know his necessities, nor how to be profitable to him; especially, when they would all be equally determined to love innumerable multitudes, whose equal virtues would have the same pretensions to their love.

The *universal benevolence* toward all men, we may compare to that principle of *gravitation*, which perhaps extends to all bodies in the universe; but increases as the distance is diminished, and is strongest when bodies come to touch each other. Now this increase, upon nearer approach, is as necessary as that there should be any attraction at all. For a general attraction, equal in all distances, would by the contrariety of such multitudes of equal forces, put an end to all regularity of motion, and perhaps stop it altogether. Beside this general attraction, the learned in these subjects show us a great many other attractions among several sorts of bodies, answering to some particular sorts of passions, from some special causes. And that attraction or force by which the parts of each body cohere, may represent the self-love of each individual.

These different sorts of love to persons according to their nearer approaches to ourselves by their benefits, is observable in the high degree of love, which heroes and lawgivers universally obtain in their own countries, above what they find abroad, even among those who are not insensible of their virtues; and in all the strong ties of friendship, acquaintance, neighbourhood, partnership; which are exceedingly necessary to the order and happiness of human society.

III. From considering that natural gratitude, and love toward our benefactors, which was already shown to be disinterested, we are easily led to consider another determination of our minds, equally natural with the former, which is to desire and delight in the good opinion and love of others, even when we expect no other advantage from them, except what flows from this constitution, whereby *honour* is made an *immediate good*. This desire of honour I would call *ambition*, had not custom joined some evil ideas to that word, making it denote such a violent desire of honour, and of power also, as will make us stop at no base means to obtain them. On the other hand, we are by nature subjected to a grievous sensation of misery, from the unfavourable opinions of others concerning us, even when we dread no other evil from them. This we call *shame*; which in the same manner is constituted an *immediate evil*, as we said, *honour* was an *immediate good*.

Now, were there no moral sense, or had we no other idea of actions but as advantageous or hurtful, I see no reason why we should be delighted with honour, or subjected to the uneasiness of shame; or how it could ever happen, that a man, who is secure from punishment for any action, should ever be uneasy at its being known to all the world. The world may have an opinion of him as pernicious to his neighbours; but what subjects his ease to this opinion of the world? Why, perhaps, he shall not be so much trusted henceforward in business, and so suffer loss. If this be the only reason of shame, and it has no immediate evil or pain in it, distinct from fear of loss, then, wherever we expose ourselves to loss, we should be ashamed, and endeavour to conceal the action: and yet it is quite otherwise.

A merchant, for instance, lest it should impair his credit, conceals a shipwreck, or a very bad market, which he has sent his goods to. But is this the same with the passion of *shame*? Has he that anguish, that dejection of mind, and self-condemnation, which one shall have whose *treachery* is detected? Nay, how will men sometimes glory in their losses, when in a cause imagined morally good, though they really weaken their credit in the merchant's sense; that is, the opinion of their wealth, or fitness for business? Was any man ever *ashamed* of impoverishing himself to serve his country, or his friend?

* * *

VIII. Let us next consider another determination of our mind, which strongly proves benevolence to be *natural* to us, and that is *compassion*; by which we are disposed to study the interest of others, without any views of private advantage. This needs little illustration. Every mortal is made uneasy by any grievous misery he sees another involved in, unless the person be imagined morally evil: nay, it is almost impossible for us to be unmoved, even in that case. Advantage may make us do a cruel action, or may overcome pity; but it scarce ever extinguishes it. A sudden passion of hatred or anger may represent a person as absolutely evil, and so extinguish pity, but when the passion is over, it often returns. Another *disinterested* view may even in cold blood overcome pity; such as love to our country, or zeal for religion. Persecution is generally occasioned by love of virtue, and a desire of the eternal happiness of mankind, although our folly makes us choose absurd means to promote it; and is often accompanied with pity enough to make the persecutor uneasy, in what, for prepollent reasons, he chooses; unless his opinion leads him to look upon the heretic as absolutely and entirely evil.

* * *

How independent this disposition to compassion is on custom, education, or instruction, will appear from the prevalence of it in women and children, who are less influenced by these. That children delight in some actions which are cruel and tormenting to animals which they have in their power, flows not from malice, or want of compassion, but from their ignorance of those signs of pain which many creatures make; together with a curiosity to see the various contortions of their bodies. For when they are more acquainted with these creatures, or come by any means to know their sufferings, their compassion often becomes too strong for their reason; as it generally does in beholding executions, where as soon as they observe the evidences of distress, or pain in the malefactor, they are apt to condemn this necessary method of self-defence in the State. Some have alleged, that 'however the sight of another's misery some way or other gives us pain, yet the very feeling of compassion is also attended with pleasure: this pleasure is superior to the pain of sympathy, and hence we desire to raise compassion in ourselves, and incline to indulge it.' Were this truly the case, the *continuation of the suffering* would be the natural desire of the compassionate, in order to continue this state, not of pure pleasure indeed, but of pleasure superior to all pains.

Section VI:
Concerning the Importance of this Moral Sense to the present Happiness of Mankind, and its Influence on Human Affairs

III. There is a further consideration which must not be passed over, concerning the *external beauty* of persons, which all allow to have a great power over human minds. Now it is some apprehended *morality*, some natural or imagined indication of concomitant virtue, which gives it this powerful charm above all other kinds of *beauty*. Let us consider the characters of beauty, which are commonly admired in countenances, and we shall find them to be sweetness, mildness, majesty, dignity, vivacity, humility, tenderness, good-nature; that is, that certain airs, proportions, je ne sais quoi's, are natural indications of such virtues, or of abilities or dispositions toward them. As we observed above, of misery or distress appearing in countenances; so it is certain, almost all habitual dispositions of mind form the countenance in such a manner, as to give some indications of them to the spectator. Our violent passions are obvious at first view in the countenance; so that sometimes no art can conceal them: and smaller degrees of them give some less obvious turns to the face, which an accurate eye will observe. Now, when the natural air of a face approaches to that which any passion would form it unto, we make a conjecture from this concerning the leading disposition of the person's mind.

* * *

v. Here we may remark the manner in which nature leads mankind to the continuance of their race, and by its strongest power engages them to what occasions the greatest toil and anxiety of life; and yet supports them under it with an inexpressible delight. We might have been excited to the propagation of our species, by such an uneasy sensation as would have effectually determined us to it, without any great prospect of happiness; as we see *hunger* and *thirst* determine us to preserve our bodies, tho' few look upon eating and drinking as any considerable happiness. The *sexes* might have been engaged to concurrence, as we imagine the brutes are, by desire only, or by a love of sensual pleasure. But how dull and insipid had life been, were there no more in *marriage!* Who would have had resolution enough to bear all the cares of a *family*, and education of *children*? Or who, from the general motive of benevolence alone, would have chosen to subject himself to natural affection toward an offspring, when he could so easily foresee what troubles it might occasion?

This inclination therefore of the sexes, is founded on something stronger, and more efficacious and joyful, than the solicitations of uneasiness, or the bare desire of sensible pleasure. Beauty gives a favourable presumption of good moral dispositions, and acquaintance confirms this into a real love of esteem, or begets it, where there is little beauty. This raises an expectation of the greatest moral pleasures along with the sensible, and a thousand tender sentiments of humanity and generosity; and makes us impatient for a society which we imagine big with unspeakable moral pleasures: where nothing is indifferent, and every trifling service, being an evidence of this strong love and esteem, is mutually received with the rapture and gratitude of the greatest benefit, and of the most substantial obligation; and where prudence and good-nature influence both sides, this society may answer all their expectations.

Nay, let us examine those of looser conduct with relation to the *fair sex*, and we shall find, that love of sensible pleasure is not the chief motive of debauchery, or false gallantry. Were it so, the meanest prostitutes would please as much as any. But we know sufficiently, that men are fond of *good-nature, faith, pleasantry of temper, wit*, and many other *moral qualities*, even in a *mistress*. And this may furnish us with a reason for what appears pretty unaccountable, viz. 'that *chastity* itself has a powerful charm in the eyes of the dissolute, even when they are attempting to destroy it.'

This powerful determination even to a *limited benevolence,* and other moral sentiments, is observed to give a strong bias to our minds toward a universal goodness, tenderness, humanity, generosity, and contempt of private good in our whole conduct; besides the obvious improvement it occasions in our external deportment, and in our relish of beauty, order, and harmony. As soon as a heart, before hard and obdurate, is softened in this flame, we shall observe, arising along with it, a love of poetry, music, the beauty of nature in rural scenes, a contempt of other selfish pleasures of the external senses, a neat dress, a humane deportment, a delight in, and emulation of, everything which is gallant, generous, and friendly.

* * *

VII. We have found this *sense** to be the foundation also of the chief pleasures of *poetry*. We hinted, in the former Treatise, at the foundation of delight in the numbers, measures, metaphors, similitudes.[†] But as the contemplation of *moral objects*, either of vice or virtue, affects us more strongly, and moves our passions in a quite different and a more powerful manner, than natural beauty, or what we commonly call deformity; so the most moving beauties bear a relation to our *moral sense*, and affect us more vehemently, than the representations of natural objects in the liveliest descriptions. Dramatic and epic poetry are entirely addressed to this sense, and raise our passions by the fortunes of characters, distinctly represented as morally good or evil; as might be seen more fully, were we to consider the passions separately.

Where we are studying to raise any desire, or admiration of an object really beautiful, we are not content with a bare narration, but endeavour, if we can, to present the object itself, or the most lively image of it. And hence the *epic poem*, or *tragedy*, gives a far greater pleasure than the writings of *philosophers*, tho' both aim at recommending virtue. The representing actions themselves, if the representation be judicious, natural, and lively, will make us admire the good, and detest the vicious, the inhuman, the treacherous and cruel, by means of our moral sense, without any reflections of the poet to guide our sentiments. It is for this reason that Horace has justly made knowledge in *morals* so necessary to a *good poet*.

* * *

* [The moral sense.]
† See Treatise I, Sect. II, Art. XIII; Sect. IV, Art. III.

Section VII:

A Deduction of Some Complex Moral Ideas; viz. of Obligation, and Right, Perfect, Imperfect, and External, Alienable, and Unalienable, from this Moral Sense

I. To conclude this subject, we may, from what has been said, see the true original of moral ideas, viz. *this moral sense of excellence in every appearance, or evidence of benevolence*. It remains to be explained, how we acquire more particular ideas of virtue and vice, abstracting from any *law*, human, or divine.

If any one ask, can we have any sense of *obligation*, abstracting from the *laws* of a *superior*? we must answer according to the various senses of the word *obligation*. If by *obligation*, we understand a determination, without regard to our own interest, to approve actions, and to perform them; which determination shall also make us displeased with ourselves, and uneasy upon having acted contrary to it: in this meaning of the word *obligation*, there is *naturally* an obligation upon all men to *benevolence*; and they are still under its influence, even when by false, or partial opinions of the natural tendency of their actions, this moral sense leads them to evil; unless by long inveterate habits it be exceedingly weakened; for it scarce seems possible wholly to extinguish it. Or, which is to the same purpose, this internal sense, and instinct of benevolence, will either influence our actions, or make us very uneasy and dissatisfied; and we shall be conscious, that we are in a base unhappy state, even without considering any *law* whatsoever, or any external advantages lost, or disadvantages impending from its sanctions. And farther, there are still such indications given us of what is in the whole beneficent, and what not, as may probably discover to us the true tendency of every action; and let us see, some time or other, the evil tendency of what upon a partial view appeared good: or if we have no friends so faithful as to admonish us, the persons injured will not fail to upbraid us. So that no mortal can secure to himself a perpetual serenity, satisfaction, and self-approbation, but by a serious inquiry into the tendency of his actions, and a perpetual study of universal good, according to the justest notions of it.

But if, by *obligation*, we understand a motive from self-interest, sufficient to determine all those who duly consider it, and pursue their own advantage wisely, to a certain course of actions; we may have a sense of such an obligation, by reflecting on this *determination* of our *nature* to approve *virtue*, to be pleased and happy when we reflect upon our having done virtuous actions, and to be uneasy when we are conscious of having acted otherwise; and also by considering how much superior we esteem the happiness of virtue to any other enjoyment.* We may likewise have a sense of this sort of obligation, by considering those reasons which prove a constant course of *benevolent* and *social* *actions*, to be the most probable means of promoting the *natural good* of every *individual*; as Cumberland and Pufendorf have proved: and all this without relation to a *law*.

But farther, if our moral sense be supposed exceedingly weakened, and the selfish passions grown strong, either through some general corruption of nature, or inveterate habits; if our understanding be weak, and we be often in danger of being hurried by our passions into precipitate and rash judgments, that malicious actions shall promote our advantage more than beneficence; in such a case, if it be inquired what is necessary to engage men to beneficent actions, or induce a steady sense of an obligation to act for the public good; then, no doubt, 'a law with sanctions, given by a superior being, of sufficient power to make us happy or miserable, must be necessary to counterbalance those apparent motives of interest, to calm our passions, and give room for the recovery of our moral sense, or at least for a just view of our interest.'

* * *

III. We are often told, 'that there is no need of supposing such a *sense* of *morality* given to men, since *reflection* and *instruction* would recommend the same actions from arguments of *self-interest*, and engage us, from the acknowledged principle of *self-love*, to the practice of them, without this unintelligible determination to benevolence, or the occult quality of a moral sense.'

It is perhaps true, that reflection, and reason might lead us to approve the same actions as *advantageous*. But would not the same reflection and reason likewise generally recommend the same meats to us, which our *taste* represents as pleasant? And shall we thence conclude, that

* See above, Sect. VI, Art, I, II.

we have no *sense* of tasting, or that such a sense is useless? No: the use is plain in both cases. Notwithstanding the mighty *reason* we boast of above other animals, its processes are too slow, too full of doubt and hesitation, to serve us in every exigency, either for our own preservation, without the *external senses*, or to influence our actions for the good of the whole, without this *moral sense*. Nor could we be so strongly determined at all times to what is most conducive to either of these ends, without these expeditious monitors, and importunate solicitors; nor so nobly rewarded, when we act vigorously in pursuit of these ends, by the calm dull reflections of self-interest, as by those delightful sensations.

This *natural determination* to approve and admire, or hate and dislike actions, is, no doubt, an occult quality. But is it any way more mysterious, that the idea of an action should raise esteem or contempt, than that the motion or tearing of flesh should give pleasure or pain; or the act of volition should move flesh and bones? In the latter case, we have got the brain, and elastic fibres, and animal spirits, and elastic fluids, like the Indian's elephant, and tortoise, to bear the burden of the difficulty: but go one step farther, and you find the whole as difficult as at first, and equally a mystery with this determination to love and approve, or condemn and despise actions and agents, without any views of *interest*, as they appear *benevolent*, or the contrary.

Some also object, that according to this account, brutes may be capable of virtue; and this is thought a great absurdity. But it is manifest, that, 1. brutes are not capable of that, in which this scheme places the highest virtue, to wit, the *calm motions of the will* toward the good of others; if our common accounts of brutes are true, that they are merely led by particular passions toward present objects of sense. Again, it is plain there is something in certain tempers of brutes, which engages our liking, and some lower good-will and esteem, though we do not usually call it virtue, nor do we call the sweeter dispositions of children virtue; and yet they are so very like the lower kinds of virtue, that I see no harm in calling them virtues. What if there are low virtues in creatures void of reflection, incapable of knowing laws, or of being moved by their sanctions, or by example of rewards or punishments? Such creatures cannot be brought to a proper trial or judgment: laws, rewards, or punishments won't have these effects upon them, which they may have upon rational agents. Perhaps they are no farther rewarded or punished than by the immediate pleasure or pain of their actions, or what men immediately inflict upon them. Where is the harm of all this, that there are lower virtues, and lower vices, the rewarding or punishing of which, in creatures void of reason and reflection, can answer no wise end of government?

* * *

IV. The writers upon opposite schemes, who deduce all ideas of good and evil from the private advantage of the actor, or from relation to a law, and its sanctions, either known from reason or revelation, are perpetually recurring to this moral sense which they deny; not only in calling the laws of the Deity *just* and *good*, and alleging *justice* and *right* in the Deity to govern us; but by using a set of words which import something different from what they will allow to be their only meaning. *Obligation*, with them, is only such a constitution, either of nature, or some governing power, as makes it advantageous for the agent to act in a certain manner. Let this definition be substituted, wherever we meet with the words, *ought, should, must*, in a moral sense, and many of their sentences would seem very strange; as that the Deity *must* act rationally, *must* not, or *ought* not to punish the innocent, *must* make the state of the virtuous better than that of the wicked, *must* observe promises; substituting the definition of the words, *must, ought, should*, would make these sentences either ridiculous, or very disputable.

V. But that our first ideas of moral good depend not on *laws*, may plainly appear from our constant inquiries into the *justice* of *laws themselves*; and that not only of human laws, but of the divine. What else can be the meaning of that universal opinion, 'that the *laws* of God are *just*, and *holy*, and good?' Human laws may be called *good*, because of their conformity to the divine. But to call the laws of the supreme Deity *good*, or *holy*, or *just*, if all goodness, holiness, and justice be constituted by *laws*, or the *will* of a *superior* any way revealed, must be an insignificant tautology, amounting to no more than this, 'that God *wills* what he *wills*. Or that his *will* is conformable to his *will*.'

It must then first be supposed, that there is something in actions which is apprehended *absolutely good*; and this is *benevolence*, or desire of the *public natural happiness* of *rational agents*; and that our *moral sense* perceives this *excellence*: and then we call the *laws* of the Deity *good*, when we imagine that they are contrived to promote the *public good* in the most effectual and impartial manner. And the Deity is called *morally good*, when we apprehend that his *whole providence* tends to the universal happiness of his *creatures*; whence we conclude his *benevolence*, and *desire* in their happiness.

Some tell us, 'that the goodness of the divine laws consists in their conformity to some essential rectitude of his nature.' But they must excuse us from assenting to this, till they make us understand the meaning of this metaphor, *essential rectitude*; and till we discern whether any thing more is meant by it than a perfectly wise, uniform, impartial benevolence.

Hence we may see the difference between *constraint* and *obligation*. There is indeed no difference between *constraint*, and the second sense of the word *obligation*, viz. a constitution which makes an action eligible from self-interest, if we only mean *external interest*, distinct from the delightful consciousness which arises from the moral sense. The reader need scarcely be told, that by *constraint*, we do not understand an *external force* moving our limbs without our consent; for in that case we are not *agents* at all; but that *constraint* which arises from the threatening and presenting some *evil*, in order to make us act in a certain manner. And yet there seems an universally acknowledged difference between even this sort of *constraint* and *obligation*. We never say, we are *obliged* to do an action which we count base, but we may be *constrained* to it: we never say, that the divine laws, by their sanctions, *constrain* us, but *oblige* us; nor do we call obedience to the Deity *constraint*, unless by a metaphor, though many own they are influenced by fear of punishments. And yet supposing an almighty evil being should require, under grievous penalties, treachery, cruelty, ingratitude, we would call this *constraint*. The difference is plainly this: when any sanctions co-operate with our moral sense, in exciting us to actions which we count morally good, we say we are *obliged*; but when sanctions of rewards or punishments oppose our moral sense, then we say we are *bribed* or *constrained*. In the former case we call the lawgiver *good*, as designing the public happiness; in the latter we call him *evil*, or *unjust*, for the supposed contrary intention. But were all our ideas of moral good or evil derived solely from opinions of private advantage or loss in actions, I see no possible difference which could be made in the meaning of these words.

VI. From this sense too we derive our ideas of *rights*. Whenever it appears to us, that a faculty of doing, demanding, or possessing any thing, universally allowed in certain circumstances, would in the whole tend to the general good, we say, that one in such circumstances has a right to do, possess, or demand that thing. And according as this tendency to the public good is greater or less, the right is greater or less.

The *rights* called *perfect*, are of such necessity to the public good, that the universal violation of them would make human life intolerable; and it actually makes those miserable, whose rights are thus violated. On the contrary, to fulfil these rights in every instance, tends to the public good, either directly, or by promoting the innocent advantage of a part . . . Instances of perfect rights are those to our lives; to the fruits of our labours; to demand performance of contracts upon valuable considerations, from men capable of performing them; to direct our own actions either for public, or innocent private good, before we have submitted them to the direction of others in any measure: and many others of like nature.

Imperfect rights are such as, when universally violated, would not necessarily make men miserable. These rights tend to the improvement and increase of positive good in any society, but are not absolutely necessary to prevent universal misery. The violation of them only disappoints men of the happiness expected from the humanity or gratitude of others; but does not deprive men of any good which they had before . . . Instances of imperfect rights are those which the poor have to the charity of the wealthy; which all men have to offices of no trouble or expense to the performer; which benefactors have to returns of gratitude, and such-like.

The violation of imperfect rights only argues a man to have such weak benevolence, as not to study advancing the positive good of others, when in the least opposite to his own: but the violation of perfect rights argues the injurious person to be positively evil or cruel; or at least so immoderately selfish, as to be indifferent about the positive misery and ruin of others, when he imagines he can find his interest in it. In violating the former, we show a weak desire of public happiness, which every small view of private interest over-balances; but in violating the latter, we show ourselves so entirely negligent of the misery of others, that views of increasing our own good overcome all our compassion toward their sufferings. Now as the absence of good is more easily borne than the presence of misery; so our good wishes toward the positive good of others, are weaker than our compassion toward their misery. He then who violates imperfect rights, shows that his self-love overcomes only the desire of positive good to others; but he who violates perfect rights, betrays such a selfish desire of advancing his own positive good, as overcomes all compassion toward the misery of others.

* * *

XIII. It has often been taken for granted in these papers, 'that the Deity is morally good'; though the reasoning is not at all built upon this supposition. If we inquire into the reason of the great agreement of mankind in this opinion, we shall perhaps find no demonstrative arguments *a priori*, from the idea of an *independent being*, to prove his *goodness*. But there is abundant probability, deduced from the whole frame of nature, which seems, as far as we know, plainly contrived for the good of the whole; and the casual evils seem the necessary concomitants of some mechanism designed for prepollent good. Nay, this very moral sense, implanted in rational agents, to approve and admire whatever actions flow from a study of the good of others, is one of the strongest evidences of goodness in the Author of nature.

But these reflections are not so universal as the opinion, nor are they often inculcated. What then more probably leads mankind into that opinion, is this: the obvious frame of the world gives us ideas of *boundless wisdom* and *power* in its Author. Such a being we cannot conceive indigent, and must conclude *happy*, and in the *best state* possible, since he can still gratify himself. The best state of rational agents, and their greatest and most worthy happiness, we are necessarily led to imagine must consist in *universal efficacious benevolence*: and hence we conclude the Deity *benevolent* in the most *universal impartial manner*. Nor can we well imagine what else deserves the name of *perfection* more than *benevolence*, and those capacities or abilities which are necessary to make it *effectual*; such as *wisdom* and *power*: at least we can have no more lovely conception of it.

TREATISE III:
AN ESSAY ON THE NATURE AND CONDUCT
OF THE PASSIONS AND AFFECTIONS

The Preface

Some strange love of simplicity in the structure of human nature, or attachment to some favourite hypothesis, has engaged many writers to pass over a great many *simple perceptions*, which we may find in ourselves. We have got the number five fixed for our external senses, though a larger number might perhaps as easily be defended. We have multitudes of perceptions which have no relation to any external sensation; if by it we mean perceptions immediately occasioned by motions or impressions made on our bodies, such as the ideas of number, duration, proportion, virtue, vice, pleasures of honour, of congratulation; the pains of remorse, shame, sympathy, and many others. It were to be wished, that those who are at such pains to prove a beloved maxim, that 'all ideas arise from *sensation* and *reflection*,' had so explained themselves, that none should take their meaning to be, that all our ideas are either *external sensations*, or *reflex acts* upon *external sensations*: or if by *reflection* they mean an inward power of perception, as Mr Locke declares expressly, calling it *internal sensation*, that they had as carefully examined into the several kinds of internal perceptions, as they have done into the external sensations: that we might have seen whether the former be not as natural and necessary and ultimate, without reference to any other, as the latter. Had they in like manner considered our *affections* without a previous notion, that they were all from *self-love*, they might have felt an *ultimate desire* of the happiness of others as easily conceivable, and as certainly implanted in the human breast though perhaps not so strong as self-love.

* * *

One may easily see from the great variety of terms, and diversity of schemes invented, that all men feel something in their own hearts recommending virtue, which yet it is difficult to explain. This difficulty probably arises from our previous notions of a small number of senses, so that we are unwilling to have recourse in our theories to any more; and rather strain out some explication of moral ideas, with relation to some of the natural powers of perception universally acknowledged. The like difficulty attends several other perceptions, to the reception of which philosophers have not generally assigned their distinct senses; such as natural beauty, harmony, the perfection of poetry, architecture, designing, and such like affairs of genius, taste, or fancy; the explications or theories on these subjects are in like manner full of confusion and metaphor.

* * *

Section I
A General Account of our several Senses and Desires, Selfish or Public

I. 'Objects, actions, or events obtain the name of *good*, or *evil*, according as they are the causes, or occasions, mediately, or immediately, of a grateful, or ungrateful *perception* to some sensitive nature.' To understand therefore the several kinds of good, or evil, we must apprehend the several powers of perception or *senses* natural to us.

* * *

If we may call 'every determination of our minds to receive ideas independently on our will, and to have perceptions of pleasure and pain, A SENSE,' we shall find many other *senses* beside those commonly explained. Though it is not easy to assign accurate divisions on such subjects, yet we may reduce them to the following classes, leaving it to others to arrange them as they think convenient. A little reflection will show that there are such *natural powers* in the human mind, in whatever order we place them. In the 1st class are the *external senses*, universally known. In the 2nd, the pleasant perceptions arising from regular, harmonious, uniform objects; as also from grandeur and novelty. These we may call, after Mr Addison, the pleasures of the *imagination*; or we may call the power of receiving them, an *internal sense*. Whoever dislikes this name may substitute another. 3. The next class of perceptions we may call a *public sense*, viz. 'our determination to be pleased with the happiness of others, and to be uneasy at their misery.' This is found in some degree in all men, and was sometimes called κοινονοημοσύνη, or *sensus communis* by some of the ancients. This inward pain of compassion cannot be called a sensation of sight. It solely arises from an opinion of misery felt by another, and not immediately from a visible form. The same form presented to the eye by the exactest painting, or the action of a player, gives no pain to those who remember that there is no misery felt. When men by imagination conceive real pain felt by an actor, without recollecting that it is merely feigned, or when they think of the real story represented, then, as there is a confused opinion of real misery, there is also pain in compassion. 4. The fourth class we may call the *moral sense*, by which 'we perceive virtue or vice, in ourselves, or others.' This is plainly distinct from the former class of perceptions, since many are strongly affected with the fortunes of others, who seldom reflect upon virtue or vice, in themselves, or others, as an object: as we may find in natural affection, compassion, friendship, or even general benevolence to mankind, which connect our happiness or pleasure with that of others, even when we are not reflecting upon our own temper, nor delighted with the perception of our own virtues. 5. The fifth class is a *sense of honour*, which makes the approbation, or gratitude of others, for any good actions we have done, the necessary occasion of pleasure; and their dislike, condemnation, or resentment of injuries done by us, the occasion of that uneasy sensation called *shame*, even when we fear no further evil from them.

There are perhaps other perceptions distinct from all these classes, such as some ideas 'of decency, dignity, suitableness to human nature in certain actions and circumstances; and of an indecency, meanness and unworthiness, in the contrary actions or circumstances, even without any conception of *moral* good, or evil.' Thus the pleasures of sight, and hearing, are more esteemed than those of taste or touch: the pursuits of the pleasures of the imagination, are more approved than those of simple external sensations. Plato makes one of his dialogists*

* Hippias Major.

account for this difference from a constant opinion of innocence in this sort of pleasures, which would reduce this perception to the moral sense. Others may imagine that the difference is not owing to any such reflection upon their innocence, but that there is a different sort of perceptions in these cases, to be reckoned another class of sensations.

* * *

II. Desires arise in our mind, from the frame of our nature, upon apprehension of good or evil in objects, actions, or events, to obtain for ourselves or others the agreeable sensation, when the object or event is good: or to prevent the uneasy sensation, when it is evil. Our original desires and aversions may therefore be divided into five classes, answering to the classes of our senses. 1. The desire of sensual pleasure, (by which we mean that of the external senses, of taste and touch chiefly); and aversion to the opposite pains. 2. The desires of the pleasures of imagination or internal sense,* and aversion to what is disagreeable to it. 3. Desires of the pleasures arising from public happiness, and aversion to the pains arising from the misery of others. 4. Desires of virtue, and aversion to vice, according to the notions we have of the tendency of actions to the public advantage or detriment. 5. Desires of honour, and aversion to shame.

And since we are capable of reflection, memory, observation, and reasoning about the distant tendencies of objects and actions, and not confined to things present, there must arise, in consequence of our original desires, 'secondary desires of every thing imagined useful to gratify any of the primary desires, and that with strength proportioned to the several original desires, and the imagined usefulness, or necessity of the advantageous object.' Thus as soon as we come to apprehend the use of wealth or power to gratify any of our original desires, we must also desire them. Hence arises the universality of these desires of wealth and power since they are the means of gratifying all other desires. How foolish then is the inference, some would make, from the universal prevalence of these desires, that human nature is wholly selfish, or that each one is only studious of his own advantage; since wealth or power are as naturally fit to

* See Treat. I.

gratify our public desires, or to serve virtuous purposes, as the selfish ones?'

*   *   *

Let it be premised, that there is a certain pain or uneasiness accompanying most of our violent desires. Though the object pursued be good, or the means of pleasure, yet the desire of it generally is attended with an uneasy sensation. When an object or event appears evil, we desire to shun or prevent it. This desire is also attended with uneasy sensation of impatience: Now this sensation immediately connected with the desire, is a distinct sensation from those which we dread, and endeavour to shun. It is plain then,

I. 'That no desire of any event is excited by any view of removing the uneasy sensation attending this desire itself.' Uneasy sensations previously felt, will raise a desire of whatever will remove them; and this desire may have its concomitant uneasiness. Pleasant sensations expected from any object may raise our desire of it; this desire too may have its concomitant uneasy sensations: But the uneasy sensation, accompanying and connected with the desire itself, cannot be a motive to that desire which it presupposes. The sensation accompanying desire is generally uneasy, and consequently our desire is never raised with a view to obtain or continue it; nor is the desire raised with a view to remove this uneasy sensation, for the desire is raised previously to it. This holds concerning all desire public or private.

There is also a peculiar pleasant sensation of joy, attending the gratification of any desire, beside the sensation received from the object itself, which we directly intended. 'But desire does never arise from a view of obtaining that sensation of joy, connected with the success of gratification of desire; otherwise the strongest desires might arise toward any trifle, or an event in all respects indifferent: since, if desire arose from this view, the stronger the desire were, the higher would be the pleasure of gratification; and therefore we might desire the turning of a straw as violently as we do wealth or power.' This expectation of that pleasure which merely arises from gratifying of desire, would equally excite us to desire the misery of others as their happiness; since this pleasure of gratification might be obtained from both events alike.

II. It is certain that 'that desire of the happiness of others which we account virtuous, is not directly excited by prospects of any secular advantage, wealth, power, pleasure of the external senses, reward from the Deity, or future pleasures of self-approbation.' To prove this let us consider, 'that no desire of any event can arise immediately or directly from an opinion in the agent, that his having such a desire will be the means of private good.' This opinion would make us wish or desire to have that advantageous desire or affection; and would incline us to use any means in our power to raise that affection: but no affection or desire is raised in us, directly by our volition or desiring it. That alone which raises in us from self-love the desire of any event, is an opinion that that event is the means of private good. As soon as we form this opinion, a desire of the event immediately arises: but if having the desire, or the mere affection, be imagined the means of private good, and not the existence of the event desired, then from self-love we should only desire or wish to have the desire of that event, and should not desire the event itself, since the event is not conceived as the means of good.

* * *

III. 'There are in men desires of the happiness of others, when they do not conceive this happiness as the means of obtaining any sort of happiness to themselves.' Self-approbation, or rewards from the Deity, might be the ends, for obtaining which we might possibly desire or will from self-love, to raise in ourselves kind affections; but we could not from self-love desire the happiness of others, except we imagined their happiness to be the means of our own. Now it is certain that sometimes we may have this subordinate desire of the happiness of others, conceived as the means of our own; as suppose one had laid a wager upon the happiness of a person of such veracity, that he would own sincerely whether he were happy or not; when men are partners in stock, and share in profit or loss; when one hopes to succeed to, or some way to share in the prosperity of another; or if the Deity had given such threatenings, as they tell us Telamon gave his sons when they went to war, that he would reward or punish one according as others were happy or miserable: in such cases one might have this subordinate desire of another's happiness from self-love. But as we are sure the

Deity has not given such comminations, so we often are conscious of
the desire of the happiness of others, without any such conception of it
as the means of our own; and are sensible that this subordinate desire is
not that virtuous affection which we approve. The virtuous benevolence
must be an ultimate desire, which would subsist without view to
private good. Such ultimate public desires we often feel, without any
subordinate desire of the same event, as the means of private good. The
subordinate may sometimes, nay often does concur with the ultimate;
and then indeed the whole moment of these conspiring desires may be
greater than that of either alone: but the subordinate alone is not that
affection which we approve as virtuous.

iv. This will clear our way to answer the chief difficulty: 'May not our
benevolence be at least a desire of the happiness of others, as the means
of obtaining the pleasure of the public sense, from the contemplation of
their happiness?' If it were so, it is very unaccountable, that we should
approve this subordinate desire as virtuous, and yet not approve the like
desire upon a wager, or other considerations of interest. Both desires
proceed from self-love in the same manner. In the latter case the desires
might be extended to multitudes, if any one would wager so capriciously;
and, by increasing the sum wagered, the motive of interest might, with
many tempers, be made stronger than that from the pleasures of the
public sense.

Do not we find that we often desire the happiness of others without
any such selfish intention? How few have thought upon this part of
our constitution which we call a public sense? Were it our only view, in
compassion to free ourselves from the pain of the public sense; should the
Deity propose it to our choice, either to obliterate all ideas of the person
in distress, or to harden our hearts against all feelings of compassion, on
the one hand, while yet the object continued in misery; or on the other
hand to relieve him from it; should we not upon this scheme be perfectly
indifferent, and choose the former as soon as the latter? Should the Deity
assure us that we should be immediately annihilated, so that we should
be incapable of either pleasure or pain, but that it should depend upon
our choice at our very exit, whether our children, our friends, or our
country should be happy or miserable; should we not upon this scheme be
entirely indifferent? Or, if we should even desire the pleasant thought of

their happiness, in our last moment, would not this desire be the faintest imaginable?

It is true, our public sense might be as acute at our exit as ever; as a man's taste of meat or drink and his sensations of hunger and thirst might be as lively the instant before his dissolution as in any part of his life. But would any man have as strong desires of the means of obtaining these pleasures, only with a view to himself, when he was to perish the next moment? Is it supposable that any desire of the means of private pleasure can be as strong when we only expect to enjoy it a minute, as when we expect the continuance of it for many years? And yet, it is certain, any good man would as strongly desire at his exit the happiness of others, as in any part of his life, which must be the case with those who voluntarily hazard their lives, or resolve on death for their country or friends. We do not therefore desire it as the means of private pleasure.

* * *

The occasion of the imagined difficulty in conceiving disinterested desires, has probably been from the attempting to define this simple idea, desire. It is called an uneasy sensation in the absence of good. Whereas desire is as distinct from any sensation, as the will is from the understanding or senses. This every one must acknowledge, who speaks of desiring to remove uneasiness or pain.

* * *

Section II
Of the Affections and Passions: the Natural Laws of Pure Affection: the Confused Sensations of the Passions, with their Final Causes

II . . . There is a distinction to be observed on this subject, between 'the *calm desire* of good, and aversion to evil either selfish or public, as they appear to our reason or reflection; and the *particular passions* towards objects immediately presented to some sense.' Thus nothing can be more distinct than the *general calm desire* of private good of any kind, which alone would incline us to pursue whatever objects were apprehended as the means of good, and the particular *selfish passions*, such as ambition, covetousness, hunger, lust, revenge, anger, as they arise upon particular occasions. In like manner our public desires may be distinguished into the *general calm desire* of the happiness of others, or aversion to their misery upon reflection; and the *particular affections* or *passions* of love, congratulation, compassion, natural affection. These particular affections are found in many tempers, where, through want of reflection, the general calm desires are not found: nay, the former may be opposite to the latter, where they are found in the same temper. Sometimes the calm motion of the will conquers the passion, and sometimes is conquered by it. Thus lust or revenge may conquer the calm affection toward private good, and sometimes are conquered by it. Compassion will prevent the necessary correction of a child, or the use of a severe cure, while the calm parental affection is exciting to it. Sometimes the latter prevails over the former. All this is beautifully represented in the 9th book of Plato's *Republic*. We obtain command over the particular passions, principally by strengthening the general desires through frequent reflection, and making them habitual, so as to obtain strength superior to the particular passions.*

Again, the *calm public desires* may be considered as 'they either regard the good of particular persons or societies presented to our senses; or that of some more abstracted or general community, such as a species or system.' This latter sort we may call *universal calm benevolence*. Now it is plain, that not only *particular kind passions*, but even *calm particular benevolence* do not always arise from, or necessarily presuppose, the *universal benevolence*; both the former may be found in persons of little reflection, where the latter is wanting: and the former two

---

* The Schoolmen express this distinction by the *appetitus rationalis*, and the *appetitus sensitivus*. All animals have in common the external senses suggesting notions of things as pleasant or painful; and have also the *appetitus sensitivus*, or some instinctive desires and aversions. Rational agents have, superadded to these, two higher analogous powers; viz. the understanding, or reason, presenting farther notions, and attended with a higher sort of sensations; and the *appetitus rationalis*. This latter is a 'constant natural disposition of soul to desire what the understanding, or these sublimer sensations, represent as good, and to shun what they represent as evil, and this either when it respects ourselves or others.' This many call the *will* as distinct from the passions. Some later writers seem to have forgot it, by ascribing to the understanding not only ideas, notions, knowledge; but action, inclinations, desires, prosecution, and their contraries.

may be opposite to the other, where they meet together in one temper. So the *universal benevolence* might be where there was neither of the former; as in any superior nature or angel, who had no particular intercourse with any part of mankind.

Our moral sense, though it approves all particular kind affection or passion, as well as calm particular benevolence abstractedly considered; yet it also approves the restraint of limitation of all particular affections or passions, by the calm universal benevolence. To make this desire prevalent above all particular affections, is the only sure way to obtain constant self-approbation.

* * *

Section III:
Particular Divisions of the Affections and Passions

* * *

Since our moral sense represents virtue as the greatest happiness to the person possessed of it, our public affections will naturally make us desire the virtue of others. When the opportunity of a great action occurs to any person against whom we are no way prejudiced, we wish he would attempt it, and desire his good success. If he succeeds we feel joy; if he is disappointed, or quits the attempt, we feel sorrow. Upon like opportunity of, or temptation to a base action, we have aversion to the event: If he resists the temptation, we feel joy; if he yields to it, sorrow. Our affections toward the person arise jointly with our passions about this event, according as he acquits himself virtuously or basely.

* * *

Section IV:

How Far our several Affections and Passions are in our Power, either to Govern Them when Raised, or to Prevent their Arising: with some General Observations about their Objects

* * *

II. The government of our passions must then depend much upon our opinions: but we must here observe an obvious difference among our desires, viz. that 'some of them have a previous, painful, or uneasy sensation, antecedently to any opinion of good in the object; nay, the object is often chiefly esteemed good, only for its allaying this pain or uneasiness; or if the object gives also positive pleasure, yet the uneasy sensation is previous to, and independent of this opinion of good in the object.' 'These desires we may call appetites.' 'Other desires and aversions necessarily presuppose an opinion of good and evil in their objects; and the desires or aversions, with their concomitant uneasy sensations, are produced or occasioned by this opinion or apprehension.' Of the former kind are hunger and thirst, and the desires between the sexes; to which desires there is an uneasy sensation previous, even in those who have little other notion of good in the objects, than allaying this pain or uneasiness. There is something like to this in the desire of society, or the company of our fellow-creatures.

* * *

In other desires the case is different. No man is distressed for want of fine smells, harmonious sounds, beautiful objects, wealth, power, or grandeur, previously to some opinion formed of these things as good, or some prior sensation of their pleasures. In like manner, virtue and honour as necessarily give us pleasure, when they occur to us, as vice and contempt give us pain; but, antecedently to some experience or opinion of this pleasure, there is no previous uneasy sensation in the absence, as there is in the absence of the objects of appetite. The necessity of these sensations previous to our appetites, has been considered already. The sensations accompanying or subsequent to our other desires, by which they are denominated passions, keep them in a just balance with our appetites, as was before observed.

But this holds in general, concerning all our desires or aversions, that according to the opinion or apprehension of good or evil, the desire or aversion is increased or diminished: every gratification of any desire gives at first pleasure; and disappointment pain, generally proportioned to the violence of the desire. In like manner, the escaping any object of aversion, tho' it makes no permanent addition to our happiness, gives at first a pleasant sensation, and relieves us from misery, proportioned to the degree of aversion or fear. So when any event, to which we had an aversion, befalls us, we have at first misery proportioned to the degree of aversion. So that some pain is subsequent upon all frustration of desire or aversion, but it is previous to those desires only, which are called appetites.

* * *

TREATISE IV:
ILLUSTRATIONS ON THE MORAL SENSE

Introduction

The differences of actions from which some are constituted morally good and others morally evil have always been accounted a very important subject of inquiry and, therefore, every attempt to free this subject from the usual causes of error and dispute, the confusion of ambiguous words, must be excusable.

In the following discourse *happiness* denotes pleasant sensation of any kind, or a continued state of such sensations; and *misery* denotes the contrary sensations.

Such actions as tend to procure happiness to the agent are called for shortness, privately useful, and such actions as procure misery to the agent, privately hurtful.

Actions procuring happiness to others may be called publicly useful and the contrary actions publicly hurtful. Some actions may be both publicly and privately useful and others both publicly and privately hurtful.

These different natural tendencies of actions are universally acknowledged and in proportion to our reflection upon human affairs we shall enlarge our knowledge of these differences.

When these natural differences are known, it remains to be inquired into, first, 'What quality in any action determines our *election* of it rather than the contrary?' Or, if the mind determines itself, 'What motives or desires excite to an action, rather than the contrary, or rather than to the omission?' Second, 'What quality determines our *approbation* of one action rather than of the contrary action?'

The words *election* and *approbation* seem to denote simple ideas known by consciousness which can only be explained by synonymous words or by concomitant or subsequent circumstances. *Election* is purposing to do an action rather than its contrary, or than being inactive. *Approbation* of our own action denotes, or is attended with, a pleasure in the contemplation of it, and in reflection upon the affections which inclined us to it. Approbation of the action of another has some little pleasure attending it in the observer and raises love toward the agent in whom the quality approved is deemed to reside, and not in the observer who had a satisfaction in the act of approving.*

The qualities moving to *election*, or *exciting to action*, are different from those moving to *approbation*. We often do actions which we do not approve and approve actions which we omit. We often desire that an agent had omitted an action which we approve and wish he would do an action which we condemn. Approbation is employed about the actions of others where there is no room for our election.

Now in our search into the qualities exciting either our election or approbation let us consider the several notions advanced of moral good and evil in both these respects and what senses, instincts, or affections must be necessarily supposed to account for our approbation of election.

There are two opinions on this subject entirely opposite: the one that of the old Epicureans, as it is beautifully explained in the first book of Cicero, *de Finibus*; which is revived by Hobbes, Rochefoucauld, and others of the last century, and followed by many better writers: 'that all the desires of the human mind, nay of all thinking natures, are reducible to *self-love*, or *desire* of *private happiness*: that from this desire all actions of any agent do flow.' Our Christian moralists of this scheme introduced other sorts of happiness to be desired, but still it is the 'prospect of private happiness, which, with some of them, is the sole motive of election. And that, in like manner, what determines any agent to approve his own action, is its tendency to his private happiness in the whole, though it may bring present pain along with it; that the approbation of the action of another is from an opinion of its tendency to the happiness of the approver, either immediately or more remotely: that each agent may discover it to be the surest way to promote his private happiness, to do publicly useful actions and to abstain from those which are publicly hurtful; that the neglecting to observe this, and doing publicly hurtful actions, does mischief to the whole of

* See Treat. II, Sect. 1, par. ult.

mankind, by hurting any one part; that every one has some little damage by this action; such an inadvertent person might possibly be pernicious to any one, were he in his neighborhood: and the very example of such actions may extend over the whole world, and produce some pernicious effects upon any observer. That therefore every one may look upon such actions as hurtful to himself, and in this view does disapprove them, and hates the agent. In the like manner, a publicly useful action may diffuse some small advantage to every observer, whence he may approve it and love the agent.'

This scheme can never account for the principal actions of human life, such as the offices of friendship, gratitude, natural affection, generosity, public spirit, compassion. Men are conscious of no such intentions, or acute reflections about these actions. Ingenious speculative men, in their straining to support an hypothesis, may contrive a thousand subtle selfish motives which a kind generous heart never dreamed of. In like manner, this scheme can never account for the sudden approbation, and violent sense of something amiable, in actions done in distant ages and nations while the approver has perhaps never thought of these distant tendencies to his happiness. Nor will it better account for our want of approbation towards publicly useful actions done casually, or only with intention of private happiness to the agent. And then, in these actions reputed generous, if the agent's motive was only a view to his own pleasure, how come we to approve them more than his enriching himself or his gratifying his own taste with good food? The whole species may receive a like advantage from both and the observer an equal share.

Were our approbation of actions done in distant ages and nations occasioned by this thought, that such an action done toward our selves would be useful to us, why do not we approve and love in like manner any man who finds a treasure, or indulges himself in any exquisite sensation, since these advantages or pleasures might have been conferred on ourselves and tend more to our happiness than any actions in distant ages?

The sanctions of laws may make any agent choose the action required under the conception of useful to himself, and lead him into an opinion of private advantage in it and of detriment in the contrary actions; but what should determine any person to approve the actions of others, because of a conformity to a law, if approbation in any person were only an opinion of private advantage?

The other opinion is this, 'that we have not only *self-love*, but *benevolent affections* also toward others, in various degrees, making us desire their happiness as an *ultimate end*, without any view to private happiness: that we have a *moral sense* or determination of our mind, to *approve* every *kind affection* either in ourselves or others, and all publicly useful actions which we imagine flow from such affection, without our having a view to our private happiness, in our approbation of these actions.'

These two opinions seem both intelligible, each consistent with itself. The former seems not to represent human nature as it is, the other seems to do it.

There have been many ways of speaking introduced, which seem to signify something different from both the former opinions. Such as these, that 'Morality of actions consists in *conformity to reason* or *difformity from* it': that 'Virtue is acting according to the *absolute fitness and unfitness of things*, or agreeably to the natures or relations of things,' and many others in different authors. To examine these is the design of the following sections and to explain more fully how the moral sense alleged to be in mankind must be presupposed even in these schemes.

Section I:
Concerning the Character of Virtue, Agreeable to Truth or Reason

Since reason is understood to denote our power of *finding out true proposition*, reasonableness must denote the same thing, with *conformity to true propositions, or to truth.*

Reasonableness in an action is a very common expression, but yet upon inquiry it will appear very confused, whether we suppose it the motive to *election*, or the quality determining *approbation*.

There is one sort of *conformity to truth* which neither determines to the one or the other: viz., that conformity which is between every true proposition and its object.* This sort of conformity can never make us

* [Hutcheson is here thinking of Wollaston.]

choose or approve one action more than its contrary, for it is found in all actions alike. Whatever attribute can be ascribed to a generous kind action the contrary attribute may as truly be ascribed to a selfish cruel action. Both propositions are equally true, and the two contrary actions, the objects of the two truths, are equally conformable to their several truths with that sort of conformity which is between a truth and its object. This conformity then cannot make a difference among actions, or recommend one more than another either to election or approbation, since any man may make as many truths about villainy as about heroism by ascribing to it contrary attributes.

For instance, these are truths concerning the preservation of property, 'It tends to the happiness of human society. It encourages industry. It shall be rewarded by God.' These are also truths concerning robbery. 'It disturbs society. It discourages industry. It shall be punished by God.' The former three truths have that sort of conformity to its objects which is common to all truths with their objects. The moral difference cannot therefore depend upon this conformity, which is common to both.

The number of truths in both cases may be plainly the same, so that a good action cannot be supposed to agree to more truths than an evil one, nor can an evil action be disagreeable to any truth or compages of truths made about it; for whatever propositions do not agree with their objects are not truths.

If *reasonableness*, the character of virtue, denote some other sort of conformity to truth, it were to be wished that these gentlemen who make it the original idea of moral good, antecedent to any sense or affections would explain it, and show how it determines us, antecedently to a sense, either to election or approbation.

They tell us, 'We must have some *standard* antecedently to all sense or affections since we judge even of our senses and affections themselves and approve or disapprove them. This standard must be our *reason*, conformity to which must be the original idea of moral good.'

But what is this *conformity of actions to reason*? When we ask the reason of an action, we sometimes mean, 'What truth shows a quality in the action, exciting the agent to do it?' Thus, why does a luxurious man pursue wealth? The reason is given by this truth, 'Wealth is useful to purchase pleasures.' Sometimes for a reason of actions we show the truth expressing a quality engaging our approbation. Thus the reason of hazarding life in just war is that 'It tends to preserve our honest countrymen or evidences public spirit.' The reason for temperance and against luxury is given thus, 'Luxury evidences a selfish base temper.' The former sort of reasons we will call exciting and the latter justifying. Now we shall find that all *exciting reasons* presuppose *instincts* and *affections* and the *justifying* presuppose a *moral sense*.

As to *exciting reasons*, in every calm rational action some end is desired or intended. No end can be intended or desired previously to some one of these classes of affections, *self-love, self-hatred*, or desire of private misery (if this be possible), *benevolence* toward others, or malice. All affections are included under these. No *end* can be previous to them all. There can therefore be no *exciting reason* previous to *affection*.

* * *

But are there not also exciting reasons, even previous to any end, moving us to propose one end rather than another? To this Aristotle long ago answered 'that there are *ultimate ends* desired without a view to any thing else, and *subordinate ends* or objects desired with a view to something else.' To *subordinate ends* those *reasons* or *truths* excite which show them to be conducive to the *ultimate end*, and show one object to be more effectual than another. Thus subordinate ends may be called *reasonable*. But as to the *ultimate ends*, to suppose exciting reasons for them, would infer that there is no ultimate end but that we desire one thing for another in an infinite series.

Thus ask a being who desires *private happiness* or has *self-love*, 'What reason excites him to desire wealth?' He will give this reason, 'that wealth tends to procure *pleasure* and *ease*'. Ask his reason for desiring pleasure or happiness. One cannot imagine what propositions he could assign as his exciting reason. This proposition is indeed true, 'There is an *instinct* or *desire* fixed in his nature determining him to pursue his *happiness*.' But it is not this reflection on his own nature, or this proposition, which excites or determines him, but the instinct itself. This is a truth, 'Rhubarb strengthens the stomach,' but it is not a proposition which strengthens the stomach, but the quality in that medicine. The effect is not produced by propositions showing the cause but by the cause itself.

In like manner, what reason can a *benevolent being* give as *exciting* him to *hazard his life* in just war? This perhaps, 'Such conduct tends to the happiness of his country.' Ask him, 'Why he serves his country?' He will say, 'His country is a very valuable part of mankind.' Why does he study the happiness of mankind? If his *affections* be really *disinterested* he can give no *exciting reason* for it. The *happiness of mankind* in general, or of any valuable part of it, is an *ultimate end* to that series of desires.

* * *

Should any one ask even concerning these two *ultimate ends, private good and public*, is not the latter more reasonable than the former? – what means the word *reasonable* in this question? If we are allowed to presuppose *instincts* and *affections*, then the truth just now supposed to be discoverable concerning our state, is an exciting reason to serve the public interest, since this conduct is the most effectual means to obtain both ends. But I doubt if any truth can be assigned which excites in us either the desire of private happiness or public. For the former none ever alleged any exciting reason: and a benevolent temper finds as little reason exciting him to the latter, which he desires without any view to private good. If the meaning of the question be this, 'Does not every *spectator approve* the pursuit of public good more than private?' – the answer is obvious, that he does: but not for any reason or truth but from a *moral sense* 'in the constitution of the soul.'

This leads to consider *approbation* of actions, whether it be for *conformity to any truth*, or *reasonableness*, that actions are ultimately approved, independently of any *moral sense*? Or if all *justifying reasons* do not presuppose it?

If conformity to truth, or reasonable, denote nothing else but that 'an action is the object of a true proposition,' it is plain that all actions should be approved equally, since as many truths may be made about the worst, as can be made about the best. See what was said above about exciting reasons.

But let the *truths* commonly assigned as justifying be examined. Here it is plain, 'a truth showing an action to be fit to attain an end,' does not justify it; nor do we approve a subordinate end for any truth which only shows it to be fit to promote the ultimate end; for the worst actions may be conducive to their ends, and *reasonable* in that sense. The justifying reasons then must be about the ends themselves, especially the ultimate ends. The question then is, 'Does a conformity to any truth make us approve an ultimate end, previously to any moral sense?' For example, we approve pursuing the public good. For what reason? Or what is the truth for conformity to which we call it a reasonable end? I fancy we can find none in these cases, more than we could give for our liking any pleasant fruit.

The reasons assigned are such as these, 'It is the end proposed by the Deity.' But why do we approve concurring with the divine ends? This reason is given, 'He is our benefactor.' But then, for what *reason* do we approve concurrence with a benefactor? Here we must recur to a *sense*. Is this the reason moving to approbation, 'Study of public good tends to the advantage of the approver'? Then the quality moving us to approve an action is its being advantageous to us and not conformity to a truth. This scheme is intelligible but not true in fact. Men approve without perception of private advantage and often do not condemn or disapprove what is plainly pernicious, as in the execution of a just sentence which even the sufferer may approve.

If any allege, that this is the justifying reason of the pursuit of public good, 'that it is best all be happy', then we approve actions for their tendency to that state which is best and not for conformity to reason. But here again, what means *best*? morally best, or naturally best? If the former, they explain the same word by itself in a circle, if they mean the latter, that 'It is the most happy state where all are happy', then, most happy, for whom? the system, or the individual? If for the former, what reason makes us approve the happiness of a system? Here we must recur to a sense or kind affections. Is it most happy for the individual? Then the quality moving approbation is again tendency to private happiness, not reasonableness.

There are some other reasons assigned in words differing from the former, but more confused, such as these. 'It is our *duty* to study public good. We are *obliged* to do it. We owe obedience to the Deity. The whole is to be preferred to a part.' But let these words, *duty, obligation, owing* and the meaning of that gerund 'or participle', *is to be preferred*, be explained and we shall find ourselves still at a loss for exciting reasons previously to affections or justifying reason without recourse to a moral sense.

When we say one is *obliged* to an action we either mean, 1. that the action is *necessary to obtain happiness to the agent*, or to avoid misery or, 2. that *every spectator*, or he himself upon reflection, *must approve* his action, and disapprove his omitting it, if he considers fully all its circumstances. The *former meaning* of the word obligation presupposes *selfish affections*, and the sense of private happiness; the *latter meaning* includes the *moral sense*. Mr Barbeyrac, in his annotations upon Grotius, makes obligation denote an indispensable necessity to act in a certain manner. Whoever observes his explication of this necessity (which is not natural, otherwise no man could act against his obligation) will find that it denotes only 'such a constitution of a powerful superior as will make it possible for any being to obtain happiness or avoid misery but by such a course of action.' This agrees with the former meaning, though sometimes he also includes the latter.

Many other confused definitions have been given of obligation by no obscure names in the learned world. But let any one give a distinct meaning different from the two above-mentioned. To pursue them all would be endless; only let the definitions be substituted in place of the word obligation, in other parts of each writer, and let it be observed whether it makes good sense or not.

Before we quit this character *reasonableness* let us consider the arguments brought to prove that there must be some *standard* of moral good *antecedent to any sense*. Say they, 'Perceptions of sense are *deceitful*; we must have some perception or idea of virtue more *stable and certain*. This must be *conformity to reason*. Truth discovered by our reason is certain and invariable. That then alone is the original idea of virtue, agreement with reason.' But in like manner our sight and sense of beauty is deceitful and does not always represent the true forms of objects. We must not call that beautiful or regular, which pleases the sight, or an internal sense, but beauty in external forms, too, consists in conformity to reason. So our taste may be vitiated. We must not say that savour is perceived by taste but must place the original idea of grateful savours in conformity to reason and of ungrateful in contrariety to reason. We may mistake the real extent of bodies, or their proportions, by making a conclusion upon the first sensible appearance. Therefore ideas of extension are not originally acquired by a sense but consist in conformity to reason.

If what is intended in this conformity to reason be this, 'that we should call no action virtuous unless we have some reason to conclude it to be virtuous, or some truth showing it to be so,' this is very true. But then, in like manner, we should count no action vicious unless we have some reason for counting it so, or when it is truth 'that it is vicious.' If this be intended, by *conformity to truth*, then at the same rate we may make conformity to truth the *original idea of vice* as well as virtue, nay, of every attribute whatsoever. That taste alone is sweet which there is reason to count sweet; that taste alone is bitter, concerning which it is true that it is bitter; that form alone is beautiful, concerning which it is true that it is beautiful; and that alone deformed, which is truly deformed. Thus virtue, vice, sweet, bitter, beautiful, or deformed, originally denote conformity to reason, antecedently to perceptions of any sense. The idea of virtue is particularly that concerning which it is truth, that it is virtue; or virtue is virtue; a wonderful discovery!

So when some tell us, 'that truth is naturally pleasant, and more so than any sensible perception; this must therefore engage men more than any other motive, if they attend to it,' let them observe that as much truth is known about vice as virtue. We may demonstrate the public miseries which would ensue upon perjury, murder, and robbery. These demonstrations would be attended with that pleasure which is peculiar to truth, as well as the demonstrations of the public happiness to ensue from faith, humanity and justice. There is equal truth on both sides.

We may transiently observe what has occasioned the use of the word *reasonable* as an epithet of *only virtuous actions*. Though we have instincts determining us to desire ends without supposing any previous reasoning, yet it is by use of our reason that we find out the means of obtaining our ends. When we do not use our reason we often are disappointed of our end. We therefore call those actions which are effectual to their ends reasonable in one sense of that word.

Again, in all men there is probably a moral sense, making publicly useful actions, and kind affections, grateful to the agent and to every observer. Most men who have thought of human actions agree that the publicly useful are in the whole also privately useful to the agent, either in this life or the next. We conclude that all men have the same affections and sense. We are convinced by our reason that it is by publicly useful actions alone that we can promote all our ends. Whoever then acts in contrary manner we presume is mistaken, ignorant of, or inadvertent to, these truths which he might know; and say he acts unreasonably. Hence some have been led to imagine some reasons either exciting or justifying previously to all affections or a moral sense.

Two arguments are brought in defence of this epithet, as antecedent to any sense, viz., 'that we judge even of our affections and senses themselves, whether they are morally good or evil.'

The second argument is, 'that if all moral ideas depend upon the constitution of our sense then all constitutions would have been alike reasonable and good to the Deity, which is absurd.'

As to the first argument, it is plain we judge of our own *affections*, or those of others, by our *moral sense*, by which we approve kind affections, and disapprove the contrary. But none can apply moral attributes to the very *faculty* of perceiving moral qualities, or call his moral sense morally good or evil, any more than he calls the power of tasting sweet or bitter; or of seeing, straight or crooked, white or black.

Every one judges the *affections* of others by his own *sense*, so that it seems not impossible that in these senses men might differ as they do in taste. A sense approving benevolence would disapprove that temper which a sense approving malice would delight in. The former would judge of the latter by his own sense, so would the latter of the former. Each one would at first view think the sense of the other perverted. But, then, is there no difference? Are both senses equally good? No, certainly, any man who observed them would think the sense of the former more desirable than of the latter: but this is because the moral sense of every man is constituted in the former manner. But were there any nature with no moral sense at all observing these two persons, would he not think the state of the former preferable to that of the latter? Yes, he might, but not from any perception of moral goodness in the one sense more than in the other. Any rational nature observing two men thus constituted with opposite senses might by reasoning see, not moral goodness in one sense more than in the contrary, but a tendency to the happiness of the person himself, who had the former sense in the one constitution, and a contrary tendency in the opposite constitution. Nay, the persons themselves might observe this, since the former sense would make these actions grateful to the agent which were useful to others, who, if they had a like sense would love him and return good offices; whereas the latter sense would make all such actions as are useful to others, and apt to engage their good offices, ungrateful to the agent; and would lead him into publicly hurtful actions, which would not only procure the hatred of others, if they had a contrary sense, but engage them out of their self-love to study his destruction, though their senses agreed. Thus any observer, or the agent himself with this latter sense, might perceive that the pains to be feared, as the consequence of malicious actions, did over-balance the pleasures of this sense; so that it would be to the agent's interest to counteract it. Thus one constitution of the moral sense might appear to be more advantageous to those who had it, than the contrary; as we may call that sense of tasting healthful which made wholesome meat pleasant; and we would call a contrary taste pernicious. And yet we should no more call the moral sense morally good or evil than we call the sense of tasting savoury or unsavoury, sweet or bitter.

But must we not own that we judge of all our *senses* by our *reason* and often correct their reports of the magnitude, figure, colour, taste of objects, and pronounce them right or wrong as they agree or disagree with reason? This is true. But does it then follow that extension, figure, colour, taste, are not *sensible ideas* but only denote *reasonableness*, or agreement with reason? Or that these qualities are perceivable antecedently to any sense by our power of finding out truth? Just so a compassionate temper may rashly imagine the correction of a child or the execution of a criminal to be cruel and inhuman; but by reasoning may discover the superior good arising from them in the whole; and then the same moral sense may determine the observer to approve them. But we must not hence conclude that it is any *reasoning* antecedent to a *moral sense* which determines us to approve the study of public good, any more than we can in the former case conclude that we perceive extension, figure, colour, taste, antecedently to a sense. All these sensations are often corrected by reasoning, as well as our approbations of actions as good or evil and yet no body ever placed the original idea of extension, figure, colour, or taste, in conformity to reason.

* * *

As to the second argument, what means 'alike reasonable or good to the Deity'? Does it mean, 'that the Deity could have had no reasons exciting him to make one constitution rather than another'? It is plain, if the Deity had nothing essential to his nature, resembling or analogous to our sweetest and most kind affections, we can scarce suppose he could have any reason exciting him to any thing he has done. But grant such a disposition in the Deity, and then the manifest tendency of the present constitution to the happiness of his creatures was an exciting reason for choosing it before the contrary. Each sort of constitution might have given men an equal immediate pleasure in present self-approbation for any sort of action; but the actions approved by the present sense procure all pleasures of the other senses and the actions which would have been approved by a contrary moral sense would have been productive of all torments of the other senses.

If it be meant, 'that upon this supposition, that all our approbation presupposes in us a moral sense, the Deity could not have approved one constitution more than another,' where is the consequence? Why may not the Deity have something of a superior kind, analogous to our moral sense, essential to him? How does any constitution of the senses of men hinder the Deity to reflect and judge of his own actions? How does it affect the divine apprehension which way soever moral ideas arise with men?

If it means 'that we cannot approve one constitution more than another, or approve the Deity for making the present constitution,' this consequence is also false. The present constitution of our moral sense determines us to approve all *kind affections*. This constitution the Deity must have foreseen as *tending* to the *happiness* of his creatures; it does therefore evidence *kind affection* or *benevolence* in the Deity, this therefore we must *approve*.

* * *

Section II:
Concerning that Character of Virtue and Vice, the Fitness or Unfitness of Actions

We come next to examine some other explications of morality which have been much insisted on of late.* We are told, 'that there are *eternal and immutable differences* of things, absolutely and antecedently; that there are also *eternal and unalterable relations* in the natures of the things themselves from which arise *agreements* and *disagreements*, *congruities* and *incongruities*, *fitness* and *unfitness* of the application of circumstances to the qualifications of persons; that actions agreeable to these relations are morally good, and that the contrary actions are morally evil.' These expressions are sometimes made of the same import with those more common ones, 'acting agreeably to the eternal reason and truth of things.' It is asserted that God who knows 'all these relations, etc., does guide his actions by them, since he has no wrong affection (the word 'wrong' should have been first explained) and that in like manner these *relations*, etc., *ought* (another unlucky word in morals) to determine the choice of all rationals, abstracting from any views of interest. If they do not, these creatures are insolently *counteracting their Creator* and, as far as they can, *making things to be what they are not* which is the greatest impiety.'

That things are now different is certain. That ideas, to which there is no object yet existing conformable, are also different, is certain. That upon comparing two ideas there arises a relative idea, generally when the two ideas compared have in them any modes of the same simple idea, is also obvious. Thus every extended being may be compared to any other of the same kinds of dimensions; and relative ideas be formed of greater, less, equal, double, triple, subduple, etc., with infinite variety. This may let us see that relations are not *real qualities* inherent in external natures but only *ideas* necessarily accompanying our *perception* of two objects at once and comparing them. Relative ideas continue when the external objects do not exist, provided we retain the *two ideas*. But what the *eternal relations*, in the natures of things, do mean is not so easy perhaps to be conceived.

* See Dr Samuel Clarke's Boyle's Lectures and many late authors.

To show particularly how far morality can be concerned in relations, we may consider them under these three classes. 1. The *relations* of *inanimate objects* as to their *quantity*, or active and passive powers, as explained by Mr Locke. 2. The *relations* of *inanimate objects* to *rational agents*, as to their active or passive powers. 3. The *relations* of *rational agents* among themselves founded on their powers or actions past or continued. Now let us examine what fitnesses or unfitnesses arise from any of these sorts of relations in which the morality of actions may consist, and whether we can place morality in them without presupposing a moral sense. It is plain that ingenious author says nothing against the supposition of a moral sense. But many imagine that his account of moral ideas is independent upon a moral sense and therefore are less willing to allow that we have such an immediate perception, or sense of virtue and vice. What follows is *not intended* to *oppose his scheme*, but rather to suggest what seems a *necessary explication* of it by showing that it is *not otherwise intelligible* but upon supposition of a *moral* sense.

1. Relations of inanimate objects being known, puts it in the power of a rational agent often to diversify them, to change their forms, motions or qualities of any kind, at his pleasure. But nobody apprehends any virtue or vice in such actions where no relation is apprehended to a rational or sensitive being's happiness or misery; otherwise we should have got into the class of virtues all the practical mathematics and the operations of chemistry.

2. As to the relations of inanimate objects to rational agents, the knowledge of them equally puts it in one's power to destroy mankind as to preserve them. Without presupposing affections this knowledge will not excite to one action rather than another; nor without a moral sense will it make us approve any action more than its contrary. The relation of corn to human bodies being known to a person of kind affections was perhaps the exciting reason of teaching mankind husbandry. But the knowledge of the relations of arsenic would excite a malicious nature, just in the same manner, to the greatest mischief. A sword, a halter, a musket, bear the same relation to the body of an hero which they do to a robber. The killing of either is equally agreeable to these relations, but not equally good. The knowledge of these relations neither excites to actions nor justifies

them without presupposing either affections or a moral sense. Kind affections with such knowledge makes heroes; malicious affections, villains.

3. The last sort of relations is that among rational agents, founded on their actions or affections, whence one is called Creator, another creature, one benefactor, the other beneficiary (if that word may be used in this general sense), the one parent, the other child, the one governor, the other subject, etc. Now let us see what fitnesses or unfitnesses arise from these relations.

There is certainly, independently of fancy or custom, a *natural tendency* in some actions *to give pleasure*, either to the agent or others, and a contrary tendency in other actions to give pain, either to the agent or others. This sort of relation of actions to the agents or objects is indisputable. If we call these relations fitnesses, then the most contrary actions have equal fitnesses for contrary ends; and each one is unfit for the end of the other. Thus *compassion* is fit to *make others happy* and unfit to make others miserable. *Violation of property* is *fit to make men miserable*, and unfit to make them happy. Each of these is both fit and unfit, with respect to different ends. The *bare fitness then to an end is not the idea of moral goodness.*

Perhaps the virtuous fitness is that of ends. The fitness of a subordinate end to the ultimate cannot constitute the action good unless the ultimate end be good. To keep a conspiracy secret is not a good end, though it be fit for obtaining a farther end, the success of the conspiracy. The moral fitness must be that of the ultimate end itself. The public good alone is a fit end, therefore the means fit for this end alone are good.

What means the fitness of an ultimate end? For what is it fit? Why, it is an ultimate end, not fit for anything farther, but absolutely fit. What means that word fit? If it notes a simple idea it must be the perception of some sense. Thus we must recur, upon this scheme too, to a moral sense.

If fitness be not a simple idea, let it be defined. Some tell us that it is 'an agreement of an affection, desire, action, or end, to the relations of agents.' But what means agreement? Which of these four meanings has it? 1. We say one quantity agrees with another of equal dimensions every way. 2. A corollary agrees with a theorem when our knowing the latter to be truth leads us to know that the former is also a true proposition. 3. Meat agrees with that body which it tends to preserve. 4. Meat agrees with the taste of that being in whom it raises a pleasant perception. If any one of these are the meanings of agreement in the definition then one of these is the idea of fitness. 1. That an action or affection is of the same bulk and figure with the relation. Or, 2. when the relation is a true proposition, so is the action or affection or, 3. the action or affection tends to preserve the relation and contrary actions would destroy it so that, for instance, God would be no longer related to us as Creator and Benefactor when we disobeyed him. Or, 4. the action raises pleasant perceptions in the relation. All these expressions seem absurd.

These gentlemen probably have some other meanings to these words fitness or agreement. I hope what is said will show the need for explication of them, though they be so common. There is one meaning perhaps intended, however it be obscurely expressed, 'that certain affections or actions of an agent, standing in a certain relation to other agents, are approved by every observer, or raise in him a grateful perception, or move the observer to love the agent.' This meaning is the same with the notion of pleasing a moral sense.

Whoever explains virtue or vice by justice or injustice, right or wrong, uses only more ambiguous words, which will equally lead to acknowedge a moral sense.

Section III:
Mr Wollaston's Significancy of Truth, as the Idea of Virtue, Considered

Mr Wollaston* has introduced a new explication of moral virtue, viz., significancy of truth in actions, supposing that in every action there is some significancy like that which moralists and civilians speak of in their tacit conventions and *quasi contractus*.

* * *

To do actions from which the observer will form false opinions, while yet the agent is not understood to profess any intention of communicating to him his opinions or designs, is never of itself imagined evil, let the signs be natural or instituted, provided there be no malicious intention,

---

* In his *Religion of Nature Delineated*.

or neglect of public good. It is never called a crime in a teacher to pronounce an absurd sentence for an instance; in a nobleman to travel without coronets; or a clergyman in lay-habit for private conveniency, or to avoid troublesome ceremony; to leave lights in a lodge to make people conclude there is a watch kept. This significancy may be in any action which is observed; but as true conclusions argue no virtue in the agent, so false ones argue no vice.

* * *

Mr Wollaston acknowledges that there may be very little evil in some actions signifying falsehood, such as throwing away that which is of but little use or value. It is objected to him that there is equal contrariety to truth in such actions as in the greatest villainy. He, in answer to it, really unawares gives up his whole cause. He must own that there may be the strictest truth and certainty about trifles, so there may be the most obvious falsehood signified by trifling actions. If, then, significancy of falsehood be the very same with moral evil, all crimes must be equal. He answers, that crimes increase according to the importance of the truth denied; and so the virtue increases as the importance of the truths affirmed.

Then,

> *Virtue* and *Vice* increase as the *importance* of propositions is affirmed or denied.
> But *signification of truth and falsehood* does not so increase.
> Therefore, *signification of truth or falsehood*, are not the same with *virtue* or *vice*.

But what is this *importance of truth*? Nothing else but the moment or quantity of good or evil, either private or public, which should be produced by actions concerning which these true judgments are made. But it is plain, the signification of truth or falsehood is not varied by this importance. Therefore virtue or vice denote something different from this signification.

But farther, the importance of actions toward public good or evil is not the idea of virtue or vice. Nor does the one prove virtue in an action, any farther than it evidences kind affections, or the other vice, farther than it evidences either malice or want of kind affections. Otherwise a casual invention, an action wholly from views of private interest, might be as virtuous as the most kind and generous offices. And chance medley, or kindly intended, but unsuccessful attempts, would be as vicious as murder or treason.

* * *

Section IV:
Showing the Use of Reason Concerning Virtue and Vice, upon Supposition that we Receive these Ideas by a Moral Sense

* * *

Perhaps what has brought the epithet *reasonable*, or *flowing from reason*, in opposition to what flows from *instinct*, *affection*, or *passion*, so much into use, is this, 'that it is often observed that the very best of our particular affections or desires, when they are grown violent and passionate through the confused sensations and propensities which attend them, make us incapable of considering calmly the whole tendency of our actions and lead us often into what is absolutely pernicious, under some appearance of relative or particular good.' This indeed may give some ground for distinguishing between *passionate actions* and those from *calm desire* or *affection* which employs our *reason* freely, but can never set rational actions in opposition to those from instinct, desire or affection. And it must be owned that *the most perfect virtue* consists in the *calm*, *unpassionate benevolence*, rather than in particular affections.

If one asks, 'How do we know that our affections are right when they are kind?' what does the word 'right' mean? Does it mean what we approve? This we know by consciousness of our sense. Again, how do we know that our sense is right, or that we approve our approbation? This can only be answered by another question, viz., 'How do we know we are pleased when we are pleased?' Or does it mean, 'How do we know that we shall always approve what we now approve?' To answer this, we must first know that the same constitution of our senses shall always remain and, again, that we have applied ourselves carefully to consider the natural tendency of our actions. Of the continuance of the same constitution of our sense we are as sure as of the continuance of gravitation or any other law of nature.

The tendency of our own actions we cannot always know, but we may know certainly that we heartily and sincerely study to act according to what, by all the evidence now in our power to obtain, appears as most probably tending to public good. When we are conscious of this sincere endeavour, the evil consequences which we could not have foreseen never will make us condemn our conduct. But without this sincere endeavour we may often approve at present what we shall afterwards condemn.

If the question means, 'How are we sure that what we approve, all others shall also approve?' of this we can be sure upon no scheme. But it is highly probable that the senses of all men are pretty uniform, that the Deity also approves kind affections, otherwise he would not have implanted them in us nor determined us by a moral sense to approve them. Now since the probability that men shall judge truly, abstracting from any presupposed prejudice, is greater than that they shall judge falsely, it is more probable, when our actions are really kind and publicly useful, that all observers shall judge truly of our intentions, and of the tendency of our actions, and consequently approve what we approve ourselves, than that they shall judge falsely and condemn them.

If the meaning of the question be, 'Will the doing what our moral sense approves tend to our happiness and to the avoiding misery?' it is thus we call a taste wrong when it makes that food at present grateful which shall occasion future pains or death. This question concerning our self-interest must be answered by such reasoning as was mentioned above to be well managed by our moralists both ancient and modern.

Thus there seems no part of that reasoning which was ever used by moralists to be superseded by supposing a moral sense. And yet without a moral sense there is no explication can be given of our ideas of morality, nor of that reasonableness supposed antecedent to all instincts, affections, or sense.

'But may there not be a *right* or *wrong state* of our *moral sense*, as there is in our other *senses*, according as they represent their objects to be as they really are, or represent them otherwise?' So may not our moral sense approve that which is vicious, and disapprove virtue, as a sickly palate may dislike grateful food, or a vitiated sight misrepresent colours or dimensions? Must we not know therefore antecedently what is morally good or evil by our reason before we can know that *our moral sense is right*?

To answer this, we must remember that of the sensible ideas, some are allowed to be only perceptions in our minds, and not images of any like external quality, as colours, sounds, tastes, smells, pleasure, pain. Other ideas are images of something external, as duration, number, extension, motion, rest. These latter, for distinction, we may call *concomitant ideas of sensation*, and the former *purely sensible*. As to the purely sensible ideas, we know they are altered by any disorder in our organs and made different from what arise in us from the same objects at other times. We do not denominate objects from our perceptions during the disorder, but according to our ordinary perceptions, or those of others in good health. Yet nobody imagines that therefore colours, sounds, tastes, are not sensible ideas. In like manner many circumstances diversify the concomitant ideas, but we denominate objects from the appearances they make to us in an uniform medium, when our organs are in no disorder, and the object not very distant from them. But none therefore imagines that it is reason and not sense which discovered these concomitant ideas, or primary qualities.

Just so in our ideas of actions. These three things are to be distinguished, 1. the idea of the external motion, known first by sense, and its tendency to the happiness or misery of some sensitive nature, often inferred by argument or reason, which on these subjects, suggests as invariable eternal or necessary truths as any whatsoever, 2. apprehension or opinion of the affections in the agent, inferred by our reason. So far the idea of an action represents something external to the observer, 'really existing whether he had perceived it or not, and having a real tendency to certain ends.' The perception of approbation or disapprobation arising in the observer, according as the affections of the agent are apprehended kind in their just degree, or deficient, or malicious. This approbation cannot be supposed an image of any thing external, more than the pleasures of harmony, of taste, of smell. But let none imagine that calling the ideas of virtue and vice perceptions of a sense upon apprehending the actions and affections of another, does diminish their reality, more than the like assertions concerning all pleasure and pain, happiness or misery. Our reason often corrects the report of our senses about the natural tendency of the external action and corrects rash conclusions about the affections of the agent. But whether our moral sense be subject to such a disorder as to have different perceptions from the same apprehended affections in an agent, at different times, as the eye may have of the colours of an unaltered object, it is not easy to determine. Perhaps it will be hard to find any instances of such a change. What reason could correct if it fell into such a disorder I know not, except suggesting to its remembrance its former approbations and representing the general sense of mankind. But this does not prove ideas of virtue and vice to be previous to a sense, more than a like correction of the ideas of colour in a person under the jaundice proves that colours are perceived by reason previously to sense.

If any say, 'This moral sense is not a *rule*' what means that word? It is not a straight rigid body. It is not a general proposition, showing what means are fit to obtain an end. It is not a proposition asserting that a superior will make those happy who act one way and miserable who act the contrary way. If these be the meanings of rule, it is no rule; yet by reflecting upon it our understanding may find out a rule. But what rule of actions can be formed without relation to some end proposed? Or what end can be proposed without presupposing instincts, desires, affections, or a moral sense, it will not be easy to explain.

Section V:
Showing that Virtue may have Whatever is Meant by Merit; and be Rewardable, upon the Supposition, that it is Perceived by a Sense, and Elected from Affection or Instinct

Some will not allow any *merit* in actions flowing from kind instincts: '*merit*, say they, attends actions to which we are excited by *reason* alone, or to which we *freely* determine ourselves. The operation of instincts or affections is *necessary*, and not *voluntary*; nor is there more merit in them than in the shining of the sun, the fruitfulness of a tree, or the overflowing of a stream, which are all publicly useful.'

But what does *merit* mean? or *praise-worthiness*? Do these words denote the 'quality in actions, which gains approbation from the observer, according to the present constitution of the human mind?' Or, secondly, are these actions called meritorious, 'which, when any observer does approve, all other observers approve him for his approbation of it; and would condemn any observer who did not approve these actions?' These are the only meanings of *meritorious*, which I can conceive as distinct from *rewardable*, which is considered hereafter separately. Let those who are not satisfied with either of these explications of *merit*, endeavour to give a definition of it reducing it to its simple ideas: and not, as a late author has done, quarrelling these descriptions, tell us only that it is *deserving or being worthy of approbation*, which is defining by giving a synonymous term.

* * *

Perhaps by meritorious is meant the same thing with another word used in like manner, viz. *rewardable*. Then indeed the quality in which merit or rewardableness is founded, is different from that which is denoted by merit in the former meanings.

Rewardable, or *deserving reward*, denotes either that quality which would incline a superior nature to make an agent happy: or, secondly, that quality of actions which would make a spectator approve a superior nature, when he conferred happiness on the agent, and disapprove that superior, who inflicted misery on the agent, or punished him. Let any one try to give a meaning to the word *rewardable* distinct from these, and not satisfy himself with the words *worthy of*, or *deserving*, which are of very complex and ambiguous signification.

* * *

A SYSTEM OF MORAL PHILOSOPHY
BOOK I

Chapter IV
Concerning the Moral Sense, or Faculty of Perceiving Moral Excellence, and its Supreme Objects

1. Altho' we have kind affections ultimately aiming at the good of others, the success of which is joyful to us, yet our approbation of moral conduct is very different from liking it merely as the occasion of pleasure to ourselves in gratifying these kind affections. As we do not approve all conduct which gives us this pleasure, so we approve sometimes such conduct as does not give it; and our approbation of the good conduct which gives this pleasure is not proportioned to the pleasure it gives us. Thus many inventions, and much art and industry which does good to the persons or country we love, is not approved as virtuous: we approve generous attempts tho' unsuccessful; we approve the virtues of enemies, which may hurt the chief objects of our love. We equally approve the virtues or generous designs of good men in former ages toward their contemporaries, or in the remotest nations, toward their countrymen, for whom our affections are very faint and weak, as if the like were done to our friends, or country, the objects of our strongest affections.

Again . . . Tho' the approbation of moral excellence is a grateful action or sensation of the mind, 'tis plain the good approved is not this tendency to give us a grateful sensation. As, in approving a beautiful form, we refer the beauty to the object; we do not say that it is beautiful because we reap some little pleasure in viewing it, but we are pleased in viewing it because it is antecedently beautiful. Thus, when we admire the virtue of another, the whole excellence, or that quality which by nature we are determined to approve, is conceived to be in that other; we are pleased in the contemplation because the object is excellent, and the object is not judged to be therefore excellent because it gives us pleasure.

II. Much less is it the approved species of virtue, that it is an affection or action which gives pleasure to the agent. It always may indeed give him pleasure upon reflection, by means of this moral faculty: but 'tis plainly *then* that we most admire the virtue of another when we attend to its labours, dangers, difficulties, pains; and have no thought of any present or future pleasures of the agent.

'Tis strange that men should be at a loss to discern what form, or conception, or species it is, under which they approve esteem or admire their own affections and conduct, or that of others; and disapprove and condemn the contrary. One would think it manifest that the notion under which one approves virtue, is neither its tendency to obtain any benefit or reward to the agent or to the approver. The approver never expects a reward for the virtue of another; he approves where he sees no interest of his own promoted: and he would less approve such actions as are beneficent, the more he considered them as advantageous to the agent, and imagined him influenced by the views of his own advantage. Actions are conceived rewardable because they are good, not good because they are to be rewarded. Both the spectator and the agent value good actions the more in point of virtue, the more expensive or disadvantageous they are to the agent; and both will disapprove as immoral some actions which the one will allure to by bribes, and the other undertake; both conceiving them in this manner advantageous.

Now, if direct explicit opinions of tendencies to the advantage of the approver or agent do not raise moral approbation, much less can we suppose that any confused imaginations, or vague associations of ideas, about such advantages to the approver or the agent, can be the form under which virtue is approved.

'Tis also obvious that the notion under which we approve virtue is not its tendency to procure honour. A prospect of honour may be a motive to the agent, at least to external actions: but the tendency of an action to procure honour cannot make another approve it, who derives no honour from it. Our very desire of gaining honour, and the disposition in spectators to confer it, must presuppose a moral sense in both. And any views an agent may have to obtain self-approbation must also presuppose a moral sense. We cannot therefore say an action is judged good because it gains to the agent the pleasure of self-approbation; but it gains to him this pleasure because it was antecedently good, or had that quality which by the constitution of this sense we must approve.

* * *

JURISPRUDENCE, POLITICS AND ECONOMICS

A SHORT INTRODUCTION TO MORAL PHILOSOPHY BOOK II: ELEMENTS OF THE LAW OF NATURE

(Reprinted from the English translation, 1st edition, 1747)

A SYSTEM OF MORAL PHILOSOPHY

(Book III, Chapters III–VIII, reprinted from the posthumous 1st edition, 1755)

A SYSTEM OF MORAL PHILOSOPHY

(Book II, Chapter XII, reprinted from the posthumous 1st edition, 1755)

A SHORT INTRODUCTION TO MORAL PHILOSOPHY

BOOK II:
ELEMENTS OF THE LAW OF NATURE

Chapter I
Of the Law of Nature

That we may show how all the several parts of life may be brought into a conformity to nature, and the better discern the several rights and duties of mankind, we shall premise the more general doctrine in morals, explaining some pretty complex notions and terms constantly occurring; and this is the subject of this and the two following chapters.

In the preceding book we showed, how from the very structure of our nature we derived our first notions of right and wrong, virtuous and vicious, in our affections and actions: and that it was then *right* and *just* that any person should act, possess, or demand from others, in a certain manner, 'when his doing so tended either directly to the common interest of all, or to the interest of some part or some individual, without occasioning any detriment to others.' And hence we say in such cases that a man *has a right* thus to act, possess or demand: and whoever would obstruct or hinder him thus to act or possess, or would not comply with such demand, is said to do an *injury* or *wrong*.

But resuming this matter a little higher; 'tis plain that this structure of our nature exhibits clear evidence of the will of God and nature about our conduct, requiring certain actions and prohibiting others. The notion of a *law* to which our actions may be compared, is, no doubt, *artificial*, formed upon observation: and yet it has in all ages been so obvious and familiar to men that it may also be called natural. For the notion of a *just power*, or *right of governing* others, is obviously intimated, from that power nature has invested the parent with, over his children, so manifestly tending to their good. And this too is known to all by constant experience, that the bulk of mankind don't by any nice reasonings or observation of their own discover what is advantageous or hurtful in life; nay, that the greater part of the practical sagacity and wisdom of the generality depends upon the discoveries and instructions of a few, who have had greater penetration and sagacity: and since 'tis commonly known, and even the men of less sagacity acknowledge it, that there are great diversities of genius, and that some few have superior abilities to the common herd: that moral principle implanted in all must also recommend it as advantageous to all, that large societies of men united for their common interest, should commit the administration of their common concerns to a council of a few of the wiser sort, and compel any who may thereafter be refractory to submit to their orders, who have thus obtained a just right of governing. Hence the notion of *just power*, or of a *right of governing*, is among the most common and familiar with mankind, when from the very plan and model of power constituted, there is tolerable precaution taken that the rulers shall have either no inducements to abuse it to the detriment of the whole body, or no hopes of doing so with impunity. Hence the notion of *law* too is obvious to all, to wit, 'The will of those vested with just power of governing, declared to their subjects, requiring certain actions and forbidding others with denunciations of rewards or punishments.'

II. Now since 'tis generally agreed among men, that the Deity is endued with the highest goodness, as well as with wisdom and power; it must obviously follow that an universal compliance with the will of God must tend both to the general good, and to that of each individual; to which compliance also we are most sacredly bound in gratitude, as we were created by him, and are constantly deriving good from his munificent hand: it must also in like manner follow, that all disobedience to the will of God must be opposite to the common felicity, and show a base ungrateful mind. Now these considerations plainly show that it is perfectly just and right in the Deity to assume to himself the government of his rational creatures, and that his *right* is founded upon his own *moral excellencies*.

But since no man can give sufficient evidence to the satisfaction of all, that he is possessed even of superior wisdom, and much less of his stable inflexible goodness; since ambitious dissimulation would always make the greatest show of goodness, if this were a sure step to ascent to power; nor can men search into each others hearts to detect such hypocrisy: and since no power generally suspected and dreaded can make a people, who are diffident of their most important interests, easy or happy; no man can justly assume to himself power over others upon any persuasion of his own superior wisdom or goodness, unless the body of the people are also persuaded of it, or consent to be subjected to such power, upon some reasonable security given them, that the power entrusted shall not be abused to their destruction.

III. And further since it was God our Creator who implanted this sense of right and wrong in our souls, and gave us these powers of reason, which observing our own constitution, and that of persons and other things around us, discovers what conduct tends either to the common prosperity of all, or that of individuals, and what has a contrary tendency; and shows also that all sorts of kind offices generally tend to the happiness of the person who discharges them, and the contrary offices to his detriment: all these precepts or practical dictates of *right reason* are plainly so many *laws*,* enacted, ratified by penalties, and promulgated by God in the very constitution of nature. [As words or writing are not essential to the nature of a law, but only the most convenient way of notifying it.]

In every law there are two parts, the *precept* and the *sanction*. The precept shows what is required or forbidden; and the sanctions contain the rewards or punishments abiding the subjects, as they observe or violate the precept. In civil laws, beside the peculiar rewards or *premiums* proposed in some of them, there is this general reward understood in them all, that by obedience we obtain the defence and protection of the state, with the other common advantages of a civilized life, and the rights of citizens. The penalties of human laws are generally expressed. The sanctions of the law of nature are known and promulgated in like manner with the preceptive part. The *rewards* are all those internal joys and comfortable hopes which naturally attend a virtuous course; and all these external advan-

---

* On this subject see Cumberland's *Prolegomena*, or introduction, and Ch. I. Concerning the law of nature.

tages whether immediately arising from good actions, or generally obtained by the good-will and approbation of others, or of the Deity, whether in this life or in a future state. The *penalties* are all those evils internal or external, which naturally ensue upon vice; such as remorse, solicitude, and distressing fears and dangers: in fine, all these evils which right reason shows may probably be expected to ensue through the just resentment of the Deity or of our fellow-creatures.

iv. The divine laws according to the different manners of promulgation are either *natural* or *positive*. *Natural* laws are discovered by our reason observing the natures of things. *Positive* laws are revealed only by words or writing. Laws may again be divided according to the matter of them into the *necessary* and the *not-necessary*. Every sort of law indeed should have in view some real benefit to the state: but some laws point out the sole and necessary means of obtaining some great benefit, or of averting some great evil; so that contrary or even different laws could not answer the necessary purpose of society: while others only fix upon the most convenient means, where many others might have tolerably answered the end; or, where there is a variety of means equally apposite, yet fix upon one set of them, when 'tis necessary that multitudes should agree in using the same means. Such is the case in appointing *set times* and *places*, and other *circumstances*, where matters of common concern are to be transacted jointly by many. These latter sort of laws are also called *positive* as to their matter, and the former *natural*, in the same respect.

v. Laws generally respect alike a whole people, or at least all of a certain class or order; this holds as to all natural laws. But sometimes civil laws are made in singular cases, respecting only one person; these the Romans called *privilegia*; which were either out of singular favour, or singular resentment. If such *privileges* are granted for extraordinary merits, and have no pernicious tendency toward the body, they are very justifiable. Cases may happen too, tho' seldom, in which it may be just to bring to punishment some very artful dangerous criminal by a special law, which is not to be made a precedent in the ordinary procedure of justice.

Equity is sometimes understood as something distinct from *strict law*, being 'the reasonable wise correction of any imperfection in the words of the law, by their being either not sufficiently extended, or too extensive in regard to the true reason or design of the law.' This equity has place only as to laws promulgated in words; for the law of nature determines all points not by words but by right reason, and what is humane and good.

VI. The doctrine of *dispensations* was brought in by the canon-law. A dispensation is 'the exempting one out of special favour from the obligation of a law.' Dispensations are either from the preceptive part, or from the sanction, in remitting the penalty. Where the penalty is remitted or altered in such a manner as consists with the common safety, and does not weaken the authority and influence of the law, it is not to be blamed. Such a dispensing power for singular important reasons is frequently vested in the supreme rulers or magistrates of states. But for previous exemptions from the preceptive part of any wise law they can never be reasonable.

But first, we don't count it a dispensation when any one, using his own right and the ordinary power vested in him by law, frees another from some legal obligation, or imposes a new one. As when a creditor remits a debt; or the supreme governor commissions subjects to act in his name what he has a right to execute, tho' without such commission these subjects had acted illegally in doing so.

Again, sometimes by laws, whether divine or human, an external impunity may be justly and wisely granted to such conduct as is very vicious and culpable; if either through the stupidity or depravity of the people such vices could not be restrained without much greater inconvenience than what arises from the permission of them. But this comes not up to the notion of dispensation.

But in the third place, no grant or permission of any governor, human or divine, can make evil malevolent affections become morally good or innocent, or benevolent ones become evil: nor can the moral nature of actions flowing from them be any more altered by mere command or permission. The *dispensations* therefore, the *Canonists* intend, are then only justifiable, when the laws themselves are bad or imprudent, of which the canon-law contains a great multitude.

VII. The *law of nature* as it denotes a large collection of precepts is commonly divided into the *primary* and *secondary*; the former they suppose immutable, the latter mutable. This division is of no use as some explain it,* that the primary consists of self-evident propositions, and the secondary of such as require reasoning. Many of those they count primary require reasoning: nor are just conclusions more mutable than the self-evident premises. The only useful sense of this distinction is, when such precepts as are absolutely necessary to any tolerable social state are called the *primary*; and such as are not of such necessity, but tend to some considerable improvement or ornament of life are called *secondary*. But these latter in the sight of God and our own consciences are not mutable, nor can be transgressed without a crime, more than the primary; altho' there may be many political constitutions where the violation of these secondary precepts passes with impunity.

From the doctrine of the former book it must appear, that all our duties, as they are conceived to be enjoined by some divine precept, are included in these two general laws, the one that 'God is to be worshipped with all love and veneration': and in consequence of it, that 'he is to be obeyed in all things.'

The second is, that 'we ought to promote as we have opportunity the common good of all, and that of particular societies or persons, while it no way obstructs the common good, or that of greater societies.'

Chapter II
Of the Nature of Rights, and their Several Divisions

Since it is manifestly necessary to the common interest of all that large numbers of men should be joined together in amicable societies, and as this is the sum of all our duties toward men that we promote their happiness as we have opportunity; it must follow that all actions by which any one procures to himself or his friends any advantage, while he obstructs no advantage of others, must be lawful: since he who profits one part without hurting any other plainly profits the whole. Now since there are many enjoyments and advantages naturally desired by all, which one may procure to himself, his family or friends, without hurting others, and which 'tis plainly the interest of society that each one should be allowed to procure, without any obstruction

---

* See Vinnius's comment on the Instit. lib. i. 2. II. The same distinction is variously explained by other authors; but scarce any of them so explain it as to make it of importance.

from others (since otherways no friendly, peaceable society could be maintained): we therefore deem that each man has a *right* to procure and obtain for himself or his friends such advantages and enjoyments; which right is plainly established and secured to him by the second general precept above mentioned, enjoining and confirming whatever tends to the general good of all, or to the good of any part without detriment to the rest. In all such cases therefore men are said to act according to their *right*. And then, as the several offices due to others are recommended to us by the sense of our own hearts; so others in a social life have a claim to them, and both desire, and naturally or justly expect them from us, as some way due to them: in consequence of this it must appear, that the several rules of duty, or special laws of nature, cannot be delivered in a more easy manner than by considering all the several *claims* or *rights* competent either to individuals, to societies, or to mankind in general as a great body or society; all which are the matter of some special laws.

The several rights of mankind are therefore first made known, by the natural feelings of their hearts, and their natural desires, pursuing such things as tend to the good of each individual or those dependent on him: and recommending to all certain virtuous offices. But all such inclinations or desires are to be regulated by right reason, with a view to the general good of all.

Thus we have the notion of *rights* as moral qualities, or *faculties*, granted by the law of nature to certain persons. We have already sufficiently explained how these notions of our *rights* arise from that *moral sense* of right and wrong, natural to us previous to any consideration of law or command. But when we have ascended to the notion of a divine natural law, requiring whatever tends to the general good, and containing all these practical dictates of right reason, our definitions of moral qualities may be abridged by referring them to a law; and yet they will be of the same import; if we still remember that the grand aim of the law of nature is the general good of all, and of every part as far as the general interest allows it.

A right therefore may be defined 'a faculty or claim established by law to act, or possess, or obtain something from others'; tho' the primary notion of right is prior to that of a law, nor does it always include a reference to the most extensive interest of the whole of mankind.

For by our natural sense of right and wrong, and our sympathy with others, we immediately approve any persons procuring to himself or his friends any advantages which are not hurtful to others, without any thought either about a law or the general interest of all. For as the general happiness is the result of the happiness of individuals; and God has for the benefit of each individual, and of families, implanted in each one his private appetites and desires, with some tender natural affections in these narrower systems: actions flowing from them are therefore naturally approved, or at least deemed innocent, and that immediately for themselves; unless they should appear hurtful to others, or opposite to some nobler affection. Hence every one is conceived to have a *right* to act or claim whatever does no hurt to others, and naturally tends to his own advantage, or to that of persons dear to him.

And yet this we must still maintain, that no private right can hold against the general interest of all. For a regard to the most extensive advantage of the whole system ought to control and limit all the rights of individuals or of particular societies.

II. Now since a friendly society with others, and a mutual intercourse of offices, and the joint aids of many, are absolutely necessary not only to the pleasure and convenience of human life, but even to the preservation of it; which is so obvious that we need not reason upon it. Whatever appears necessary for preserving an amicable society among men must necesarily be enjoined by the law of nature. And in whatever circumstances the maintaining of peace in society requires, that certain actions, possessions, or claims should be left free and undisturbed to any one, he is justly deemed to have a *right* so to act, possess, or claim from others. As some law answers to each right, so does an *obligation*. This word has two senses, 1. We are said to be *obliged* to act, or perform to others, 'when the inward sense and conscience of each one must approve such action or performance, and must condemn the contrary as vicious and base': in like manner we conceive an obligation to omit or abstain. This sort of obligation is conceived previous to any thought of the injunction of a law. 2. Obligation is sometimes taken for 'a motive of interest superior to all motives on the other side, proposed to induce us to certain actions or performances, or omissions of action.' Such motives indeed must arise from the laws of an omnipotent Being. This latter meaning seems chiefly intended in these metaphorical definitions of great authors, who would have all obligation to arise from the law of a superior, '*a bond of right binding us by a necessity of acting or abstaining*' or an '*absolute necessity imposed upon a man, to act in certain manner.*'

III. Rights according as they are more or less necessary to the preservation of a social life are divided into *perfect* and *imperfect*. Perfect rights are of such necessity that a general allowing them to be violated must entirely destroy all society: and therefore such rights ought to be maintained to all even by violence: and the severest punishments inflicted upon the violation of them.

Imperfect rights or claims are sometimes indeed of the greatest consequence to the happiness and ornament of society, and our obligation to maintain them, and to perform to others what they thus claim, may be very sacred: yet they are of such a nature that greater evils would ensue in society from making them matters of compulsion, than from leaving them free to each one's honour and conscience to comply with them or not. 'Tis by a conscientious regard to these imperfect rights or claims of others, which are not matters of compulsion, that virtuous men have an occasion of displaying their virtues, and obtaining the esteem and love of others.

Yet the boundaries between perfect and imperfect rights are not always easily seen. There is a sort of scale or gradual ascent, through several almost insensible steps, from the lowest and weakest claims of humanity to those of higher and more sacred obligation, till we arrive at some imperfect rights so strong that they can scarce be distinguished from the perfect, according to the variety of bonds among mankind, and the various degrees of merit, and claims upon each other. Any innocent person may have some claim upon us for certain offices of humanity. But our fellow-citizen or neighbour would have a stronger claim in the like case. A friend, a benefactor, a brother, or a parent would have still a stronger claim, even in these things which we reckon matters of imperfect obligation.

There is also a third kind of right, or rather an external show of it, which some call an *external right*: when some more remote considerations of distant utility require that men should not be restrained in certain actions, enjoyments; or demands upon others, which yet are not consistent with a good conscience, or good moral dispositions. These external shows of right, which will never satisfy a good man as a foundation of conduct, often arise from imprudent contracts rashly entered into by one of the parties, and often even from the wisest civil laws.

'Tis plain here, that there can be no opposition either between two perfect rights or two imperfect ones. But imperfect rights may be contrary to these called external. Since however the imperfect rights are not matters of just force or compulsion; wars, which are violent prosecutions or defences of some alleged rights, cannot be just on both sides.

IV. Rights are also divided into the *alienable*, and such as *cannot be alienated* or transferred. These are alienable, where the transfer can actually be made, and where some interest of society may often require that they should be transferred from one to another. Unless both these qualities concur, the right is to be deemed inalienable. 'Tis plain therefore, for instance, that for defect of both these qualities, our opinions in matters of religion are inalienable; and so are our internal affections of devotion; and therefore neither of them can be matters of commerce, contract, or human laws. No man can avoid judging according to the evidence which appears to him; nor can any interest of society require one to profess hypocritically contrary to his inward sentiments; or to join in any external worship which he judges foolish or impious, and without the suitable affections.

From the general account given of the nature of right, these must be the two fundamental precepts of a social life; first, that 'no man hurt another' or occasion any loss or pain to another which is neither necessary nor subservient to any superior interest of society. The second is 'that each one on his part, as he has opportunity, should contribute toward the general interest of society'; at least by contributing toward the interest of his friends or family. And he who innocently profits a part, contributes also in fact to the good of the whole.

* * *

Chapter IV
Concerning the Natural Rights of Individuals

We have already shown that the several duties of life may be naturally explained by explaining the several *rights* belonging to men, and the corresponding obligations, in all the several states and relations they stand in to each other. By a *state* we understand 'some permanent condition one is placed in, as it includes a series of rights and obligations.' Our state is either that of the *freedom in which nature placed us*; or an *adventitious* state, introduced by some human acts or institution.

The state of *natural liberty*, is 'that of those who are subjected to no human power:' which plainly obtained at first in the world, among persons adult and exempt from the parental power. This state too must always subsist among some persons, at least among the sovereign princes of independent states, or among the states themselves, with respect to each other.

The character of any state is to be taken from the rights and laws which are in force in it, and not from what men may do injuriously contrary to the laws. 'Tis plain therefore from the preceding account of our nature and its laws, that the state of nature is that of peace and good-will, of innocence and beneficence, and not of violence, war, and rapine: as both the immediate sense of duty in our hearts, and the rational considerations of interest must suggest to us.*

For let us observe what's very obvious, that without society with a good many of our fellows, their mutual aids, and an intercourse of friendly offices, mankind could neither be brought to life or preserved in it; much less could they obtain any tolerably convenient or pleasant condition of life. 'Tis plain too that no one has such strength that he could promise to himself to conquer all such as he may desire to wrong or spoil, and all such enemies as he may raise up against himself by an injurious course of life; since an honest indignation at wrongs will make many more enemies to him than those he immediately injures: and there are few who won't find considerable strength to avenge themselves or their neighbours, when they have conceived a just indignation. And then men have it generally in their power much

---

* This suffices to overturn the fallacious reasonings of Hobbes upon the state of nature as a state of war of all against all.

more certainly and effectually to make others uneasy and miserable, than to make others easy and happy. External prosperity requires a perfectly right state of the body, and all its tender and delicate parts, many of which may be disturbed and destroyed by very small forces; it requires also a considerable variety of external things, which may be easily damaged, taken away, or destroyed. A just consideration of this infirm, uncertain condition of mankind, so that their prosperity may so easily be disturbed, must engage every wise man rather to cultivate peace and friendship with all, as far as possible, than to provoke any by unnecessary enmity or injury.

II. The rights of men according as they immediately and principally regard either the benefit of some *individual*, or that of some *society* or body of people, or of *mankind* in general as a great community, are divided into *private*, *public*, and *common to all*. The *private* rights of individuals are pointed out by their senses and natural appetites, recommending and pursuing such things as tend to their happiness: and our moral faculty of conscience shows us, that each one should be allowed full liberty to procure what may be for his own innocent advantage or pleasure, nay that we should maintain and defend it to him.

To discover therefore these *private rights* we should first attend to the several natural principles or appetites in men,* and then turn our views toward the general interests of society, and of all around them: that where we find no obstruction to the happiness of others, or to the common good, thence ensuing, we should deem it the *right* of each individual to do, possess, or demand and obtain from others, whatever may tend to his own innocent advantage or pleasure.

Private rights are either *natural* or *adventitious*. The former sort, nature itself has given to each one without any human grant or institution. The adventitious depend upon some human deed or institution.

III. The private natural rights are either *perfect* or *imperfect*. Of the perfect kind these are the chief, 1. A right to life, and to retain their bodies unmaimed. 2. A right to preserve their chastity. 3. A right to an unblemished character for common honesty, so as not to be deemed unfit for human society. 4. A right of liberty, or of acting according

---

* See Grotius, *de Jure Belli*, etc. I. c. 2. l.

to one's own judgment and inclination within the bounds of the law of nature. 5. A right over life, so far that each one, in any honourable services to society or his friends, may expose himself not only to dangers, but to certain death, when such public good is in view as overbalances the value of his life. This is our conscience, or moral sense, and love of virtue will strongly recommend to us in many cases. 6. There is also a sense deeply infixed by nature, of each one's *right of private judgment*, or of judging for himself in all matters of duty, especially as to religion; for a base judgment or opinion cannot of itself be injurious to others: and 'tis plain no man can without guilt counteract his own conscience; nor can there be any virtue in dissimulation or hypocrisy, but generally there is great guilt in it. Our sentiments therefore about religion and virtue cannot be matter of commerce or contract, so as to give others a right over them. Such commerce is no way requisite for any good in society; nor is it in one's power to judge or think as another shall command him. All engagements or contracts of this kind are null and void. Suppose one has judged amiss and has false opinions: yet while he injures no man, he is using his own *external right*; that is, tho' he acts amiss, yet much greater evils would ensue if any power were vested in others to compel him by penalties or threatenings of tortures, either to a change of his sentiments, or to a profession of it.

Each one also has a natural right to the use of such things as nature intended to remain common to all; that he should have the same access with others, by the like means, to acquire adventitious rights; and that he should find equal treatment with his equals. Men have likewise rights to marriage with such as are willing to inter-marry with them, provided they be under no prior bonds of marriage, or hindered by any other just impediment: nor can any third person or society which has not acquired any just power over the parties, pretend a right to obstruct their designs of inter-marriage; or to hinder any who are not their subjects from entering into any other innocent associations or commerce of any kind for their own behoof.

The sense of every one's heart, and the common natural principles, show that each one has these perfect rights; nor without maintaining them can there be any social life: so that they are also confirmed by considerations of common utility, and our more extensive affections.

IV. In this respect all men are originally *equal*, that these natural rights equally belong to all, at least as soon as they come to the mature use of reason; and they are equally confirmed to all by the law of nature, which requires that we should consult the interest of each individual as far as the common utility will allow; and maintain to the feeble and weak their small acquisitions or advantages, as well as their greater acquisitions or advantages to the ingenious and active. For 'tis plainly for the common good, that no mortal endued with reason and forethought should without his own consent, or crime, be subjected to the will of his fellow, without regard to his own interest, except in some rare cases, that the interest of a society may make it necessary. None of mankind are so stupid and thoughtless about their own interests, as not to count it next to death to have themselves and all that's dear to them, subjected to another's pleasure or caprice, and thus exposed to the greatest contumelies. Nature makes none masters, none slaves: and yet the wiser and better sort of men have many imperfect rights superior to those of others, and superior offices and services of humanity are due to them.

But as nature has set no obvious or acknowledged marks of superior wisdom and goodness upon any of mankind; and often weak men may have high notions of their own wisdom; and the worst of men may make the greatest shows of goodness, which their fellows cannot discover to be hypocritical; 'tis plain that no pretences of superior wisdom or goodness will justify a man in his assuming power over others without their own consent; this would be plainly eversive [subversive] of the common interest, and the source of perpetual wars.

V. To every imperfect right of individuals there answers a like *obligation* or duty which our conscience plainly enjoins, and in some cases most sacredly. These are the chief imperfect rights: each one may justly claim such offices as are profitable to him, and no burden or expense to the performer. Nay every innocent person has a right to such offices of others, as are of high advantage to him, and of small burden or expense to the performers. This is particularly the case of men under great calamities, needing the charitable aids of others. Men of eminent characters, tho' under no calamity, have a right to some higher offices from others, as particularly to their friendly suffrages for their advantage or promotion. Each one whose vices have not made him infamous has a right to be admitted on equitable terms into any societies civil or religious, which are instituted in his neighbourhood, for his more convenient subsistence, or his improvement in piety. And lastly each one, who has not forfeited by some crime, has a right to be treated on an equal footing of humanity with his equals, and with others in proportion to their merits.

VI. Concerning beneficence and liberality, these general maxims are evident,* that the importance of any benefit to the receiver, is proportioned jointly to the quantity of the benefit and his indigence: and that benefits are less burdensome to the giver the smaller their value is and the greater his wealth. Hence liberality may be exceedingly advantageous in many cases to him that receives it, and yet of small or no burden to the giver.

Beneficence, which is peculiarly becoming a good man, and eminently displays the goodness of his heart, ought to be practised with these cautions; first, that it doesn't hurt the persons it is employed about or the community. Secondly, that it be proportioned to our fortunes, so as not to exhaust its own fountain. Thirdly, that it be proportioned to the merits or claims of others. Among these claims we regard, first, the moral characters of the objects, and next their kind affections towards us, and thirdly the social intercourses we have had with them, and lastly the good offices we formerly received from them. None of these considerations are to be neglected, and least of all the last one; since there is no obligation more sacred than that of gratitude, none more useful in life; nor is any vice more odious than ingratitude, or more hurtful in society. When therefore in certain cases we cannot exercise all the beneficence we desire, offices of gratitude should take place of other offices of liberality.

* * *

Chapter VI
The Methods of Acquiring Property

Property is either *original* or *derived*. The original property arises from the first occupation of things formerly common. The derived is that which is transferred from the first proprietors.

* This is taken from Cicero, *de Officiis*, Lib. I.14, 15, etc.

Whosoever either from a desire of preserving himself, or profiting any who are dear to him, first occupies any of the spontaneous fruits of the earth, or things ready for human use on which no culture was employed, either by first discovering them with intention immediately to seize them, or by any act or labour of his catching or enclosing them so that they are most easily attainable and secured for human life, is deemed justly the proprietor for these reasons; that if any other person, capable of subsisting otherways, would wrest from him what he had thus acquired, and defeat and disappoint his labours, he would plainly act inhumanly, break off all friendly society, and occasion perpetual contention. What this person pretends to now, he may attempt anew every hour: and any other person may do the same with equal right: and thus all a man's pains in acquiring any thing may be defeated, and he be excluded from all enjoyment of anything unless he perpetually defend his acquisitions by violence.

'Tis trifling to imagine that property is any physical quality or bond between a man and certain goods, and thence to dispute that there's no such force or virtue in first espying, touching, striking, or enclosing anything, as to constitute a sacred right of property; or to debate which of all these actions has the greatest virtue or force. For in all our inquiries into the grounds or causes of property, this is the point in question, 'what causes or circumstances show, that it is human and equitable toward individuals, and requisite also to the maintainance of amicable society, that a certain person should be allowed the full use and disposal of certain goods; and all others excluded from it?' and when these are discovered, our road is cleared to find out the causes and rules about property.

II. Thus therefore we should judge about the different methods of occupation: that 'tis inhuman and unjust, without the most urgent necessity, to obstruct the innocent labours others have begun and persist in, or by any speedier attempt of ours to intercept their natural profits. If therefore any person in search for things requisite for himself, first discovers them with intention immediately to seize or pursue them, one who had employed no labour about them, nor was in search for them, would act unjustly and inhumanly, if by his greater swiftness he first seized them for himself. If severals at once were searching for such things, and at once discover them by sight, they will be

common among them, even altho' one swifter than the rest first
touched them; unless by civil laws or custom such points be otherways
determined. If one first espies them, and another conscious of his
design, but also in search for such things for himself, first seizes them,
the things will be common to both, or in joint property: for there are
no more potent reasons of humanity on one side than on the other. If
one by his labour or ingenuity encloses or ensnares any wild animals,
or so wearies them out in the chase that they can now easily be taken;
'tis a plain wrong for another to intercept them, tho' the former had
neither seen nor touched them. If it is known to many that certain
lands or goods lie common to be occupied by any one; and severals,
not conscious of each other's designs, at once are preparing to occupy
them, and set about it: by the custom which has obtained, he that
first arrives at them is the proprietor. But, abstracting from received
customs and laws, such things should be common to all who without
fraud or imprudent negligence employed their labours in occupying
them, whether they came earlier or later; and should either be held in
common, or divided among them in proportion to expense and pains
prudently employed by each of them for this purpose. Nay tho' each of
them were aware of the designs of the rest; 'tis right that each should
proceed and acquire a joint title with others. Nor should those who
without any fault of their own came too late, or such whose wise and
vigorous attempts have been retarded by accidents, be precluded from
their share.

    In such disputable cases we should first inquire what reasons
of humanity give the preference to any one above the rest; and this
chiefly, 'that the natural fruits of no man's honourable or innocent
labours should be intercepted; or any honest industrious attempts
defeated.' If this plea belongs alike to all, the goods should be deemed
in joint property of all. If some accidents or circumstances make
the point very doubtful; and some sorts of goods can neither be
held in common, nor divided or sold without great loss; we should
follow some implicit conventions of men, appearing by the laws or
customs which prevail; and assign the property to him who has on
his side such circumstances the regarding of which prevents many
inextricable disputes and violent contentions. Hence it is that law and
custom so generally favour the first seizer, the public purchaser, and

the person to whom goods have been publicly delivered. And this conduces to the common utility.

If different persons intending to occupy agree that the whole should fall to him who first occupies; they ought also to specify the manner of occupation; otherways different methods may be deemed equally valid, and constitute a joint property. These rules seem the most conducive to peace.

No doubt inextricable questions may arise about what the several parties insisting on their utmost rights may do, without being chargeable with injustice. But such as sincerely aim at acting the virtuous part, will always easily discern what equity and humanity require, unless they are too much influenced by selfishness. Nor have we reason to complain, that, in these and such like cases, nature has not precisely enough fixed the boundaries, to let us see how very near we may approach to fraud or injury, without actually incurring the charge of it; when we are so loudly exhorted to every thing honourable, liberal and beneficent.

III. But as man is naturally endued with provident forethought, we may not only justly occupy what's requisite for present use, but may justly store up for the future; unless others be in some extraordinary distress. There are also many things requiring a very long course of labour to cultivate them, which after they are cultivated yield almost a perpetual and copious use to mankind. Now that men may be invited to such a long course of labour, 'tis absolutely requisite that a continual property be allowed them as the natural result and reward of such laborious cultivation. This is the case in clearing woody grounds for tillage or pasture; preparing vineyards, oliveyards, gardens, orchards; in rearing or breaking of beasts for labour.

Property is deemed to begin as soon as one begins the culture of what before was unoccupied; and it is completed when the cultivator has marked out such a portion as he both can and intends to cultivate, by himself or such as he can procure to assist him. As 'tis plainly unjust to obstruct any innocent labours intended, or to intercept their fruits.

But the abilities of the occupier with his assistants must set bounds to his right of occupation. One head of a family, by his first arriving with his domestics upon a vast island capable of supporting a thousand families, must not pretend to property in the whole. He may acquire as much as there is any probability he can cultivate, but what is beyond this remains common. Nor can any state, on account of its fleets first arriving on a vast continent, capable of holding several empires, and which its colonies can never sufficiently occupy, claim to itself the dominion of the whole continent. This state may justly claim as much as it can reasonably hope to cultivate by its colonies in any reasonable time: and may no doubt extend its bounds beyond what it can cultivate the first ten or twelve years; but not beyond all probable hopes of its ever being able to cultivate. The just reasonable time to be allowed to the first occupiers, must be determined by prudent arbiters, who must regard, not only the circumstances of this state, but of all others who may be concerned, according as they are more or less populous, and either need new seats for their colonies, or have already sufficient lands for their people. If many neighbouring states are too populous, they may justly occupy the uncultivated parts of such a new discovered continent, leaving sufficient room for the first occupiers; and that without the leave of the first discoverers. Nor can the first discoverers justly demand that these colonies sent by other states should be subjected to their empire. 'Tis enough if they agree to live amicably beside them as confederated states. Nay as in a free democracy, 'tis often just to prevent such immoderate acquisitions of wealth by a few, as may be dangerous to the public, even tho' these acquisitions are a making without any private injuries: so neighbouring states may justly take early precautions, even by violence if necessary, against such acquisitions of any one, as may be dangerous to the liberty and independency of all around them; when sufficient security cannot be obtained in a gentler way. Nothing can be more opposite to the general good of mankind than that the rights, independency, and liberty of many neighbouring nations should be exposed to be trampled upon by the pride, luxury, ambition, or avarice of any nation.

'Tis plain however, that both individuals and societies should be allowed to acquire stores of certain goods far beyond all their own consumption; since these stores may serve as matter of commerce and barter to obtain goods of other kinds they may need.

IV. From these principles about property it appears, that such things as are inexhaustible by any use, are not matters of occupation or property, so that others could be excluded from them: for this further reason too, that such things can scarce be improved by any human labour. If indeed for the more safe use of any of them labour or expenses are requisite; those who wisely employ labour or expense for this purpose, may justly require that all others who use them should in a just proportion contribute to make compensation. The *air*, the *light*, *running water*, and *the ocean* are thus common to all, and cannot be appropriated: the same is the case of *straits* or *gulfs*. And yet if any state is at the expense to build fortified harbours or to clear certain seas from pirates for the behoof of all traders, they may justly insist on such taxes upon all traders who share the benefit as may proportionally defray the said expenses, as far as they really are for the benefit of all traders, but no further. Now no man should be excluded from any use of things thus destined for perpetual community, unless this use requires also some use of lands which are in property.

These reasonings also show that all things were left by God to men in that community called *negative*, not *positive*. *Negative community* is 'the state of things exposed to be appropriated by occupation.' Positive is 'the state of things in the joint property of many:' which therefore no person can occupy or acquire without the consent of the joint proprietors. At first any one might justly have occupied what he wanted, without consulting the rest of mankind; nor need we have recourse to any old conventions of all men, to explain the introduction of property.

v. The goods called by the civilians *res nullius*, which, as they say, are not in property, and yet not exposed to occupation;* such as temples, the fortifications of cities, and burial-places, are truly the property either of larger societies, or of families; altho' this property is often so restricted by superstitious laws, that it can be turned to no other use. 'Tis vain to imagine that any such things afford use to the Deity, or that his supreme right over all can be enlarged or diminished by any human deed.

The goods belonging to states† are not in the property or patrimony of any individuals, nor come into their commerce. But they are the property of the community, which may transfer

---

* Of these there are 3 classes, *sacrae, sanctae, religiosae*. Of which follow three examples in order.

† *Res publicae*, or *res populi*.

them as it pleases. Such are public theatres, high-ways, porticos, aqueducts, bagnios.

Things formerly occupied may return into the old state of community if the proprietor throw them away, or abandon his property; and this intention of abandoning may sometimes sufficiently appear by a long neglect of claiming it, when there is nothing to obstruct his recovery. A long possession in this case will give another a just title. Goods unwillingly lost fall also to the fair possessor, when the proprietor cannot be found. There are also other reasons why civil laws have introduced other sorts of *prescription* for the common utility, and to prevent inextricable controversies.

In the occupying of lands, a property is also constituted in such things as cannot be used without some use of the ground; such as lakes, and rivers as far as they flow within the lands in property, nay such parts also of things otherwise fit for perpetual community, as cannot be left open to promiscuous use without endangering our property; such as *bays* of the sea running far into our lands, and parts of the ocean contiguous to the coast, from whence our possessions might be annoyed. But by occupying lands we acquire no property in such wild creatures as can easily withdraw themselves beyond our bounds, and are no way enclosed or secured by our labour. And yet the proprietor may justly hinder others from trespassing upon his ground for fowling, hunting, or fishing.

All natural, accidental, or artificial improvements, or adventitious increase, are called accessions, such as fruits of trees, the young of cattle, growth of timber, and artificial forms. About which these general rules hold, 1. 'All accessions of our goods which are not owing to any goods or labours of others, are also our property; unless some other person has acquired some right which limits our property.'

2. When without the fraud or fault of any of the parties, the goods or labours of different persons have concurred to make any *compound*, or have improved any goods, 'these goods are in joint property of all those whose goods and labours have thus concurred; and that in proportion to what each one has contributed.' Such goods therefore are to be used by them in common, or by turns for times in the said proportion, or to be thus divided among them, if they will admit division without loss.

3. But if they admit no such common or alternate use, or division,

they to whom they are least necessary should quit their shares to the person who needs them most, for a reasonable compensation, to be estimated by a person of judgment and integrity.

4. When by the fraud or gross fault of another, his goods or labours are intermixed with my goods, so that they are less fitted for my purpose; the persons by whose gross fault this has happened is bound to compensate my loss* or make good to me the value of my goods, nay all the profit[t] I could have made had they been left to me entire as they were; and let him keep to himself the goods he has made unfit for my purpose. But if by the intermeddling of others my goods are made more convenient for me, my right remains; and I can be obliged to compensate to them no further than the value of the improvement to my purpose, or as far as I am enriched.

Full property originally contains these several rights: first, that of retaining possession; 2. and next, that of taking all manner of use; 3. that also of excluding others from any use; 4. and lastly, that of transferring to others as the proprietor pleases, either in whole or in part, absolutely, or under any lawful condition, or upon any event or contingency, and of granting any particular lawful use to others. But property is frequently limited by civil laws, and frequently by the deeds of some former proprietors.

* * *

Chapter IX
Of Contracts in General

Since a perpetual commerce and mutual aids are absolutely necessary for the subsistence of mankind not to speak of the conveniencies of life, God has indued men not only with reason but the powers of speech; by which we can make known to others our sentiments, desires, affections, designs, and purposes. For the right use of this faculty we have also a sublime sense implanted, naturally strengthened by our keen desires of knowledge, by which we naturally approve veracity, sincerity, and

---

* This *pensatio damni*, which is often due when there was no fraud in the case.

[t] *Pensare quod interest*, which always includes the former, and often extends much further.

fidelity; and hate falsehood, dissimulation, and deceit. Veracity and faith in our engagements, beside their own immediate beauty thus approved, recommend themselves to the approbation and choice of every wise and honest man by their manifest necessity for the common interest and safety; as lies and falsehood are also manifestly destructive in society.

In an intercourse of services, in commerce, and in joint labour, our sentiments, inclinations and designs must be mutually made known: and 'when we affirm to others that we will pay or perform any thing, with that professed view, that another shall pay or perform something on his part' then we are said to promise or contract. A covenant or contract is the 'consent of two or more to certain terms, with a view to constitute or abolish some obligation.' Nor does the law of nature distinguish between *contracts* and *pactions.**

Contracts are of absolute necessity in life, and so is the maintaining of faith in them. The most wealthy must need the goods and labours of the poor, nor ought they to expect them gratuitously. There must be conferences and bargains about them, that the parties may agree about their mutual performances. Suppose all men as just and good as one could desire, nay ready for all kind offices: yet without contracts no man can depend upon the assistance of others. For when I need the aid of a neighbour, he may be engaged in some more important services to a third person, or in some services to those who can give him a recompense more requisite in his affairs.

The sacred obligation of faith in contracts appears, not only from our immediate sense of its beauty, and of the deformity of the contrary, but from the mischiefs which must ensue upon violating it. 'Tis plainly more contrary to the social nature, and frequently a baser injury, to break our faith, than in other equal circumstances to have omitted or declined a duty we owe another way. By violating our faith we may quite defeat the designs of such as trusted to our integrity, and might have otherwise obtained the aid they wanted: and, from the necessity of commerce, it must appear, that the rights founded on contracts are of the *perfect* sort, to be pursued even by force.

* The difference between *contractus* and *pactum* is found in any Civil-law dictionary.

The perfidious for his part breaks of all social commerce among men.

II. And further; tho' a good man would not take any advantage of another's weakness or ignorance in his dealings, nay would frequently free another from a bargain which proved highly inconvenient to him, and not very necessary to himself, provided any loss he sustained were made good; yet there is such a manifest necessity of maintaining faith in commerce, and of excluding the cavils which might be made from some smaller inconveniences to one or other of the parties, that in the proper matters of commerce, the administration of which the law of nature commits to human prudence, our covenants tho' rashly made must be valid, and constitute at least such external rights to others, as must for the common utility be maintained, tho' perhaps a good man would not insist on them. But if the person who claims them persists in his claim to the utmost, we can have no right to oppose him violently; but ought to observe our covenants; according to an old rule, that 'what ought not to have been done, yet in many cases when done is obligatory.'

The proper *matters of commerce* are our labours and goods, or in general, all such things as must be frequently interchanged among men for the interest of society; and by a commerce in which we neither directly violate that pious reverence due to God, nor the perfect right of another; and about which no special law of God deprives us of the right of transacting.

III. We must distinguish from contracts *the bare declarations of our future intentions*; which neither transfer any right to others nor bind us to continue in the same purpose. What come nearer to contracts are these *imperfect promises*, in which from custom 'tis understood, that we convey no right to others to oblige us to performance, but only bind ourselves in honour and veracity; and that too only upon condition, that the person to whom we make such promises so behave as to be worthy of the favour designed him, and don't by his bad conduct give us just cause of altering our intentions: and in this point the promiser reserves to himself the right of judging; nor does he bring himself under an higher perfect obligation, than that of compensating any loss the other may sustain, even tho' he should without cause alter his purpose.

IV. The circumstances to be considered in explaining the nature of contracts and the just exceptions against their obligation, relate either to the *understanding*, or the *will*, the two internal principles of action, or the *matter* about which they are made.

As to the *understanding*; the common interest, as well as humanity, requires, that no person should sustain any damage on account of any ignorance in his own affairs which is no way faulty. And hence the contracts of minors unacquainted with the nature of the business, are not obligatory; nor of those seized with madness or dotage, nor of idiots, nor even of men quite disordered by drunkenness so as to have lost the use of their reason. And altho' there may be a great crime in drunkenness which may justly be punished; yet this is no reason why the fraudulent and covetous should be allowed to make a prey of them. The case is very different as to crimes or injuries done by men intoxicated. For tho' we are not bound with respect to others to preserve ourselves always in a condition fit for transacting of business, yet we are bound to preserve ourselves innocent continually, and to avoid doing injuries. If one of the parties was not aware that the other was intoxicated; this latter will be bound to make good any loss the other sustained by his non-performance of the contract. But there are many degrees of intoxication, some of which tho' they may abate our caution and prudence, yet don't deprive us of the necessary use of reason. If all these degrees also made contracts void, there could be no sure transactions among men. Questions concerning these degrees, must be decided in the several cases by the judgment of prudent arbitrators.

The same might be said concerning the imprudence of youth, previous to civil laws: since the degree of prudence requisite for commerce appears in different persons at very different ages. That therefore commerce may be ascertained, and such endless evasions prevented, 'tis absolutely necessary that in every society some certain age be agreed upon, to which whosoever attains must be deemed his own master, and capable of managing his own business. This age must be determined with this view, that as few as possible of ripe judgment be excluded from the administration of their own affairs, and yet as few as possible admitted before the maturity of judgment. The medium fixed by the Roman law is as good as any; that minors before fourteen years of age in males, and twelve in females, should have no management of their affairs, but be under the natural guardianship of their parents; or, if they are dead, under that of the guardians their parents or the law has appointed: and after these years, till twenty-one, or as it was in their earlier times, till twenty-five, they should be so subjected to curators, that no deed of theirs intended to bind themselves or their fortunes, should be deemed valid without the consent of their curators.

'Tis on one hand unjust that minors should sustain losses in contracts; but 'tis on the other hand unjust that they should be enriched at the expense of others. If therefore any contract has been made with them, and something paid or performed by the other party, if it is not detrimental to them to confirm the contract, they ought to do it when they come to maturity: if it be found detrimental, they should restore or compensate what was received on that account, or as far as they were profited. Minors before the legal years often have sufficient judgment in certain matters; and when it is so, nor was there any thing fraudulent or faulty on the other side, they are bound before God and their own consciences by their contracts, even as the adult.

When parents or curators are at hand, one can scarce without a gross fault enter into any important contracts with a minor without their consent. As generally the passions of the young are impetuous and incautious; they are rash in promising, keen in their desires, improvident, liberal, full of hopes and void of all suspicion.

v. He who was engaged into a contract by any mistake or error about the very nature of the object or goods, or these qualities which are chiefly regarded in them, is not bound: and whatever he has paid on that account should be restored. But no man has this plea who was engaged only by a secret expectation of such qualities as he did not openly insist on, or of such as are not commonly expected in such goods. If the mistake was about some different matter or event, which moved him to the bargain; when the mistake is discovered, humanity may require it of the other party to set him free, especially if he is ready to compensate any damage occasioned by his mistake. But this is not a matter of perfect obligation, unless the person in the mistake made it an express condition of the bargain.

The nature of the goods, and the qualities upon which their value depends, and the defects of such qualities, are, as they speak, *essential points* in contracts. Where one of the parties has been in a mistake about them he is not bound. Where the mistake has been only about the current price; the person deceived and sustaining the loss has a perfect right to have the price reduced to equality; which if the other party refuses the bargain may be made void.

Whoever by any fault or rashness of his caused the mistake of the other party, or fell into a mistake himself, is bound to compensate any loss the other thereby sustains: but he that dealt fraudulently, is bound further to make good any profit the other could have made, had the bargain been executed with integrity. Any promises or contracts obtained from us by the fraud of the person with whom we contracted, are plainly void; because through his fraud we wanted the due knowledge requisite in contracting, and he is bound to compensate our damage occasioned by his fraud, which is easiest done by making the bargain void.

Where the fraud of a third person has moved us to a contract without any collusion with the other party; the bargain is valid. But we have a right of demanding compensation of any loss from that third person who deceived us.

vi. We always deem that all such voluntarily consent who voluntarily use such signs of consenting as by custom import it. Nor could there be any faith maintained, if we allowed exceptions from a secret dissent contrary to our expressions.

Words and writing are the fittest methods of declaring consent: but any other sign agreed upon by the parties, or received by common custom is sufficient. Nay some actions in certain circumstances are justly deemed to declare consent, when they are such as no man of common sense or equity would do, unless he also consented to certain terms. From such actions therefore we justly conclude a person's consent, unless he timously premonish all concerned of the contrary. Covenants or contracts founded on consent thus declared are called *tacit*: which are distinguished from another set of obligations, to be presently explained, said to arise *after the manner of contracts*, by this, that in tacit contracts the obligation is prevented by an express declaration to the contrary; but not in the others.

Beside the principal expressed articles in contracts, there are frequently others plainly understood as adjected from the very nature of the transactions, or from the prevailing custom among all who are engaged in such business.

The consent of both parties, of the receiver as well as the giver, is necessary in all translation either of property or any other rights, whether gratuitous or not. For from one's intention of bestowing any thing on a friend, we cannot conclude any design of throwing it away in case he don't accept, or of forcing it upon him. But a lower sort of evidence will serve to prove a consent to accept any thing valuable; and we may always presume upon it, if the thing was previously requested; provided the offer answer the request.

But as in full property there is included a right of disposing under any lawful conditions, or upon any contingency; and of giving in trust to a friend, till some future event happens: inheritances and legacies may thus be left with trustees, till it be found whether the heirs designed, or the legatees are willing to accept. Nay goods may thus be kept in favours of persons not yet existing; as it is unjust to hinder the proprietor to appoint his goods thus to be reserved for the offspring of his friends if they shall happen to have any: and 'tis injurious toward such offspring to have defeated or intercepted any benefits destined for them by their deceased parents, kinsmen, or friends. And yet no heir or legatee can be forced to be proprietor of any thing thus left to him without his own consent. Mankind however, and each one as he has opportunity, when no special trustee is appointed, ought to take this care of infants, or persons unborn, to preserve such inheritances or legacies for their behoof, till they can accept them.

VII. As the obligation of contracts plainly depends on the consent of the parties, and without it is void; so when it was only given under certain conditions, if they don't exist, there's no obligation. But such conditions must be known as such on both sides, otherways there could be no faith in our transactions. These conditions therefore alone are of such force as that their non-existence makes the transaction void, which were either expressly made conditions by one or other of the parties, or which the person who insists on them did in conscience believe the other party understood as adjected from the nature of the affair; and not every one which one of the parties might secretly expect would exist, tho' the like is not ordinarily expected in such transactions. Whatever indeed one party has undertaken for to the other, or positively affirmed to him to engage him to the bargain, *that* the other party may justly be deemed to have made a condition of his consenting.

In the known division of contracts into *absolute* and *conditional*, by a condition is understood 'some event yet uncertain to one or both the parties, distinct from the prestations covenanted, upon the existence of which the validity of the contract depends.' A condition known to be naturally impossible, shows that there is no engagement. We shall presently speak of another sort of impossibility from the prohibition of law, or moral turpitude. But a vicious action of any third person, to be done without any aid of the parties contracting, may be a just condition; provided nothing in the contract give any invitation to such actions.

Conditions in the power of either party are called *voluntary*; others are *involuntary*; and some are of a mixed nature. But neither side is understood to be obliged to make these conditions called voluntary or mixed to exist, for then they would be absolute covenants of the bargain.

VIII. The due freedom of consent may be taken away by fear. But of this there are two sorts, one denoting a suspicion that when one party has fulfilled his part of the bargain, the other party won't fulfil his: the other denotes a terror occasioned by some great evil threatened. As to the former sort these observations seem just: 1. He that voluntarily contracts with openly unjust and impious men, whose characters he previously knew, is plainly obliged by his contract, as he must have tacitly renounced any exception from their character which was previously known. But 2ly. If he only comes to the knowledge of their characters after the contract, 'tis not indeed void; but he may justly delay performing on his part, till they give such security for the performance of theirs as a wise arbiter judges sufficient. To maintain that all contracts entered into with the unjust, or heretical or impious, are void, would destroy all faith among men; since there are no such obvious characteristics to distinguish the good from the bad as all will agree in: and considering the weaknesses of mankind, they have always had the most opposite opinions about the moral and religious characters of men around them; as in all ages there have been the greatest diversities and contrarieties of opinions.

As to the second sort of fear; when I have been forced into a contract by fear of evil threatened; there are two cases, according as the evil is unjustly threatened either by him I contract with, or by a third person without any collusion with the person I contract with. In the later case when by contract I obtain the aid of an innocent man against dangers threatened by another; no doubt I am bound; unless there be something very exorbitant in the terms. For the giving aid in such perils is no doubt a most useful service well deserving compensation.

If indeed I am threatened unjustly with some great evil by any man unless I enter into a certain bargain, or make a promise, to a third person, who is in no collusion with him who threatens me, while yet I am forced to conceal from him the terror I am under; the bargain or promise is void, because by this terror I am deprived of that liberty which is necessary in commerce. But any damage this innocent person sustains by the disappointment, I am bound to make it good, as it was occasioned by me for my own safety. The same holds, when through my cowardice I have been excessively afraid without cause.

Any contracts entered into from fear of a just magistrate, or the sentence of a judge, are plainly valid, since we are deemed subjected to such civil power.

ix. But when I am forced to contract through fear of evils unjustly threatened by the very party I contract with, we must distinguish whether these evils are threatened under some such plausible show of right as might possibly impose upon an honest man, or on the other hand, by openly avowed injustice, without any such shadow of right. In the former case, tho' the author of such violence acquires no right by it, which he can use with a good conscience; yet on account of some more distant interests of mankind, he may have a sort of *external right*, with which the other party may be bound to comply. Nothing is more incident to mankind than to mistake about their rights; and hence arise wars too frequently, while yet neither side is sensible of the injustice of their cause. These wars must either be composed by treaties and contracts, or must end with the ruin of one side. Now 'tis highly eligible that they should be ended rather by some treaty: and treaties could be of no use if they still lay open to this exception of unjust force, which either side might plead whensoever they inclined to renew the old controversy. This exception therefore must not be allowed against treaties of peace, when there were any plausible pretences on both sides for the preceeding war. If indeed the terms of peace are manifestly iniquitous and oppressive, contrary to all humanity, making life quite miserable and slavish to the less fortunate side; such treaties have no plausible shows of justice, and lie open to the exception.

But where violence is used or threatened, without any pretence of right, to extort promises or contracts, they cannot be obligatory. By such violence the author of it plainly abdicates or forfeits all the rights of men; all the benefits to be claimed from the law of nature, or the humanity of his fellows; as he openly professes himself a common enemy to all, free from any social tie. The common safety therefore requires that such monsters should be cut off by any means. Suppose that such extorted promises were valid, yet whatever upon such a promise is due to the author of the violence, he is always indebted at least as much to the person thus compelled, upon account of damage done him unjustly: these two claims therefore extinguish each other by *compensation*. Nor can one here allege that by the act of promising under this terror the promiser tacitly renounces this exception of unjust force previously known; for this forced renunciation alleged is one part of the damage: and what pretence is there of alleging an obligation by tacit compact, to one who in such a cause is incapable of acquiring a right by the most express contract, and who in this very affair abdicates or forfeits all human rights?

But, however that no regard is to be had to such persons in thus trampling upon all the rights of mankind, yet when they sufficiently appear to be returning to a soberer mind, asking pardon of what's past, offering to quit their falsenesses, to deliver their arms, and to give security for their future conduct; and when such confederacies cannot be otherways destroyed without shedding much innocent blood of our citizens; the common interest may sometimes require to enter into such treaties with them, and to observe them faithfully: and as to any of our citizens who by this means are excluded from prosecuting them for reparation of damages, they ought to obtain it from the community.

x. Contracts or promises cannot be of force unless the matter of them be *possible* to the parties: and therefore no man can be obliged to what he cannot accomplish tho' he seriously desired it. If one has promised any thing, which by some subsequent accident without his fault becomes impossible, he is only obliged to restore or compensate the value of any thing he received in consideration of it. Where the fraud or other gross fault of one party either made the matter impossible, or concealed the impossibility, he is obliged to make good the profit which would otherways have arisen to the other.

The matter of contracts must also be lawful: that is, our contracts or promises should be only about the natural matters of commerce, which can be alienated, the administration of which is committed to human prudence, and not prohibited by any special law. No obligation therefore can arise from any promise, to violate directly the reverence due to God, or the perfect rights of others, or to do what any special law prohibits, or what is not committed to our power.

If therefore both parties know the unlawfulness of the terms of any contract, or ought to have known it; the contract is void. The one who employed another to commit a crime, may redemand what he gave to the person hired, before he has committed the crime. And if the crime be previously committed, the executor ought not to have the hire; nor if he previously received it, can the person who hired him redemand it. Both equally deserve the highest punishments; nor should either hold any advantage by such engagements.

If after the contract the iniquity of it appears to either side, which they had not formerly considered; before execution either of them may free himself from it: and any reward given should be restored. Nor after execution can the person employed claim his reward, unless the moral turpitude affect only the hirer and not himself; or unless his ignorance was no way culpable. But where the turpitude only affects the person who employed him, then he may justly claim his hire. 'Tis the general interest of mankind that there should be no allurements to such crimes, nor dependence upon such contracts.

But if the vice in any performance of covenant only consist in this, that a man has managed imprudently and contrary to the duty of a discreet cautious man, in these matters which naturally fall under commerce; 'tis of such importance to maintain the faith of commerce that in this case, too 'our transactions and covenants are obligatory, tho' we were faulty in entering into them.'

Covenants about the goods or actions of others which are not subjected to our power, are in the same case with those about impossibilities. Whoever has acted fraudulently in such covenants is liable to make good all the profit [that] would have accrued from the faithful performance of them: and he who has deceived others by any culpable negligence is obliged to compensate the damages.

XI. Every sort of contracts about one's goods or labours does not immediately divest him of all moral power of transacting about them in a different manner with others. This is the case only in such as convey the entire property at once, or a real right; or such as give another the whole right to one's labours for a certain time, or during life, so as to preclude his contracting with others about the same. But when one has only made a contract constituting a *personal right* against himself, he may thereafter convey a valid *real* right, to such as knew nothing about the former contract, which will take place of the personal right tho' prior. Where indeed this new grantee has acted fraudulently, being apprized of the former contract; the subsequent one should be void. For the law of nature can never confirm frauds, or any contracts* plainly contrived and designed to elude any obligations of humanity, when this design must be known to both parties in the contract. But in other cases, 'of two covenants entered into with the same person, the later derogates from the former.' But of contracts entered into about the same thing with different persons, 'such as convey a real right take place of those which only convey a personal;' provided there has been no fraud on his part to whom the real right is transferred. And lastly in contracts of the same nature entered into with different persons, 'the prior takes place of the posterior.'

XII. We may contract by *factors* or *agents*, or persons commissioned for that purpose, as well as in our own persons. Where full powers are given, and no special instructions to be shown to all he deals with, expressing the extent of our agent's commission, and how far we subject our rights to his transactions; we are deemed to be obliged to ratify what he does in our name, unless we can make proof that he acted fraudulently, or was bribed by the other party; or the manifest iniquity of his deeds satisfy a prudent arbiter that he must have been corrupted.

* Matth. xv, 5. Mark VII, II .

As to any smaller injuries we sustain, we must impute them to our agent, while we ratify what he has done with others.

But when the powers of the agent are specially declared to all concerned, what he transacts beyond these bounds does not oblige his constituent.

A SYSTEM OF MORAL PHILOSPHY
BOOK III

Chapter III
The Duties and Rights of Masters and Servants

* * *

The labours of any persons of tolerable strength and sagacity are of much more value than his bare maintenance. We see that the generality of healthy people can afford a good share of the profits of their labours for the support of a young family, and even for pleasure and gaiety. If a servant obliged himself by contract to perpetual labours for no other compensation than his bare maintenance, the contract is plainly unequal and unjust; and being of the onerous kind, where equality is professed on both sides, he has a perfect right to a further compensation, either in some *peculium*, or little stock for him and his family, or in a humane maintenance for his family.

Such a servant, whether for life or a term of years, is to retain all the rights of mankind, valid against his master, as well as all others, excepting only *that* to his labours, which he has transferred to his master: and in lieu of this he has a right to the maintenance as above mentioned, or to the wages agreed on. If by custom masters assume any reasonable jurisdiction over their domestics, not inconsistent with their safety and happiness, the servant, by voluntarily entering into the family, is deemed to have subjected himself to this jurisdiction; even as a foreigner who resides in a state, subjects himself to the laws of it as far as they relate to foreigners.

Where one has not transferred a right to all his labours, but only engaged for work of a certain kind; he is obliged to that work only; and in other respects is as free as his master. In none of these cases can the master transfer his right, or oblige the servant to serve another, unless this was expressly agreed on in the contract . . .

Men may justly be placed in a much worse condition of servitude, in consequence of damages injuriously done, or of debts incurred, which they have by their gross vices made themselves incapable of discharging. The person whom they have thus injured has a perfect right to compensation by their labours during their lives, if they cannot sooner discharge the claim. A criminal too, by way of punishment, may justly be adjudged to perpetual labours of the severest sort. In these cases, a power is founded solely for the behoof of others, to make all the profit by their labours which they can yield. Whatever humanity may be due to such unhappy servants, as they are still our fellow-creatures, yet the master's power and right being consituted only for his behoof, it is naturally alienable without their consent. But, still, in this worst condition of servitude, neither the criminal, after he has endured any public punishment which the common safety may require, nor much less the debtor, have lost any of the natural rights of mankind beside that one to their own labours . . .

As this sort of slavery has a just foundation, some nations favour liberty immoderately by never admitting the perpetual servitude of any citizen. And yet perhaps no law could be more effectual to promote general industry, and restrain sloth and idleness in the lower conditions, than making perpetual slavery of this sort the ordinary punishment of such idle vagrants as, after proper admonitions and trials of temporary servitude, cannot be engaged to support themselves and their families by any useful labours. Slavery would also be a proper punishment for such as by intemperance or other vices ruined themselves and families, and made them a public burden . . .

As to the notions of slavery which obtained among the Grecians and Romans, and other nations of old, they are horridly unjust. No damage done or crime committed can change a rational creature into a piece of goods void of all right, and incapable of acquiring any, or of receiving any injury from the proprietor; unless one should maintain that doing useless mischief, and creating excessive misery unnecessarily, can tend to the general good; and occasion no diminution of the happiness in the system, which is contradictory in the very terms.

* * *

Chapter IV
The Motives to constitute Civil Government

* * *

If all mankind were perfectly wise and good, discerning all the proper means of promoting the general happiness of their race, and inclined to concur in them, nothing further would be wanting; no other obligation or bonds than those of their own virtue and wisdom. The necessity of civil power therefore must arise either from the imperfection or depravity of men or both.

When many of the ancients speak of man as a species naturally fit for civil society, they do not mean that men as immediately desire a political union, or a state of civil subjection to laws, as they desire the free society of others in natural liberty, or as they desire marriage and offspring, from immediate instincts. 'Tis never for itself agreeable to any one to have his actions subject to the direction of others, or that they should have any power over his goods or his life. Men must have first observed some dangers or miseries attending a state of anarchy to be much greater, than any inconveniencies to be feared from submitting their affairs along with others to the direction of certain governors or councils concerned in the safety of all: and then they would begin to desire a political constitution for their own safety and advantage, as well as for the general good. As men are naturally endowed with reason, caution, and sagacity; and civil government, or some sort of political union must appear, in the present state of our nature, the necessary means of safety and prosperity to themselves and others, they must naturally desire it in this view; and nature has endowed them with active powers and understanding for performing all political offices . . .

The evils to be feared in anarchy result plainly from the weakness of men, even of those who have no unjust intentions, and partly from the unjust and corrupt dispositions which may arise in many. 'Tis wrong to assert that there is no occasion for civil polity except from human wickedness. The imperfections of those who in the main are just and good may require it.

* * *

Chapter V
The Natural Method of Constituting Civil Government and the Essential Parts of It

* * *

Civil power is most naturally founded by these three different acts of a whole people. 1. An agreement or contract of each one with all the rest, that they will unite into one society or body, to be governed in all their common interests by one council. 2. A decree or designation, made by the whole people, of the form or plan of power, and of the persons to be entrusted with it. 3. A mutual agreement or contract between the governors thus constituted and the people, the former obliging themselves to a faithful administration of the powers vested in them for the common interest, and the latter obliging themselves to obedience.

* * *

Chapter VI
The Several Forms of Polity, and their Principal Advantages and Disadvantages

* * *

'Tis obvious that when by any plan of polity these four advantages can be obtained, *wisdom* in discerning the fittest measures for the general interest; *fidelity* with *expedition* and *secrecy* in the determination and execution of them, and *concord* or *unity*; a nation must have all that happiness which any plan of polity can give it; as sufficient *wisdom* in the governors will discover the most effectual means, and *fidelity* will choose them, by *expedition* and *secrecy* they will be most effectually executed, and unity will prevent one of the greatest evils, civil wars and sedition. The great necessity of taking sufficient precaution against these mischiefs of factions and civil war leads most writers in politics into another obvious maxim, viz.

That the several parts of supreme power if they are lodged by any complex plan in different subjects, some granted to a prince, others to a senate, and others to a popular assembly, there must in such case be some *nexus imperii*, or some political bond upon them, that they may not be able or incline to act separately and in opposition to each other. Without this, two supreme powers may be constituted in the same state, which may give frequent occasions to civil wars.

* * *

Another maxim is equally certain from reason and the experience of all nations, 'That property, and that chiefly in lands, is the natural foundation upon which power must rest; though it gives not any just right to power'. Where there is property there numbers of men can be supported, and their assistance obtained as they can be rewarded for it: and where they cannot be supported and rewarded, their assistance is not to be expected. When power wants this foundation, the state must always be restless, fluctuating, and full of sedition, until either the power draws property to itself, or property obtains power. Men who have property, and can therefore obtain force, will not be excluded from some share of power. And men in power will exert it one way or other in obtaining property to support themselves; which must occasion convulsions in a state.

* * *

Pure monarchy will never continue long without crown-lands, or hereditary provinces, where the lands are either the property of the prince, or he has a power over them equivalent to property...

An hereditary aristocracy in like manner shall be exposed to constant seditions and fluctuations, unless a very large share of the lands are the property of the senators...

A democracy cannot remain stable unless the property be so diffused among the people that no such cabal of a few as could probably unite in any design, shall have a fund of wealth sufficient to support a force superior to that of the rest. And in the several complex forms of polity there must some suitable division of property be observed, otherwise they shall always be unstable and full of sedition; when power has its natural foundation of property it will be lasting, but may, in some forms be very pernicious and oppressive to the whole body of the people; and it must be the more pernicious that it will be very permanent, there being no sufficient force to overturn or control it. And this shows the great care requisite in settling a just plan, and a suitable division of property, and in taking precautions against any such change in property as may destroy a good plan: this should be the view of agrarian laws.

As 'tis manifest that in democracies, and in all democratic assemblies truly chosen by the people, and united in interest with them, there must ever be a faithful intention of the general interest, which is the interest of the whole assembly; no constitution can be good where some of the most important parts of the civil power are not committed in whole or in part to such an assembly, which ever must be faithful to that interest for which all civil polity is destined. And consequently when the situation of the people, their manners and customs, their trade or arts, do not sufficiently of themselves cause such a diffusion of property among many as is requisite for the continuance of the democratic part in the constitution; there should be such agrarian laws as will prevent any immoderate increase of wealth in the hands of a few, which could support a force superior to the whole body. 'Tis in vain to talk of invading the liberty of the rich, or the injury of stopping their progress in just acquisitions. No public interest hinders their acquiring as much as is requisite for any innocent enjoyments and pleasures of life. And yet if it did, the liberty and safety of thousands of millions is never to be put in the balance with even the innocent pleasures of a few families; much less with their vain ambition, or their unjust pleasures, from their usurped powers or external pomp and grandeur.

* * *

Chapter VII
The Rights of Governors: How Far they Extend

* * *

There is a popular outcry often raised against these tenets of the rights of resistance, as if they must cause continual seditions and rebellions: the contrary is abundantly known. Such mischiefs are more frequently occasioned by the opposite doctrines giving unbounded licence to vicious rulers, and making them expect and trust to the conscientious submission of a people, contrary to nature and common sense; when they are giving loose reins to all tyranny and oppression. 'Tis well known that men too often break through the justest persuasions of duty, under strong temptations; and much more readily will they break through such superstitious tenets, not founded in just reason. There is no hope of making a peaceful world or country, by means of such tenets as the unlimited powers of governors, and the unlawfulness of all resistance. And where the just rights of mankind are asserted and generally believed, yet there is such a general love of ease, such proneness to esteem any tolerable governors, such a fondness for ancient customs and laws, and abhorrence of what is contrary to them; such fear of dangers from any convulsions of state, and such advantages enjoyed or hoped for under the present administration, that it is seldom practicable to accomplish any changes, or to get sufficient numbers to concur in any violent efforts for that purpose, against a government established by long custom and law, even where there is just ground given for them. We see that they scarce ever are successful except upon the very grossest abuses of power, and an entire perversion of it to the ruin of a people. Mankind have generally been a great deal too tame and tractable; and hence so many wretched forms of power have always enslaved nine-tenths of the nations of the world, where they have the fullest rights to make all efforts for a change.

* * *

Chapter VIII
The Ways in which Supreme Power is Acquired;
How Far Just

* * *

Nay as the end of all political unions is the general good of those thus united, and this good must be subordinated to the more extensive interests of mankind. If the plan of the mother-country is changed by force, or degenerates by degrees from a safe, mild, and gentle limited power, to a severe and absolute one; or if under the same plan of polity, oppressive laws are made with respect to the colonies or provinces; and any colony is so increased in numbers and strength that they are sufficient by themselves for all the good ends of a political union; they are not bound to continue in their subjection, when it is grown so much more burdensome than was expected. Their consent to be subject to a safe and gentle plan of power or laws, imports no subjection to the dangerous and oppressive ones. Not to mention that all the principles of humanity require that where the retaining any right or claim is of far less importance to the happiness or safety of one body than it is dangerous and oppressive to another, the former should quit the claim, or agree to all such restrictions and limitations of it as are necessary for the liberty and happiness of the other, provided the other makes compensation of any damage thus occasioned. Large numbers of men cannot be bound to sacrifice their own and their posterity's liberty and happiness, to the ambitious views of their mother-country, while it can enjoy all rational happiness without subjection to it; and they can only be obliged to compensate the expenses of making the settlement and defending it while it needed such defence, and to continue, as good allies ready to supply as friends any loss of strength their old country sustained by their quitting their subjection to it. There is something so unnatural in supposing a large society, sufficient for all the good purposes of an independent political union, remaining subject to the direction and government of a distant body of men who know not sufficiently the circumstances and exigencies of this society; or in supposing this society obliged to be governed solely for the benefit of a distant country; that it is not easy to imagine there can be any foundation for it in justice or equity.

The insisting on old claims and tacit conventions, to extend civil power over different nations, and form grand unwieldly empires, without regard to the obvious maxims of humanity, has been one great source of human misery.

* * *

A SYSTEM OF MORAL PHILOSOPHY   193

human use.

A SYSTEM OF MORAL PHILOSOPHY
BOOK II

———

Chapter XII
The Values of Goods in Commerce and the Nature of Coin

I. In commerce it must often happen that one may need such goods of
mine as yield a great and lasting use in life, and have cost a long course
of labour to acquire and cultivate, while yet he has none of those goods
I want in exchange, or not sufficient quantities; or what goods of his I
want, may be such as yield but a small use, and are procurable by little
labour. In such cases it cannot be expected that I should exchange with
him. I must search for others who have the goods I want, and such
quantities of them as are equivalent in use to my goods, and require
as much labour to procure them; and the goods on both sides must be
brought to some estimation of value.

The natural ground of all value or price is some sort of use which
goods afford in life; this is prerequisite to all estimation. But the prices
or values in commerce do not at all follow the real use or importance
of goods for the support, or natural pleasure of life. By the wisdom and
goodness of Providence there is such plenty of the means of support,
and of natural pleasures, that their prices are much lower than of many
other things which to a wise man seem of little use. But when some
aptitude to human use is presupposed, we shall find that the prices of
goods depend on these two jointly, the *demand* on account of some
use or other which many desire, and the *difficulty* of acquiring, or
cultivating for human use. When goods are equal in these respects men
are willing to interchange them with each other; nor can any artifice
or policy make the values of goods depend on any thing else. When
there is no *demand*, there is no price, were the *difficulty* of acquiring
never so great: and were there no *difficulty* or labour requisite to
acquire, the most universal *demand* will not cause a price; as we

see in fresh water in these climates. Where the demand for two sorts of goods is equal, the prices are as the difficulty. Where the difficulty is equal, the prices are as the demand.

By the use causing a demand we mean not only a natural subserviency to our support, or to some natural pleasure, but any tendency to give any satisfaction, by prevailing custom or fancy, as a matter of ornament or distinction in the more eminent stations; for this will cause a demand as well as natural use. In like manner by difficulty of acquiring, we do not only mean great labour or toil, but all other circumstances which prevent a great plenty of the goods or performances demanded. Thus the price is increased by the rarity or scarcity of the materials in nature, or such accidents as prevent plentiful crops of certain fruits of the earth; and the great ingenuity and nice taste requisite in the artists to finish well some works of art, as men of such genius are rare. The value is also raised, by the dignity of station in which, according to the custom of a country, the men must live who provide us with certain goods, or works of art. Fewer can be supported in such stations than in the meaner; and the dignity and expense of their stations must be supported by the higher prices of their goods or services. Some other singular considerations* may exceedingly heighten the values of goods to some men, which will not affect their estimation with others. These above mentioned are the chief which obtain in commerce.

II. In settling the values of goods for commerce, they must be reduced to some common measure on both sides. Such as 'equal to the value of so many days labour, or to such quantities of grain, or to so many cattle of such a species, to such a measure or weight of certain fruits of the earth, to such weights of certain metals.' The standard or common measure would readily be taken in something of very common use for which there would be a general demand: and in fixing upon it different nations would according to their prudence or circumstances choose different materials.

The qualities requisite to the most perfect standard are these; it must be something generally desired so that men are generally willing to take it in exchange. The very making any goods the standard will of itself give them this quality. It must be portable;

---

* *Pretium affectionis.*

which will often be the case if it is rare, so that small quantities are of great value. It must be divisible without loss into small parts, so as to be suited to the values of all sorts of goods; and it must be durable, not easily wearing by use, or perishing in its nature. One or other of these prerequisites in the standard, shows the inconvenience of many of our commonest goods for that purpose. The man who wants a small quantity of my corn will not give me a work-beast for it, and his beast does not admit division. I want perhaps a pair of shoes, but my ox is of far greater value, and the other may not need him. I must travel to distant lands, my grain cannot be carried along for my support, without unsufferable expense, and my wine would perish in the carriage. 'Tis plain therefore that when men found any use for the rarer metals, silver and gold, in ornaments or utensils, and thus a demand was raised for them, they would soon also see that they were the fittest standards for commerce, on all the accounts above-mentioned. They are rare, and therefore a small quantity of them easily portable is equivalent to large quantities of other goods; they admit any divisions without loss; they are neither perishable, not easily worn away by use. They are accordingly made standards in all civilized nations.

Metals have first been used as standards by quantity or weight, without coinage. This we see in ancient histories, and in the phrases of old languages.* But this way was attended with two inconveniencies; one the trouble of making exact divisions, the other the uncertainty as to the purity of the metal. To prevent both, coinage has been introduced; in which pieces are made of very different well known sizes in the most convenient divisions: the quantity of pure metal in every piece is known; and finer methods of stamping secure us that they cannot be clipped or filed away without its being discernible at once. The public faith of the state is interposed by these stamps, both for the quantity and purity, so that there is no occasion for assays or weighing, or making divisions.

These are the sole purposes of coinage. No stamp can add any considerable value, as it is easy workmanship in such valuable materials. But it may be good evidence for the value, when it is impressed by any just and wise authority. Trading nations cannot make the comparative value of their coin with respect to other goods, greater or less than the

---

* *Impendere, expendere nummos, etc.*

value of the metal, and of the easy workmanship of coinage. Coin is ever valued as a commodity in commerce, as well as other goods; and that in proportion to the rarity of the metal, for the demand is universal. A law can only fix or alter the legal denominations of pieces or ounces; and thus indeed affect, within the state, the legal claims formerly constituted in those denominations: but commerce will always follow the natural value. If one state had all the mines in the world in its power, then by circulating small quantities, it could make the values of these metals and coins high in respect of other goods; and by circulating more of them, it could make their values fall. We say indeed commonly, that the rates of labour and goods have risen since these metals grew plenty; and that the rates of labour and goods were low when the metals were scarce; conceiving the value of the metals as invariable, because the legal names of the pieces, the pounds, shillings, or pence, continue to them always the same till a law alters them. But a day's digging or ploughing was as uneasy to a man a thousand years ago as it is now, tho' he could not then get so much silver for it: and a barrel of wheat, or beef, was then of the same use to support the human body, as it is now when it is exchanged for four times as much silver. Properly, the value of labour, grain, and cattle, are always pretty much the same, as they afford the same uses in life, where no new inventions of tillage, or pasturage, cause a greater quantity in proportion to the demand. 'Tis the metal chiefly that has undergone the great change of value, since these metals have been in greater plenty, the value of the coin is altered tho' it keeps the old names.

IV. The governors of a state which has no monopoly of silver and gold, may change the names of their coins, and cheat their subjects, or put them into a state of cheating each other in their legal demands: but in commerce coin will retain the natural value of the metal in it, with little variation. Where the legal denominations of value are considerably changed, the effects are obvious at once; and in smaller changes the effects are proportionable, tho' not so sensible.

If the legal names of our crown pieces were doubled so that the ounce of silver were called ten shillings, the nominal prices of all goods would rise as much. We should not get the barrel of wheat for the new ten shillings, as we do now in cheap years: we must give the two ounces of silver as we do now, tho' they would be called twenty shillings. Suppose people so stupid that they were contented with the same names, but half the silver. Coining with any stamp is an easy manufacture, any nation could make our crown-pieces, and get for them double the quantity of our goods they got formerly. Our own merchant therefore gets for an ounce of silver from the farmer or manufacturer what formerly cost two ounces, and yet at foreign markets he will get as many ounces for these goods as before. Now he doubles his first cost, beside his former profit. This vast gain would invite so many, and make such a demand, that the prices of all our goods would gradually rise, till they came to the same quantities of gold and silver they were at before, but with double nominal values; and then the new exorbitant gain would stop. At first our country would lose one half upon all goods bought from us by foreigners: this loss would fall upon men of estates and manufacturers at last.

As to foreign goods 'tis obvious the nominal prices of them must rise at once upon changing the names of our coin. Foreigners who do not regard our laws, or legal names of coin, must have for their goods the same pieces or ounces they got formerly. Our merchants therefore in selling goods must have as many pieces or ounces, which now bear a double name.

Again, upon lowering the legal names of coin, the nominal prices of all goods must fall. The merchant cannot afford more pieces or ounces of metal than he gave before for any goods to our farmer or manufacturer, as he will get no more at any foreign market, and this number now bears a smaller name. Foreign goods are bought abroad for the same ounces they were, and therefore the merchant can afford them here for the same ounces he formerly sold them at, and with the same profit, tho' the name be less. If one merchant refuses to sell so, another will, as all can afford it: or if all refuse, foreigners will send their goods into our country to be sold for the same ounces, now bearing a lower name.

'Tis a fundamental maxim about coin, that 'its value in commerce cannot be varied by names,' that prices of goods keep their proportion to the quantities of metal, and not to the legal names. No man values a piece more than 'tis called twenty livres, or twenty Scots pounds, than he would have done on account of the sterling name.

v. The changing considerably the legal names of coin must cause innumerable wrongs among the subjects of any state, since the real values of goods continue the same. The lowering of coins wrongs all who are indebted in legal denominations; they must pay more ounces of gold and silver than they received, or engaged for; and yet get no more ounces by any sales of their goods than they got formerly. All duties, taxes, rents, salaries payable in legal denominations are increased. More ounces are received by the creditors in such claims, and yet each ounce will purchase as much goods for the support or pleasure of life as before the change. The debtors therefore are so much wronged, and so much the creditors are unjustly enriched.

Raising the legal names has the like unjust effects on the other side. Debts, taxes, rent, salaries, specified in legal names, can then be discharged with fewer pieces or ounces; and yet the debtor gets as many ounces for any goods he sells as before; and the creditor can get no more of the goods necessary for life for an ounce than he got before. He is therefore so much wronged by the change made in the legal names.

The putting disproportioned values upon the several species of current coin must have bad effects on a country. The species under-valued at home will be carried abroad, and the species over-valued will be imported; as the former answers better at foreign markets, where the ounces of metal are regarded, and not the names, and the later answers best at home. Whatever sums are thus exchanged by foreigners, all their gain is so much loss to our country. What we export ourselves, hurts our country only by introducing perhaps a less convenient species. This disproportion often arises after the values were wisely fixed at the time they were made, if either the mines of one metal are more copious in proportion than those of the other; or there be a greater drain of one sort of metal by exportation, or by some consumption of it in the splendour of life.

An increase of both metals by copious mines, naturally abates the value of both, without any change of the names. And thus, properly speaking, the values of gold and silver are fallen within these two centuries above one half: tho' we more commonly say that the rates of goods are increased. Were the mines quite drained and the quantities of these metals much diminished by the various uses of them in plate, dress, and furniture, their value would rise again; or, we would vulgarly say, the rates of goods would fall. The standard itself is varying insensibly: and therefore if we would settle fixed salaries, which in all events would answer the same purposes of life, or support those entitled to them in the same condition with respect to others, they should neither be fixed in the legal names of coin, nor in a certain number of ounces of gold or silver. A decree of state may change the legal names; and the value of the ounces may alter by the increase or decrease of the quantities of these metals. Nor should such salaries be fixed in any quantities of more ingenious manufactures, for nice contrivances to facilitate labour, may lower the value of such goods. The most invariable salary would be so many days labour of men, or a fixed quantity of goods produced by the plain inartificial labours, such goods as answer the ordinary purposes of life. Quantities of grain come nearest to such a standard.

In matters of commerce to fix the price we should not only compute the first cost, freights, duties, and all expenses made, along with the interest of money employed in trade, but the labours too, the care, attention, accounts, and correspondence about them; and in some cases take in also the condition of the person so employed, according to the custom of our country. The expense of his station of life must be defrayed by the price of such labours; and they deserve compensation as much as any other. This additional price of their labours is the just foundation of the ordinary profit of merchants, on which account they justly demand an higher price in selling, than what answers all that was expended upon the goods. Their value *here* is augmented by those labours, as justly as by those of farmers or artisans.

As there are many contingent losses by the perishing of some goods, or their receiving damage, these losses may be justly compensated by a further augmentation of the price of such as are safe. As merchants lose sometimes by the falling of the rates of goods on hand, they may justly take the contingent advantage too of goods on hand, when the rates of such goods rise by any accident which makes them scarce. Men who are fortunate in these accidents may be much enriched, without any fraud, or extortion. The constant profit is the just reward of their labours. Thus tho' the values of what is given and received in buying and selling should still be kept equal on both sides, as we shall see presently, yet there is a natural gain in trade, viz. that additional price which the labour and attendance of the trader adds to the goods; and a contingent one, by the rising of prices.

SUGGESTIONS FOR FURTHER READING

Primary Sources

Haakonssen, Knud (General Editor), *The Complete Works of Francis Hutcheson*, Indianapolis, Liberty Fund. These are scholarly editions with introductions and extensive notes. Various dates from 2000.

Kivy, Peter (ed.), *Francis Hutcheson: An Inquiry Concerning Beauty, Order, Harmony, Design*, The Hague, Martinus Nijhoff, 1973. This is a scholarly edition of Treatise I and the *Reflections on Laughter*. There is an excellent introduction and notes by the editor.

Peach, Bernard (ed.), *Illustrations on the Moral Sense and the Correspondence between Gilbert Burnet and Francis Hutcheson*, Cambridge, MA, Harvard University Press, 1971. This is a scholarly edition of the *Illustrations* and related correspondence. There is an informative introduction and notes by the editor.

Biography

Scott, W. R., *Francis Hutcheson*, Cambridge, Cambridge University Press, 1900. Reprinted Bristol, Thoemmes Press, 1992. Despite its age this is still a reliable source of all aspects of Hutcheson's life and thought.

Secondary Sources and Commentaries

Berry, Christopher, *Social Theory of the Scottish Enlightenment*, Edinburgh, Edinburgh University Press, 1997.

Broadie, Alexander (ed.), *The Cambridge Companion to the Scottish Enlightenment*, Cambridge, Cambridge University Press, 2003.

Broadie, Alexander, *A History of Scottish Philosophy*, Edinburgh, Edinburgh University Press, 2009.

Brown, Michael, *Francis Hutcheson in Dublin, 1719–1730*, Dublin, Four Courts Press, 2002. (Contains an extensive bibliography of primary and secondary sources.)

Hook, Andrew and Sher, Richard (eds), *The Glasgow Enlightenment*, East Linton, Tuckwell Press, 1995.

Hope, V. M., *Virtue by Consensus*, Oxford, Clarendon Press, 1989.

Kivy, Peter, *The Seventh Sense: A Study of Hutcheson's Aesthetics and its Influence in Eighteenth-Century Britain*, Oxford, Clarendon Press, 2nd edition 2003.

Moore, James, 'Hume and Hutcheson', in *Hume and Hume's Connexions*, ed. M. A. Stewart and John Wright, Edinburgh, Edinburgh University Press, 1994.

Norton, D. F., *David Hume: Common-sense Moralist, Sceptical Metaphysician*, Princeton, NJ, Princeton University Press, 1982, ch. 2.

Norton, D. F., 'Francis Hutcheson in America', in *Studies on Voltaire and the Eighteenth Century*, ed. Theodore Besterman, vol. CLIV, 1976.

Raphael, D. D., *The Moral Sense*, Oxford, Clarendon Press, 1947.

Rendall, Jane, *The Origins of the Scottish Enlightenment*, London, Macmillan, 1978.

Robbins, Caroline, *The Eighteenth-Century Commonwealthman*, Cambridge, MA, Harvard University Press, 1961.

Stewart, M. A. (ed.), *Studies in the Philosophy of the Scottish Enlightenment*, Oxford, Clarendon Press, 1990, ch. 2.

INDEX